Under The Broken Scale of Justice
The Law and My Times

By Justice Nyo' WAKAI (Rtd.)

Langaa Research & Publishing CIG
Mankon, Bamenda

Publisher:
Langaa RPCIG
(*Langaa* Research & Publishing Common Initiative Group)
P.O. Box 902 Mankon
Bamenda
North West Province
Cameroon
Langaagrp@gmail.com
www.langaapublisher.com

Distributed outside N. America by African Books Collective
orders@africanbookscollective.com
www.africanbookscollective.com

Distributed in N. America by Michigan State University Press
msupress@msu.edu
www.msupress.msu.edu

ISBN:9956-558-28-1

© Justice Nyo' WAKAI 2009
First published 2009

DISCLAIMER

All views expressed in this publication are those of the author and do not necessarily reflect the views of Langaa RPCIG.

Titles by *Langaa* RPCIG

Francis B. Nyamnjoh
Stories from Abakwa
Mind Searching
The Disillusioned African
The Convert
Souls Forgotten
Married But Available

Dibussi Tande
No Turning Back. Poems of Freedom 1990-1993

Kangsen Feka Wakai
Fragmented Melodies

Ntemfac Ofege
Namondo. Child of the Water Spirits
Hot Water for the Famous Seven

Emmanuel Fru Doh
Not Yet Damascus
The Fire Within
Africa's Political Wastelands: The Bastardization of Cameroon

Thomas Jing
Tale of an African Woman

Peter Wuteh Vakunta
Grassfields Stories from Cameroon
Green Rape: Poetry for the Environment
Majunga Tok: Poems in Pidgin English
Cry, My Beloved Africa

Ba'bila Mutia
Coils of Mortal Flesh

Kehbuma Langmia
Titabet and the Takumbeng

Victor Elame Musinga
The Barn
The Tragedy of Mr. No Balance

Ngessimo Mathe Mutaka
Building Capacity: Using TEFL and African Languages as Development-oriented Literacy Tools

Milton Krieger
Cameroon's Social Democratic Front: Its History and Prospects as an Opposition Political Party, 1990-2011

Sammy Oke Akombi
The Raped Amulet
The Woman Who Ate Python
Beware the Drives: Book of Verse

Susan Nkwentie Nde
Precipice

Francis B. Nyamnjoh & Richard Fonteh Akum
The Cameroon GCE Crisis: A Test of Anglophone Solidarity

Joyce Ashuntantang & Dibussi Tande
Their Champagne Party Will End! Poems in Honor of Bate Besong

Emmanuel Achu
Disturbing the Peace

Rosemary Ekosso
The House of Falling Women

Peterkins Manyong
God the Politician

George Ngwane
The Power in the Writer: Collected Essays on Culture, Democracy & Development in Africa

John Percival
The 1961 Cameroon Plebiscite: Choice or Betrayal

Albert Azeyeh
Réussite scolaire, faillite sociale : généalogie mentale de la crise de l'Afrique noire francophone

Aloysius Ajab Amin & Jean-Luc Dubois
Croissance et développement au Cameroun : d'une croissance équilibrée à un développement équitable

Carlson Anyangwe
Imperialistic Politics in Cameroun: Resistance & the Inception of the Restoration of the Statehood of Southern Cameroons

Bill F. Ndi
K'Cracy, Trees in the Storm and Other Poems

Kathryn Toure, Therese Mungah Shalo Tchombe & Thierry Karsenti
ICT and Changing Mindsets in Education

Charles Alobwed'Epie
The Day God Blinked

G.D. Nyamndi
Babi Yar Symphony

Samuel Ebelle Kingue
Si Dieu était tout un chacun de nous?

Ignasio Malizani Jimu
Urban Appropriation and Transformation : bicycle, taxi and handcart operators in Mzuzu, Malawi

Justice Nyo' Wakai:
Under the Broken Scale of Justice: The Law and My Times

DEDICATION

TO MY PARENTS
who breathed into me the spirit
of resolute tenacity that has kept me
equal to the vicissitudes of life.

Contents

Acknowledgments	vii
Preface I	ix
Preface II	xiii
An Attorney's Prayer	xxi
Introduction	xxii

Part One	**1**
Chapter I: Lux Gentium Lex	3
Chapter II: Department Of Public Prosecutions	10
Chapter III: The Legal Profession	36
Chapter IV: Legal Cultures	50
Chapter V: Good Government And Governance	61
Chapter VI: Supremacy Of The Law	70
Part Two	**83**
Chapter VII: The Bench	85
Chapter VIII: Justice	89
Chapter IX: The Constitution	108
Chapter X: Law Reporting	116
Chapter XI: The Broken Scales Of Justice	129
Chapter XII: Signature	154

Acknowledgments

When I decided to put together all the major decisions taken during my tenure of office as President of the North West Provincial Court of Appeal, I did not expect that one day I would need them as indispensable material to write a book. It was and has always been my concern to record events that have influenced my life. If I failed to use them, others might find them useful in one form or the other.

Now that I have decided to do something, I will begin by acknowledging my indebtedness to Mr Paul Mbuyongha, the P.C. A. Personal Secretary throughout the period that I presided over the Bamenda Court of Appeal. He did all the typing. At a time when the computer had not been heard of in this part of the world, it was a feat to accomplish. To him this work owes much.

Alongside with Mr Mbuyongha is Mr Paul Langwa. Mr Langwa joined the service a few years after my assumption of office in 1977. Within a very short time, he got a hang of the registry work. He proved to be a devoted and dedicated member of my staff. Putting the decisions together, and they are several, to which I have had easy and quick reference is the handiwork of Mr Langwa. He is responsible for binding the decisions, otherwise, I would have found it very hard to access some of the decisions mentioned or discussed herein. He, like Mr Mbuyongha, should realise that they have written this book.

Mrs Tangwa Meriline Kongla is not my direct staff. She is a full time staff of an *NGO, Taso Accounting Management and Auditing Consultants (TAMAC)* headed by Mr Samuel Asobo Mbuyah a C.P.C Bali Old Boy. The Old Boy's tie induced him to accept that his organisation and the *Monie, Wakai & Associates Law Firm* should share her secretarial experience. She has been wonderful and I regard her the kingpin of the product that is now in your hands. I am extremely grateful and proud of what she has done especially coping with the legalese in some areas of the work. Same applies to Miss. Mirabel Tembei her predecessor.

Not everyone can be acknowledged in every piece of writing. Those named are but a minute few. The unnamed should know that I value their assistance in the various and different ways I received it.

Nevertheless two persons deserve special note namely, Barrister Luke K. Sendze and Professor Tazoacha Asonganyi.

Whatever merit this work may lay claim to, such claim is due to the meticulous devotion and dedication that both Barrister Luke K. Sendze and Professor Tazoacha Asonganyi put into it. Their contributions are more than succinctly to the reader than I tried to do in a jumble manner.

Because the two have succeeded where I failed to make the point, it is considered good sense to reproduce in their entireties their contributions either as previews or general comments. The reader is advised to read them in order to enhance his understanding of the book. Their contributions are not just previews but form part of this book as Prefaces.

All statements and errors of any sort found herein, whether typographical and/or misreading, I hold no person accountable but take full responsibility for them.

At the end of it all, the pillar of all my efforts remains my wife, Christine, whose concern and anxiety for my physical well being became an obsession during the long hours I spent researching for the materials that make up this little work.

Preface I

"**The Law and My Times**" is an excellent expose of the latent and sometimes overt undercurrents that helped shape the Judicial history of Cameroon during the dying days of the United Nations Trusteeship period and the early days of independence up to the present day. From the vantage positions the author was placed by virtue of the posts he occupied throughout this period, he was able to put up the narrative in this book which no doubt graphically captures the minds especially of those of us who lived the events recounted therein and helps those of later years to look at the judicial evolution of this country in its true perspective.

From the time the two sectors of Cameroon which had pre-existed under different Trusteeship masters (British and French) with different judicial cultures got united into the federal Republic of Cameroon, it was obvious that a time bomb was planted in the sense that the rivalry in Europe between the Anglophone culture and the Francophone culture was going to show its ugly head in this young vulnerable and inexperienced Federal Republic. And sure it did as can be seen by any person who scans through the pages of the wonderful book.

The conflict of judicial concepts, procedures and usages led to the judicial system of one sector trying to impose itself on the other. It is only the mature and cool heads like those of the author who from their vantage positions bent over backwards to avoid an explosion and allow a gradual evolution of the Judicial System in this country. These mature hands had an onerous task of fighting to maintain the independence of the Judiciary inherited from the colonial masters in the face of an aggressive executive power which called the shots at independence and still do so to the present day.

At independence with the connivance of the politicians, the President of the Republic who was the head of the Executive branch of Government crafted a constitution which made himself the Chief Magistrate. In that capacity he presided over the Higher Judicial Council whose members were for the most part appointed by him. This Council had the responsibility of appointing, promoting, disciplining, transferring and dismissing Magistrates. This situation seriously undermined the independence of the Judiciary and unfortunately the situation has largely remained unchanged to the present day.

Those Magistrates like the author of this book who at independence had a nostalgia for the type of Judicial independence existing during the

Trusteeship period in both sectors of Cameroon were in for a rude shock. The new constitutional dispensation had reduced them to toothless bulldogs that were only limited to talking about the independence of the Judiciary during public speeches when in fact, the Judiciary was bonded by the Executive.

The present treatise by Rtd. Justice Nyo' Wakai has graphically and in his usual precise language shown how this power in the hands of the Executive could be and was abused sometimes with reckless abandon to intimidate Magistrates who attempted to defend their independence.

The greater number of Cameroonians living today are those born into the independence period of our country who never lived the events recounted in his wonderful work. This treatise will help them understand where the Judiciary of this country came from and where it might be moving to. The eloquent constitutional provisions giving the impression that the Judiciary is a power and should be independent have since independence been mere window dressing because the practices and usages we have lived show a steady and determined effort by the executive to undermine those provisions.

The power conflict since independence which was sometime overt between the Judiciary and the executive has persisted to the present day. The independence f the Judiciary is looked upon with suspicion by the Executive which calls the shots in Cameroon. It has a nuisance value to them as they are more comfortable with absolute power which the independence of the Judiciary is incompatible with.

How could anyone dare to legally challenge any action by the omnipotent President of the Republic and before which court? Many Cameroonians even including jurists especially of the francophone sector surely thought at the time late Rt. Hon. Mr Ngom Jua as Prime Minister of West Cameroon decided to sue Barrister Gorji Dinka before a court in Buea that he was out of his mind. Worse still when he decided to appear in person before a magistrate in an attempt to defend the action this amounted to ridiculing his office. Why could he not use his enormous powers as Chief Executive of West Cameroon to take unilateral action to bring Barrister Gorji Dinka to his knees? Such thinkers felt that it was infradig for a whole Prime Minister as Chief Executive to descend so low to appear before an ordinary judge who was after all appointed by the Executive.

Outrageous as what Rt. Hon. Jua had done looked to some people, he was following the judicial tradition inherited by the former West Cameroon from the British. In this treatise anybody can see clearly that the executive was scandalized that a Procureur General who at his level is the direct representative of the Minister of Justice could be taken to Court by some godforsaken citizen. Those Magistrates, who naively thought that the beautiful laws of Cameroon gave any such right as appeared on paper ended up paying a very high price at the hands of the Executive. They were far ahead of their time.

It is hoped that with the present wind of change and the global watch over our activities by those international organs that always defend the independence of the Judiciary, the very sad experience of these dedicated magistrates will soon be past history even though it again showed its ugly head after the recent trial and conviction of a highly placed person accused of assault occasioning death at the Ngoketunjia High Court. The Magistrates who defied all types of subtle and overt pressures to bring this about were later all transferred from their stations by the Executive, transfers which were generally viewed as punitive. Politicians and the Executives should avoid such blatant attempts to undermine the independence of the Judiciary and by so doing make Cameroon a state with respect for the rule of law.

The attempt to demystify the imaginary power and immunity of some sacred cows in our public offices and bring them to succumb to the power of the Judiciary is a recent development which we hope will continue so that at least every citizen will be equal before the law. This positive trend can only have a meaning if the magistrates remain faithful to their oath and assert their independence in the proceedings that will, unless these sacred cows sit up, obviously be coming up with greater frequency than before.

We can only say bravo to those pioneer Magistrate "freedom fighters" who were living ahead of their time high price they had to pay for this notwithstanding. It is to be hoped that their example will encourage our Magistrates of the present day to continue to fight for the independence of the Judiciary and there is no doubt that the ordinary citizens of this country will support them.

The present Minister of Justice in Cameroon Mr Ahmadou Ali has time without number challenged the Magistrates to come out with any evidence that he has ever given any instructions to presiding Magistrates on how they should decide any matter before them. In other words, he has never given such instructions.

It is high time that our Magistrates of the bench especially those who have been State Counsel sometime in their career stopped imagining nonexistent instructions from the Ministry of Justice directing them on how to behave in any particular case.

By so doing they will end up retiring with their heads high as the author of this work did. It will be on retirement that they will appreciate that those of their colleagues who spent their time assisting the Executive to undermine the independence of the Judiciary while amassing wealth at the expense of their integrity will be miserable people. Our society fortunately respects those on retirement from the public service who have kept their integrity with them while in office. The author of this treatise is a living example of this hypothesis who has been treated by his former colleague Magistrates, Advocates and the public at large with a lot of difference at all times. When you are no more handling the levers of power and you can get such instant respect then your life was worth living. Bravo to those who will be encouraged by this treatise to continue the fight for the independence of the Judiciary in this country.

Luke K. Sendze,
Barmi-Njoh Chambers,
Bamenda - March 2008.

Preface II

"Nyo' Wakai: The Law and My Times" Many people do not like the courts, as attested by this remark of Jimmy Carter to his son in his book "The Living Faith": "One day I lashed out at my lawyer friends and you were there to hear me ask why legal ways are often so unfair; why instead of what is just and right, time and again money, shrewd delays, and courtroom skills seem to win…"

Although impartiality is one of the major roles of law courts, the tug-of-war that usually characterises the appointment of Supreme Court Judges in the United States, a country with a highly developed independent judiciary, confirms the verdict of legal historians that judges do not operate from reason alone; their scales of value, their passion, the response of their hearts to sets of facts and arguments, their experience, outlook and idiosyncrasies all temper the decisions they reach.

Rtd. Justice Nyo' Wakai has written his life story in the service of the Judiciary in Cameroon in "The Law and My Times", packed full of reasons for the disappointment of the Jimmy Carter, of the interplay between the head and the heart in the resolution of the dramas that we usually witness in courts. By the time those who ask the same question as Jimmy Carter finish reading this book, they will know that their worries are known in the profession because of the following advice to the advocate quoted in the book, "…*let your zeal be as warm as your blood, but let it be tempered with discretion and with self-respect, let your independence be firm, uncompromising, but let it be chastened by personal humility, let your love for liberty amount to a passion, but let it not appear to be cloak for maliciousness…*"

I remember that following the conspiracy against me in the SDF, I wrote an essay titled "Treading on Booby Traps…" in which I stated as follows: "*I never went back into the hall. I spent the rest of the evening with Justice Nyo' Wakai who pampered me like a spoilt child. I saw in all his behaviour that evening, his effort to keep me happy throughout; a translation of the kind words of congratulation he and Hon. Ngwasiri, two Founding Fathers of the party, had showered on me during the debate in NEC. During the meeting, they expressed their gratitude at the work I had done for the SDF during my 12 years of tenure as the Secretary General of the party. I will never forget the kindness shown me that evening….:*

When I wrote the statement above, I never knew that many people before me in different areas of life like the Judiciary had written virtually the same type of words of him! Reading through "The Law and My Times", I am convinced that between his "entrances and exits" in the stage of life, Justice Nyo' Wakai has been a man of innate decency and kindness. This is why I consider myself greatly honoured to have been one of the few who read through "The Law and My Times" before it got to the bookshelves.

The book is written in twelve chapters as follows:- Chapter 1: Lux Gentium Lex; Chapter 2: Department of Public Prosecutions; Chapter 3: Legal Profession; Chapter 4: Legal Culture; Chapter 5: Good Government and Governance; Chapter 6: Supremacy of the Law; Chapter 7: The Bench; Chapter 8: Justice; Chapter 9: The Constitution; Chapter 10: Law Reporting; Chapter 11: The broken Scales of Justice; and Chapter 12: Signature.

We are informed that *"this is an account by an individual of his professional experiences covering a period of his life... It is no fiction... My fervent hope is that this, in some way, will inspire future professionals in this area of human existence."* This sets the stage for the pouring out of experiences at the legal department and the bench that will inspire, jolt and tickle the reader.

The book presents the contrasting picture of those days when the judiciary could be counted on, and these days when the judiciary is "naked" and *"the cobwebs of the law catch the small flies while the big ones break through at will with impunity..."* He states: *"I recall the late President Ahidjo on one occasion of the solemn opening of the Supreme Court telling the corps of judicial officers something to this effect 'Yes, I, the President is the guarantor of your independence but that independence belongs to you and not to the President'..."* And so we see him fighting for the independence of the judiciary by insisting and obtaining from the Minister of Justice who had come to install him as Chief Justice of the North West Province in 1977 that "the Governor should not sit on the Bench, alongside the Judges". He reminded the Minister to stand while addressing the Court, but he the Chief Justice would address the court seated! It was indeed a judicial, not a civic occasion!

The overriding dominance of the administration over the judiciary is also illustrated by the 1990 liberty laws which *"have not worked out as intended by the legislator"*. This is mainly because the judicial powers given to administrative authorities were abused. The coming of the gendarmes, to West Cameroon is also used to illustrate the abuse of human rights in total disregard of the law. Unlike in West Cameroon where *"members of the public would jointly separate a street brawl and report the perpetrators to the police for investigation and possible prosecution... Cameroonians (today) are reluctant or unwilling to report criminals who commit offences for the simple reason that before they realise, the offender is walking the streets freely..."*

What we can describe as the clash of cultures came to a head around 1966 with the exodus of (foreign) legal minds due not only to the problems within the KNDP but also to the impending one-party regime that was maturing in Ahidjo's political womb. He gave birth to it on 1 September 1966. Apparently these legal minds could not stand a system where the executive would call the shots, to the exclusion of the judiciary.

The presence of "good governance" in those days and its absence these days is illustrated by what is going on in Cameroon today under what is known as "operation epervier". The operation would be a source of great fun and amusement in those days! In Southern Cameroons later called the Federated State of West Cameroon, there was a Commissions of Enquiry Ordinance (Cap 36 of the 1958 laws) which empowered the Prime Minister to appoint a commission of inquiry into any department of government to investigate possible wrongdoing. Using these powers, the PM appointed such commissions, especially into the affairs of West Cameroon Department of Lands and Surveys (notice No. 90 in West Cameroon Gazette No. 13, Vol. 7 of 1 April 1967), into the activities of the West Cameroon Development Agency as from 1959 (notice No, 61 published in West Cameroon Gazette No. 14, Vol. 8 on 27 March 1968) and into the West Cameroon Electricity Corporation (notice No, 98 published in West Cameroon Gazette No. 20, Volume 8 of 30 April 1968).

Nyo' Wakai participated in the work of these commissions as counsel from the legal department. He recalls that *"the commissions were fact-finding bodies...They reminded all public servants that public office is a public trust and that the trustee should always be reminded that the public has and will always have the power and responsibility to demand an account, and if deemed necessary, to do so publicly..."* The commissions inquired into "*...the conduct of any officer in the public service of the Federated State, or any chief or the management of any department of public welfare...*" They investigated into allegations of tribalism, nepotism and favouritism in employment; corrupt practices against the management; diversion of labour, property and funds for personal use; expenditures and justifications; personal assets of past and present members of the managerial staff and members of Boards before, during and after their tenure of office; anomalies and discrepancies in the award and execution of contracts; whether investment of funds received approval; and all other allegations of irregularities.

There is the regret that *"present day administrations or government are reluctant or find it difficult to* (imitate) *these salutary (approaches) which have worked in the past... Could one think of subjecting the SONEL, Ports Authority, SNEC,*

Cameroon Airlines, Post Office Savings Bank, SCPD, almighty SONARA and SNH with exactly the same terms of reference as were operational in the Federated State of West Cameroon?..." There is no doubt that the answer to this question can only be YES. These commissions of inquiry existed in the '60s in a government led and run by Cameroonians. Today, nearly fifty years later, we cannot pretend that this is impossible. At a future date, it would be necessary to shine the torch in various areas to lay a new foundation for good governance in Cameroon. After all, Wakai reminds us the old saying that *"history has relevance in so far as it enables us to use our knowledge of the past to tackle the problems of the present and thus fashion the shape of the future..."*

In the common law system, there was a Criminal Procedure Ordinance; in the civil law system, there was the Code d'instruction. In common law many principles evolve over the years through successive court rulings; in civil law judges generally base their decisions less on precedents set by their predecessors and more on their understanding of the written code. So which of the common law and the civil law systems is better? Nyo' Wakai thinks that none is better, since justice is ephemeral and elusive. According to him, much depends on the judges who *"being humans, have their own idiosyncrasies..can be temperamental...have feelings. ... Moral value are universally accepted while a sense of justice may be determined by an enactment... In the end a judge arrives at a decision according to his moral values or virtuous nature..."* He thinks that justice is done case by case; rather than judges resting their consciences on single cases, they should rest them on the totality of cases that come before them!

Most of the problems that burden the democratisation process in Cameroon are legal. With the failure of the judiciary to nudge the process forward, one has the impression that the judiciary has turned its back on the people. Is this apparent failure of the judiciary due to the fact that "justice may be determined by an enactment"? Are pronouncements like "the court's hands are tied" due to this? His answer is an emphatic NO! He says such pronouncements *"are not only odium but palpable nonsense...unsatisfactory malediction..."* and that in his days *"the judiciary stood out as a credible institution and absolutely beyond reproach...one cannot say this of the same institution today..."*

We are told that following unification *"we failed the test of enacting laws that reflected our new sovereignty... this made our administration (of law) look different in each component of the union..."*. Importantly, the author also admits that *"the society and its environment, the people and their interests ... their cultures and traditions all influence experiences...With two cultural heritages, attention has* therefore to be paid on the *"actual administration of justice"*. According to Dean Roscoe Pond quoted in the book, the most important thing is to *'have regard to the operation of law in human society. What end it serves and whither it is tending..."*

It is because of the foregoing that the author thinks that *"a veritable and credible justice system should be certain and predictable considering the fact that law is very much influenced by ... the society... The law in its content may mean different things to different peoples and even at different times and ages..."* This is why to him, law reporting is as important a challenge as the production of, for example, of the Criminal Procedure Code. In order to follow-up and harmonise the application of such enactments in the whole country, law reporting of the decisions reached in courts all over the country are sorely needed. This is why he says *"it would be of immense interest to know how the Court of Appeal in Bertoua interprets the controversial sections of the OHADA treaty when compared to an interpretation by the jurisdiction in Buea of similar status. The same goes for the new Criminal Procedure Code..."* To meet the Herculean challenge of Law reporting, the author suggests the setting up of something like a National Law Reporting Council. The reader will be pleased to learn that the author has *"compiled in 13 volumes these judgments of the North West Court of Appeal from 1978 – 1985..."*

Nyo' Wakai voted in the plebiscite of February 1961 before he left for London to study law. He returned to Cameroon in 1965 after being called to the English Bar by Lincoln's Inn, and took up services in Buea as Federal Counsel in 1966. Therefore Foumban and the eventual unification were of particular interest to him. He thinks that Foumban was a masquerade, since it was not really a constitutional conference to determine the form of state. Accordingly to Ahidjo, the process was *"the recovery by Cameroon (i.e. French Cameroun!) of the territorial dimension that were hers before July 1919... it was the Republic which had to transform itself into a federation, taking into account the return to it of part of its territory, a part possessing certain special characteristics..."* We are told that *"to President Ahidjo, the Republic of Cameroon (then la République du Cameroun) was the mother nation... a sovereign and legal nation to which the Southern Cameroons was eager to rejoin... the Southern Cameroonians thought that their vote would lead the parties to negotiate for a nation that would be federal in character with all the trappings of federalism... It is noteworthy that President Ahidjo hardly refers to the name of Southern Cameroons. True to his concept, Southern Cameroons was a territory to be acquired by the new sovereign state over which he was presiding at the material time..."*

Following this haphazard approach to unification, Ahidjo then proceeded to change the Federal structure of the state in 1972 by referendum, and Biya completed the project by changing by law, the name of the country to the original name of French Cameroon: The Republic of Cameroon! All this in spite of the fact that the federal constitution stated that: *"47(1): No bill to amend the constitution may be introduced if it tends to impair the unity and integrity of the Federation ... 47(3):* The amendment may be passed by a simple majority of the Federated Assembly, provided that such a majority included a majority of the membership elected from each Federated State."

Wakai is scandalised that Ahidjo was not challenged using the court systems when he *"unilaterally carried out a constitutional coup in dissolving the federation and replacing it with a centralised state"* Indeed, he thinks that the various Anglophone groups have to look critically at article 76(b) of the UN Charter and article 47 of the constitution of the Federated Republic with respect to the 1972 coup. He defines the Anglophone problem that resulted from the manipulations of Ahidjo as *"the barring of a people of a common culture and heritage in a union where they are distinct from asserting their distinctiveness and the refusal of their rightful due in the national resources of the patrimony..."*

He addresses the problems of Ordinances in our legal history by stating that although Cameroon has known no crisis since independence that put parliament out of service, the Chief Executive *'tended to request the legislative arm to surrender to him (to sign ordinances) and they too seem to do so with relish..."* Unfortunately, he does not address the problem posed by Ordinance No. 062/OF/18 of 19 March 1962 on subversion, which was in place by 1972 when the referendum was held and when law No. 84-1 of February 4, 1984 to change the name of the United Republic of Cameroon to the Republic of Cameroon came into force. The Ordinance instituted tight restraints on freedom of expression and association, allowed the security forces to act with impunity, to arrest, torture and send citizens to prison with abysmal prison conditions – all of which served to intimidate those who might voice dissent. The Ordinance established new offences termed "subversion" and "rebellion" which all prohibited free expression of opinion, making it a crime for anyone to oppose or criticize any government action. Albert Mukong and others disobeyed this to their peril! In any case, the author is right that someone would have at least challenged the violations in court. It would have been interesting to record the reaction of the court system to such a challenge!

Although the author says that *"the tapestry legal history provides rich ground for such challenges...",* it is rare even today *"to find cases where the authority or power of any institution has been challenged...Our legislators, lawyers and all those* who exercise power or authority (have to) direct the law and thereby the administration of justice...to take us to our place in the global world of tomorrow..." To him, this "laisser-faire" attitude to use the judiciary to resolve constitutional or legal issues leaves the impression that *"our judiciary is weak or lacks that clout..."* and constitutes a sorry <legacy> for a country like ours!

It can be said that this legacy and other weaknesses in our society were the challenges that provided the difference between the opposition that emerges in 1990 and the regime in place. The various slogans of "change" within the opposition gave the impression that they understood the dimension of these challenges. To prepare for the advent of a new society that would replace the old, there was need to identify the reasons that militated for the imposition of one-party rule, the repeated changes of the constitution, and the complicity of the citizens who raised no finger! Unfortunately, it appears that although the opposition imitated the regime in place by parroting concepts like the rule of law, checks and balances, parliament and all others bestowed on us by colonialism, they were hardly ever conscious of the central role of these in a democracy. Indeed, the parties did not seem to understand the true meaning from their ranks. Rhetoric like *"Politics no bi book"*, *"too much democracy is dangerous"*, etc...! Their original option for change turned out to be mere sloganeering!

This failure of the opposition is highlighted by Wakai in passing. We are told that once he entered the judiciary he was advised by Sir Dingle Foot, Q. C; not to be *"tempted to take up politics..."* We can conclude that he heard the advice, because we know that he only joined politics after his retirement. Although he was one of the founders of the SDF and played a very active role in taking the party to the height of its popularity, he did not allow his experiences in the party to colour his narrative in "The Law and MY Times". Indeed, the SDF is mentioned only once in the book when he states that *"At the time I am writing, the Social Democratic Front (SDF) is in court over the interpretation of its own constitution. What has astonished me is the fact that reasonable persons including our legal men don't see the sense in this test of the law(s). it is being passed off as an abomination intended to destabilize or attack and ridicule the party's hierarchy..."*!

An independent judiciary is vital to enforcing the law and ensuring accountability. However, the Court is not responsible for enforcing or ensuring that its orders or judgments are followed. The state machinery for enforcing such orders includes the "Procureur Général" – the Attorney Genral. In a chilling presentation of cases titled Ndifor vs the people, and Ncho No. 1 to Ncho No. 9, the attempt of the then "Procureur Général" of the North West Province to discredit and destroy the court system in the North West Province by failing to ensure that court orders were enforced, is presented. This failure to enforce court decisions generated tension and a lot of bad blood, and masters of political infighting in Yaounde and eventually he became Minster of Justice! His vantage position in Yaounde was used to successfully operate what the author refers to as the "guillotine". The author was one of the victims. His simplicity, decency, kindness, courage and popularity were the cards with which he trumped his adversaries.

Nothing wounds a man of integrity more than to find his basic honesty questioned. Under "Signature" through which he signs out "The Law and My Times", the bitter memories are signaled by the paraphrase of Shakespeare: *"Life is a stage where we are all actors with each one of us having his entrances and exits..."* This is linked up with that from Paul J. Lindell that: *"between these exits and entrances, we live in encircling gloom, an envelope of pain and distress, affliction and illness, disorder and conflict are ever with us..."*. Then Wakai informs us that *"While I enjoyed my entrances and exits, they have made me believe that there are evil powers that trot the earth untamed..."*

Man is susceptible to passion, intolerance and greed; the essence of law is to tame such evil powers. There is no doubt that "The Law and My Times" will contribute immensely to reinforcing legal practice (and Law) in Cameroon, and so confirm one of the assertions in the book that "all is well that ends well..."

Judges, legal practitioners, students, university dons and the general public that is the most concerned with the daily dramas in court rooms will treasure "The Law and My Times"

Tazoacha Asonganyi
Yaoundé, April 10, 2008.

AN ATTORNEY'S PRAYER
By Carol FILCHETT (1981)

Keep my mind always open that I might
understand___
The "scales of justice" that must balance
this land.
Help me to find realities hidden away.
And to know in all societies, "facts"
do go away.
To present a case in fairness, help me
to comply___
To your will and to your wisdom___
on these might I rely.

Introduction

This is an account by an individual of his Professional experience covering a specific period in his life. It is my story. It is not fiction. It is a story I always dreamt I should live to tell. Every attempt has been made to back up the narration with such evidence as is credible either documented or well recollected.

Much of my inspiration comes from the late Prof. Clive Parry of Cambridge University, England. I had the good fortune to be instructed by him in International Law when I attended the Government Legal Officers' course in 1974 organised by the British Overseas Development Agency. Prof. Parry was insistent in encouraging practitioners to write because they would be expressing their daily experiences. The Cameroonian Prof. E. N. Ngwafor's own written encouragement is found at the end of this book. If this work does go far, then the seed planted by the learned Professor did fall on fertile soil. But I am convinced many more of the Legal Officers who attended that six months' course have certainly preceded me because I met some of the most brilliant lawyers from different parts of the Commonwealth at the course who, equally, might have taken up the Prof.'s challenge. See the list at page _____ of this work.

Subsequently to Prof. Parry's admonition, I got an encouraging letter from Prof. Ephraim N. Ngwafor in which he said, inter alia:-

*"*It is my fervent wish that you would find your youthful retirement very rewarding. Since you have a good pen, it may not be a bad idea if you decide to do some writing"*

I know there are parts of this narration that will not go down well with some people. If you are caught in that web, so be it! To those who want to breathe the air of the time, I have gone to a great extent to reproduce documentation. These are **ipso facto.**

My fervent hope is that, this, in some way, will inspire future Professionals in this area of human existence. Namely that, what society expects of judges should be the wish generally expressed that *judges shall be judged by the informed judgment of history.*

Finally, my use of "man", "he" and "him" in this book is not meant to be exclusive of the "opposite" sex. The use is meant to be inclusive.

Bamenda, Cameroon.
October 2006.

---

* Letter dated: 23rd January 1991

Part One

Part One

CHAPTER I
LUX GENTIUM LEX

It was a bright October morning. The rains were on their way out and the dry season was about to take over control of the elements. I like this time of year because of its transition from the heavy rains to the dry and hazy weather.

The year was 1977. There was ambiance in the air. The venue was the precincts of the Court of Appeal Bamenda, housed in an old building which by its construction reminded anyone of a colonial relic. All the same to the people of the North West Province, it was not so much its magnificence as what it symbolised. To them, it was a citadel from where justice flowed pricelessly.

The audience anxiously awaited the arrival of the Minister charged with responsibility for justice. It was a cross-section of the peoples of the North West Province. For this particular ceremony, all important traditional rulers in the Province, Parliamentarians and top ranking public servants in the Province and the usual population answered present.

The day was my day. I was going to be installed as President of the North West Court of Appeal. Though my Province of origin, I had never worked in it for 23 years since leaving Cameroon Protestant College (CPC) Bali. On leaving Bali, I found employment with the Cameroon Development Corporation, Tiko, in the South West Province. I put in nine months with the corporation and moved to an opening in the civil service in Buea, capital of the Southern Cameroons, a U.N. Trust Territory administered[1] by Great Britain. For their own convenience, the British administered it as part of Nigeria, then her colony[2].

After two years in Buea, I got two years' study leave to pursue further studies in Enugu in the Nigerian College of Arts, Science and Technology in the arts subjects.

I finished in Enugu in 1959 and returned to my civil service job in Buea. I worked till 1961 when I was awarded a Southern Cameroons Government scholarship to undertake legal studies in London.

I voted in the Plebiscite of February 1961 and left for Britain on September 26 being covered by a British Passport No 262111 issued at Lagos-Nigeria on the 28th August 1961. My national status was described as a *British Protected Person*. So, I left Southern Cameroons four days to unification on October 1, 1961.

---

[1] Administered by Great Britain as a U.N. Trust Territory.
[2] Colonised by Great Britain.

I returned to Cameroon in December 1965 after being called to the English Bar at Michaelmas Term by Lincoln's Inn.

Again it was back to Buea in January 1966 as Federal Counsel in the Attorney General's Chambers. Mr Emmanuel Fonjeh Tatabod and I reported for work on January 11.

But I feel I must, for the record, recount an anecdote preceding our resumption of duty in the Attorney General's Chambers. Both of us had been among the few fortunate beneficiaries of the Southern Cameroon Government scholarship. We were, by our contract, bonded to serve the Southern Cameroons Government for at least five years after completion of our professional training. The return home was therefore to a guaranteed civil service position. Posting to Buea in the Attorney General's Chambers was a formality, that is, requiring only the necessary legal instrument.

The Hon. Sanda Oumarou of blessed memory, a francophone, was Minister of Justice and Keeper of the Seals. And the honorable Emmanuel Tabe Egbe, an Anglophone and an English trained lawyer, was Vice Minister of Justice. That was the political set up in the Ministry in Yaounde.

Unknown to us, and I can swear for myself, certain political events had taken place in the Federated State of West Cameroon.

Briefly stated, the Kamerun National Democratic Party which had spearheaded the struggle for unification had, in that year, been involved in a ferocious fracas over the succession of the Party's leadership since it was alleged that Mr John Ngu Foncha then leader should move to Yaounde to take up permanent residence as Vice President of the Federation.

In this feud, two factions emerged. One faction led by the Hon. Augustine Ngom Jua and the other by the Honourable Solomon Tandeng Muna.

You may ask why I should refer to this as concerns my appointment in the Attorney General's Chambers. Simple. Tatabod was automatically considered to be aligned to the Hon. Muna and I to the Hon. Jua. Why? Because those Anglophones in the Ministry were politically assigned on ethnic basis, the scourge of Cameroonian or African politics. Tatabod comes from the same administrative division as honourable S.T. Muna (Bamenda West) and I from that of the Hon. Jua (Wum) before it was split up into Menchum and Boyo Divisions.

On arrival back home in December of 1965, we were required to report to the Ministry in Yaounde for our postings. We did this after the Christmas break. We traveled to Yaounde on our different convenient days. I stayed with the Hon. Nzo Ekha Ngaky, an old time friend in

Cameroon Protestant College (C.P.C) Bali. He was then the Minister of Labour and Social Insurance. We spent the night discussing various subjects. It is true to say he proposed to me that I should take up private practice and that I would be given retainerships. He was one of the strong supporters of the Hon. Jua in the political duel a year or so before while the Hon. Egbe supported the Hon. Muna.

I quickly pointed out to Nzo that I was bonded to the West Cameroon government, the successor to the Southern Cameroons government and a term in the scholarship bond required that I must serve the said government for at least five years. Justice being a federal subject under the Constitution of the Federal Republic of Cameroon, I was now obliged to report to the Ministry in Yaounde. I further informed him that I had turned down a similar offer by Uniliver Limited when I worked in their head office in London in the summer of 1963.

I cannot say for certain where my friend, Mr Tatabod, stayed in Yaounde. We did not get in touch with each other while in Yaounde.

The day following my arrival in Yaounde, I reported at the Ministry, more specifically at the Vice Minister's office (cabinet) to take my posting letter. There I met Mr Stephen Okang, the head of the Vice Minister's Secretariat. I knew him well before I got my study leave. He was the Chief Clerk in the Southern Cameroons Ministry of Transport and in the Office of the Secretary to the Executive Council. He was, like all old friends, excited to see me back from Britain.

I told him I had come to take my posting letter. He was surprised. When we discussed the details, he understood. He called the Secretary who was typing a letter to bring the draft.

To my consternation and utter surprise, I noticed that the posting letter to the Attorney General's Chambers had only Tatabod's name. He told me they had information that I was being engaged by the West Cameroon government. The Hon. Jua, it should be noted, was then the Prime Minister of West Cameroon.

I told Mr Okang I was not aware of it. He went in and consulted with the Vice Minister and when he came out he instructed the Secretary to include my name in the letter to the Attorney General in Buea.

I insisted to see the Vice Minister and pay him my courtesy. In, he repeated Mr Okang's assertion. I answered him as I had answered Mr Okang.

I left Yaounde for Buea a very dispirited man wondering whether there was a future in the service for me. This attempt to politicise or tribalise our appointments was absolutely disgusting to me. After all, we were bonded to serve the Cameroon government for five years.

I kept this experience to myself for my whole career in the service. I decided to do the utmost in my power to satisfy my bosses in my work.

Throughout my service in the Legal Department, I enjoyed the confidence and I may add here the love of my bosses until I rose to head the department.

Barely two weeks of my assumption of duties in the Attorney General's chambers, I had a surprise telephone call from the Secretary to the West Cameroon Civil Service Commission. The message was short. She asked me:-

"When are you going to assume your duties in the Legal Department of the Prime Minister's Office?"

I answered that I have already resumed duties in the Attorney General's Chambers and so I was not aware of what she was talking about.

Information came to me later that Mr Emmanuel K. Mensah who was the Attorney General for West Cameroon had requested that I be posted to his Chambers as his deputy. If this is true, then the procedure was wrong. The right procedure would have been a request directed to the Ministry of Justice, justice being under the Constitution a federal responsibility. I certainly would not credit Mr Mensah with such ignorance. He was, by any standard, a brilliant lawyer; though, in my view, having a bend towards politics.

The insinuations and imputations generated by those with poisoned political minds failed woefully to glow. Neither my colleague and good friend, Mr Tatabod nor myself gave them any weight. We were more excited to put into practice our profession as we saw it in its grandeur, majesty and nobility. I remember then as now the advice of the famous and eminent English lawyer, Mr Dingle Foot, Queen's Counsel (QC). In addressing newly qualified overseas Barristers, he said:

> *"I know many of you come from the newly independent nations and you will have many opportunities open to you. I warn you, don't be tempted to take up politics especially by being offered Ministerial Posts. Ensure that you put in at least five years in your profession because that's where you will return to when everything else fails."*

That has been my guiding principle and that has made me not feel any sense of frustration when such opportunity eluded me. I have been satisfied with the practice of the law notwithstanding the frustrating moments I have had. Now at this point in my life (retirement) I follow the development of the law with keen interest.

This brief review of my professional career in the Legal and Judicial service of my country is intended to explain away the events that took place on the day of my installation in October 1977. A day full of drama.

Politically, it was blown beyond proportion. It was, as it has become customary in Cameroon : *"a son of the soil has been made Chief Justice of the Province! So, let us be glad and rejoice."*

The presiding Minister was His Excellency Joseph Charles Doumba. He is brilliant and perfectly bilingual. He speaks forcefully and confidently. He has been Secretary General of his Party, the Cameroon People's Democratic Movement (CPDM) for a long time- evidence of his political astuteness. He appreciated logical argument.

In religious parlance, one would say of him that he was the officiating minister at a religious ceremonial.

The Court hall was packed full and the sprawling crowd covered every space in the Court precincts.

Members of the Legal Department led by the Procureur Général, at the time, Mr Benjamin Mutanga Itoe as he then was, had taken their places in the court hall; so had members of the Bar. I was waiting with my team of Vice Presidents (*the American will refer to them as Associate Justices*) for the arrival of the Hon. Minister of Justice, Keeper of the Seals. On arrival the Learned Procureur Général and myself would receive His Excellency, the Minister, to whom we each would introduce separately our collaborators.

In Cameroon, waiting to receive a Minister on an official occasion is a moment of anxiety and anguish. The Chief of Cabinet of the Provincial Administrative Head who played both the role of the Director of Protocol and Security Officer keeps moving round and jostling with the crowd. This scenario was at play on this day.

Then the protocol sky broke loose. One of the Clerks of Court, Mr Paul Fungwe, ensuring that order was kept and maintained, rushed into my chambers and in the presence of my fellow Judges informed me that the Chief of Cabinet in the Governor's office was insisting that the Governor should sit on the bench alongside the Judges. Very spontaneously and without consulting my Colleagues, I rushed into the Court Hall to order the arrest of Mr Omgba. I did not, at that moment, think or bother to think of the scene I was enacting or about to enact. As soon as he saw me emerge from the entrance connecting the Chambers and the bench, he ran out of the court. He reported the incident to the Minister and his boss and of course, as usual, added some spices to it.

According to him, I had refused a place for the Governor in the front row. Instead, I had ordered that he takes his seat in the crowd. Knowing the administrative and political standing of the administrative Head of the Province, it was outrageous and could not be tolerated.

Hon. Joseph Charles Doumba knew me well when I was head of the Legal Department in Buea, South West Province, during heads of departmental meetings which were held regularly.

Then the siren signaled the arrival of the Minister and the Governor. At the precinct, the paraphernalia of introducing members of the Legal and Judicial corps took place. I escorted the Minister to my Chambers where my fellow Justices had rushed back to take their seats for a briefing session of the Minister.

Seated in the Chambers, the following dialogue ensued between the Minister and myself.

> Hon. Minister:
> *I understand you have ordered the Governor to sit in the crowd.*
> Reply:
> *Who told you that?*
> Hon. Minister:
> *The Governor's Chief of Cabinet.*
> Reply:
> *That's not true. The Chief of Cabinet insisted that the Governor should sit on the bench alongside the Justices.*
> *This is a judicial and not a civic occasion.*
> *I don't agree. When we'll be in court you'll see where the Governor is sitting with his Secretary-General and the Senior Divisional Officer (Prefet) for Mezam.*
> *Mr Minister, when you'll be speaking, you'll stand. I'll be seated when I address the court.*
> *That is a judicial ritual. If you don't agree, that is the telephone (I pointed to the phone by his side). You can ring up the President to cancel the decree appointing me. We can then go in and announce the cancellation of the ceremony.*
>
> Hon. Minister:
> *Ça c'est grave! (that is serious! – my translation)*

Then Mrs Josette Essomba, a long time Adviser in the Ministry and a native French woman, intervened.

She said:

> *Yesterday, we carried out a similar installation at Bafoussam in the adjoining West Province (Francophone) the Governor did not sit alongside the Justices (the bench) why should it happen here!*

It was, of course, a rhetorical question. That ended the debate on what I considered to be a subtle way for the executive arm of government to control the judicial arm. Not that at that date the judiciary had any power. Far from it! For me, worse days were ahead.

October 1977 as we can see, was great drama.

The following year on the occasion of the National Day i.e. May 20, I arrived at the grandstand with my colleagues of the Court of Appeal to discover that no seats were reserved for us. I advised my colleagues to keep standing. When Governor, Aboem-à-Tchoyi arrived the ceremonial grounds and saw us standing he pretended to be angry. The crowd was murmuring throughout. From that date, I never attended any official occasion until I was posted to the Supreme Court in Yaounde.

CHAPTER II
DEPARTMENT OF PUBLIC PROSECUTIONS

It is not the duty of prosecuting counsel to procure a conviction; nor should any prosecutor ever feel pride or satisfaction in the mere fact of success... Always the principle holds that Crown Counsel (State Counsel) is concerned with justice first justice second and conviction a very bad third.

As I said earlier, I came to the higher bench without serving any apprenticeship. Unlike my contemporaries, they served as trial magistrates and judges in the Courts of original jurisdictions. These were the cases of Mr George S. Ekema, Emmanuel Tatabod, Hans Ekor Tarh, Joseph P.C. Nganje, Bernard A. Muna and before all these, was Mr Emmanuel K. Mensah as they were then.

Both Mr Frederick Ngomba Eko, the first Cameroonian Procureur Général and myself formed the pillars of the Legal Department. We were the recipients of the responsibility for the department from the departing ex-patriates like Mr J. O. Quinn (as he then was) and before him Mr P.L.U. Cross, D.S.O. By 1968 Mr Quinn was appointed a Justice of the Federal Court of Justice in Yaounde cumulatively with the functions of Technical Adviser in the Ministry of Justice. He fought and succeeded in the creation of the Anglophone Section of ENAM, from which the early anglophones trained in the common law greatly benefited. Mr Eko took over from Mr Quinn.

The law reports between 1962 and 1968 were the initiative of Mr Quinn. During his tenure of office and after his departure, all efforts to continue the marvelous job of law reporting met with dismal failure. A strenuous effort was made to set up the West Cameroon Law Reporting Council but the more efforts that were made, the more frustration was encountered.

By this time our academic elite had returned home mostly trained in Britain. Doctors Peter Yana Ntamark, Fred Ngu Kisob and John Nkengong Monie were the pioneers in the field of academia.

In my opinion, the struggle to establish the Council suffered from lack of any encouragement on the part of government. In conception, it required substantial funding. It badly lacked it. Maybe *the will* to keep up the struggle by convincing the authorities to see the sense and importance in such an enterprise was lacking.

With the appointment of Mr Frederick Ngomba Eko in 1968, the Legal Department of the Federated State of West Cameroon was completely cameroonised.

Prior to 1966, the Attorney General's Chambers carried out legal functions for the government of the Federated State of West Cameroon and that of the Federal State. Typical of the common law system, the Attorney-General participated in the cabinet deliberations of the West Cameroon government. He did not do the same at Federal level where he was merely regarded as *the Director of Public Prosecutions* (DPP) in charge of West Cameroon; the Minister of Justice and Keeper of the Seals replaced him in the Federal Council of Ministers with a team of legal officers to advise him on all legal matters. In the common law system, the Attorney General combines the functions of a politician with that of a law officer.

Under the constitution of the Federal Republic of Cameroon of October 1, 1961, it was provided in Article 6: -

The powers of the Federal Authorities shall also embrace the following:
- Public liberties;
- The law of persons and property;
- The law of obligations and contracts in civil and commercial matters;
- Judicial organisation, including the rules of procedure and jurisdiction of all courts (with the exception of customary courts of West Cameroon, save as regards appeals from the decisions of such courts);
- Criminal law;

The judicial machinery was thus placed under the Federal Authority except for the Police Force.

Articles 34 and 35 of the West Cameroon Constitution of October 1, 1961 stipulated thus:
1) There shall be a police force for the State, which shall be styled *the West Cameroon Police Force.*
2) The organisation of the West Cameroon Police and its powers and duties shall be by written law.

35 (1) There shall be a Commissioner of Police whose office shall be an office in the Public Service of the State.
(2) The West Cameroon Police shall be under the command of the Commissioner of Police.

There was established a Police Council which took care of the organisation and administration of the Force and all matters relating thereto, but not matters relating to the use of the operational control of the force.

Even though the administration of justice was the responsibility of the Federal Government while the West Cameroon Police was a Federated State service, it was used to assist in the administration of justice, by the performance of legal and judicial duties.

In this regard, elements of the West Cameroon Police force, outside the usual functions of being keepers of the peace and criminal investigations, prosecuted minor offences in the Magistrates Courts (*Courts of First Instance*). In this capacity they were responsible to and came under the overall control and supervision of the Attorney – General, the Government Law Officer. The more experienced amongst them were appointed to the bench to try traffic offences and similar misdemeanours.

Generally, the duties of the police in practice were:
  (a) to prevent and detect crime;
  (b) to apprehend persons suspected of having committed a crime;
  (c) to keep the peace and order;
  (d) to protect property and the enforcement of all laws and regulations with which they are directly charged and when so required;
  (e) to perform military duties.

Most importantly, as far as the common law went, any police officer might be required to conduct in person all prosecutions before any court whether or not the charge or information is laid in his name.

To achieve this aim, the Police were generally expected to undertake intensive courses in the general principles of law. Below is the scheme or syllabuses as provided for these courses under the General Orders (popularly referred to by civil servants at the time as "G.O.") which were the rules and regulations governing the civil service.

General Orders (G.O.): under Chapter 7

Section 2: *Compulsory Examinations for Police Officers.* Officers who are required to pass.

07201: Unless specially exempted by the Governor the following Police Officers are required to pass the examinations prescribed in General Order 07202, within three years from the date of taking up their

appointments in Nigeria (by the Order in Council 1954 – Southern Cameroons) with which the examinations are associated:
a) Officers appointed to Nigeria on first appointment as Assistant Superintendents of Police or Police cadets.
b) Assistant Superintendents of Police promoted from the junior service.
c) Assistant superintendents of Police transferred from other public services at basic salaries of less than £660 who, at the date of transfer, are not confirmed officers over the age of 40.

SYLLABUSES OF EXAMINATIONS 07202
The following are the prescribed examinations for Police Officers:-

Group A: Law examination
This examination consists of two papers on the following subjects:
(i) Nigerian Criminal Law, Procedure and Evidence for which a knowledge of the following is required:
  a) The Criminal Code Ordinance, Cap. 42
  b) The Criminal Procedure Ordinance, Cap. 43
  c) The Evidence Ordinance, Cap. 63
  d) Kenny's Outline of the Criminal Law.

(ii) The main provisions of the following Nigerian Ordinances and the subsidiary legislation made thereunder:

No. of Ordinance	Title of Ordinance
Chapter 14	Arms
Chapter 33	Coins
Chapter 34	Collective Punishment
Chapter 41	Coroners
Chapter 69	Explosives
Chapter 88	Illiterates Protection
Chapter 89	Immigration
Chapter 94	Interpretation
Chapter 114	Liquor
Chapter 122	Magistrates' Courts
Chapter 123	Magistrates' Courts (Appeal only the provisions applicable to criminal matters)

Chapter 141 .... Native Children (Custody and Reformation)
Chapter 166 .... Peace Preservation
Chapter 172 .... Police
Chapter 175 .... Prevention of Crimes
Chapter 205 .... Sheriffs and Enforcement of
                                                Judgments and Orders.
Chapter 223 .... Unsettled Districts
Chapter 228 .... Weights and Measures
Chapter 230 .... West African Currency Notes
Chapter 232 .... Wild Animals Preservation
No. 43 of 1947 .... *Road Traffic, 1947.*

Group B: Examination in official publications

This examination consists of three papers on the following subjects:
  i. Colonial Regulations
  ii. General Orders
  iii. Financial Instructions

Group C: Examination in Police work

This examination consists of two papers, on the following subjects:
  i. Practical Police Work
  ii. Police Orders and Instructions.

These days the standard expected by victims of crime from the criminal justice system in which the police play a major role is the need to:
- keep the victim in touch with the progress of the investigation or court proceedings;
- ensure that information on the victim's losses and injuries is available to the court so that it can consider ordering the offender to pay compensation; and
- improve conditions at court for crime victims who have to give evidence.

I saw then as I see it now a most important role of the police as that of concern for the security of the citizen and his property. In that light the department of investigating crime is paramount. Personnel of the *Criminal Investigation* Department as it generally was known consisted of the best brains who undertook a rigorous training in not just tracking down criminals but more importantly in preventing crime. An allowance was allocated for entering public places and places of entertainment to trace a criminal unsuspiciously. He was dressed in mufti and spent freely in order to pick up information that could give him leads.

Information so obtained could forestall the commission. It could also provide evidence for the prosecution of the person of an offence. The investigator in giving evidence was not bound to disclose the source of his information. By that token, citizens were encouraged to assist the police generally in volunteering information that helped the investigator in the apprehension of a criminal or potential criminal.

The police respected the citizen in order to continue to receive co-operation from him and guaranteed the citizen's protection from any threat to his person or life for such co-operation. It was a question of mutual friendship and trust.

The *beat system* was intended to prevent the commission of crime and at the same time help to identify some criminal or potential criminal elements in various locations. This enabled the Criminal Investigation Department (CID) to identify them and follow their movements more closely.

The establishment of the business of security services today is overwhelming evidence that the system has collapsed or is not cherished by our justice system, or that we don't believe in it or simply that we cannot support it.

The practice today presumes everyone a criminal who should be incriminated on mere suspicion. Yet the system has been ridiculed by men of the underworld. The law-abiding ones amongst us fear to go about freely while the criminal elements parades our streets and quarters with impunity. They break into homes with audacity and commit crimes in broad daylight.

A common sight in our streets today is a scuffle between two individuals. The crowd stands around and applauds. The same attitude of not being involved goes for any passing member of the forces. My experience teaches me that I am far away from the time(s) when members of the public would jointly separate a street brawl and report the perpetrators to the police for an investigation and possible prosecution of the culprit or culprits. Cameroonians are reluctant or unwilling to report criminals who commit offences for the simple reason that before they realise, the offender is walking the streets freely. The law-abiding individual might end up being assaulted by the offender. We now talk of "*everyone to himself and God for us all*".

It is sad for people in my position to recount all this. We are written off as suffering from nostalgia. *The 'have beens'* as we are popularly labeled.

This point is vividly brought out in the provisions of section 198-201 of the Criminal Code which was enforceable until 1966 when the Penal Code came into force.

Section 198 punishes a public officer who refuses to perform his duty in these terms:

> "*Any person who, being a person employed in the public service, and being required by any Order, Ordinance, Law or Statute, to do any act by virtue of his employment, perversely and without lawful excuse omits or refuses to do any such act is guilty of a misdemeanour, and is liable to imprisonment for two years........"*

Section 199 is more specific to the police, generally regarded as *a peace officer* or in present day, *the generic term of law enforcing officer would be appropriate.*

The section provides:

> "*Any person who, being a peace officer, and having notice that there is a riot in his neighbourhood, without reasonable excuse omits to do his duty in suppressing such riot, is guilty of a misdemeanour, and is liable to imprisonment for two years".*

The individual citizen *per se* has his own responsibility in maintaining and keeping the peace for the betterment of society.

This responsibility is enshrined in section 200 of the Criminal Code. It stipulates:

> "*Any person who, having reasonable notice that he is required to assist any peace officer in suppressing a riot, without reasonable excuse omits to do so, is guilty of a misdeamour, and is liable to imprisonment for one year."*

We should be partners in the suppression of crime and at the same time aid in the preservation of peace in our community. Hence, the provisions of section 201 of the Code which provides:

> "*Any person who, having reasonable notice that he is required to assist any peace officer or member of the police force in arresting any person, or in preserving the peace, without reasonable excuse omits to so do, is guilty of a misdemeanour and is liable to imprisonment for one year."*

These provisions were intended, no doubt, to guarantee the protection of both the police and/or peace officers and the individual citizen. Sharing a mutual responsibility and equitable balance prevailed and the co-operation so badly needed on both sides for peace to reign in the society was thus guaranteed. It is absolutely important to note the regularity with which *peace officer* is used as against our present day preference for *forces of law and order*. This description is loaded with meaning. It invokes the idea of a permanent state of defiance of the law and the lack of order in the society.

Things have changed. The police baton has been replaced by a revolver and A.K 47 (3). The outward trappings of a law enforcement officer conjures fright in every citizen and instills fear. There is arrest and incarceration before any question is asked or a charge preferred. Peace officer in the context of the sections referred to herein before is generic in that it includes members of the police force and other officers whose duty is to enforce and preserve the public peace.

Public peace itself is understood to mean the peace and tranquility of the community in general, the good order and repose of the people composing a state or a community. It extends to order and freedom from agitation or disturbance, the security, good order and decorum guaranteed by civil society and the law.

These are ideals for which governments are instituted. These categorisations included magistrates who could arrest offenders committing or attempting to commit offences in their presence or reasonably suspected of having committed an offence.

One magistrate, Mr Savage, was well known in Victoria for arresting young women for wearing dresses he considered indecent. By such activity, Magistrate Savage was able to restore the dignity of the woman. Whether the Magistrate's conduct would be acceptable today is a matter for conjecture. Certainly, it did achieve good order and decorum as demanded of a good society.

The functions of the police force did not end with preventing crime and criminal investigation but by a Constitutional Order-in-Council, it was provided that:

"any police officer may conduct in person all prosecutions before any court whether the information or complaint was laid in his name or not".

The system produced a very efficient and effective system of administration of justice. The investigating officers were thorough; their duty and their report constituted legal opinion on the facts and the law. This was the result of their training in the fundamental principles of criminal law and procedure.

When I joined the Attorney General's Department, I discovered that some of the investigators wrote opinions that were comparable to any written by a legally trained mind. Investigators and prosecutors like Nazarius Nju Ghong, Lawrence Tafon, Barnabas Nguma and Yubin could have run a department of public prosecutions effectively at a first tier level.

All the same and despite the paucity of trained professionals, the prosecuting competence of the police was limited to the Magistrates' Court (the Court of First Instance).

Indictable offences were within the competence of trained professionals because an indictment lay to the High Court that was empowered to try more serious offences inclusive of murder that carried the death sentence.

The usefulness of the functions of the police in this area of the administration of justice cannot be overemphasised. Immediately after independence, the Southern Cameroons and subsequently the West Cameroon Federated State government, as a matter of policy, decided to embark on awarding scholarships that would, with time, provide the badly needed personnel in this area of government. Those who benefited from these awards bonded themselves to serve the State Government for a period of not less than five years. The earlier members of staff of the Legal Department were generally the beneficiaries of these awards. This position remained until the 70s when many West Cameroonians undertook legal studies locally, thanks to the many Nigerian Universities that opened up the doors to them in their Law Faculties.

On the cameroonisation of the Legal Department of West Cameroon, there was merely a skeleton professional staff but overlaid on a background of devoted and dedicated young Cameroonians.

That was our challenge as young Cameroonians. Justice was a federal subject under the constitution of October 1, 1961.

With the creation of the office of the Procureur Général for West Cameroon, it became necessary for the West Cameroon Government to set up its own Legal Division. This was done and the first person appointed to head that Division was Mr Emmanuel Kofi Mensah.

From all accounts and indications, Mr Emmanuel Kofi Mensah who was the first Cameroonian Government Counsel had considerable experience as a Federal Counsel and a presiding Magistrate. That far, all the West Cameroonian trained as lawyers were sponsored by the Southern Cameroons government.

At the time of Mr Mensah's appointment, I was fully integrated in the Procureur Général's Chambers. One bright morning, I received a phone call from the Secretary to the West Cameroon Public Service Commission requesting me to report at the commission to pick up my appointment papers as an Assistant in the Legal Division of the West Cameroon government.

As I pointed out earlier, I told her I had already started work as a Federal Counsel (F.C.) in the Procureur Général's Chambers. I remember that Mr Mensah had hinted me on his desire to have me work with him in building up the West Cameroon Legal Department.

Bearing in mind the events preceding my appointment prior to January 11, 1966, I saw a political colouring in the saga. Mr Augustine N. Jua was still Prime Minister.

I was so firm in my answer to the Secretary to the West Cameroon Public Service Commission that the matter was never raised again. Besides, with the departure of the expatriates and Mr Fred Ngomba Eko as the Procureur Général, I was content to work with him. Many people thought Mr Eko to be hard and stiff. Somehow, we got on well together and several times he would tell me: *"you are the dauphin of this department"*. Our wives got on well too in their circles. That close relationship solidified in the years 1968/69, the years of the Commissions of Inquiry following a change of government in West Cameroon as Hon. Solomon Muna was appointed Prime Minister to replace the Hon. Augustine Ngom Jua.

Whatever may be said, the police prosecutor played an important role in so far as lightening the prosecutorial work of the Legal Department was concerned. Until the 1970s the staffing situation of the department was most precarious in that at no time were there ever more than three Federal Counsel, in Buea. They had to cover the High Courts of Buea, Kumba, Mamfe, Bamenda and subsequently Mundemba after its establishment in 1976. The method of work was to start a prosecution and continue with the evidence till it was ended. Any adjournment was but to enable the presiding judge write his judgment or ruling. Since the investigator always ensured that potential witnesses were present for the hearing, many prosecutions were finished during an assize.

I wonder how this system would work today where only one day a week is allocated to particular cases. As presently operated, the practice has produced an enormous backlog and discourages potential prosecution witnesses from attending court sessions. They find it burdensome and unnecessarily disruptive of their daily business activities. The result is to keep away from attending court and consequently long adjournments with the resultant effect of *persons-awaiting-trial* having to be detained for a long time without the foggiest idea when the charges against them would be disposed of.

The legal instrument setting up the Legal Department under the common law to which I was introduced provided:[3]

---

[3] Law Officers' Ordinance – Cap. 100 section 3

> "Every person appointed as Attorney-General or Solicitor-General of the Federation (Nigeria), Attorney-General or Solicitor-General of a Region .... Legal Secretary of the Southern Cameroons or Crown Counsel, shall, so long as he continues to hold such office be deemed to be, and every person who shall have been appointed to any such office shall have been deemed to be, a barrister, advocate and solicitor of the Federal Supreme Court ex-officio and shall be entitled, and shall been deemed to have been entitled, to appear as counsel in all courts in which counsel may appear."

The Law gave precedence to these state officials if and when they entered appearance in the courts throughout the country.

When Southern Cameroons seceded from the Federation of Nigeria, West Cameroon undertook a series of adaptation of the laws. These provisions continued to be applicable in West Cameroon until replaced by new legislation. They were given constitutional recognition in Article 46 of the Constitution of the Federal Republic of Cameroon 1961 in the following terms:

> "Previous legislation of the Federated States shall remain in force in so far as it does not conflict with the provisions of this Constitution."

Relying on this provision of the Constitution, West Cameroon continued to apply and rely on the provisions of the Law Officers' Ordinance.

I assumed office as a Federal Counsel in the West Cameroon Attorney-General's Office under P.L.C Cross, who sat in the Council of Ministers of the West Cameroon government advising the federated state Government in legal matters. And yet he was a Federal Official because justice was a responsibility of the Federal Government. As should have been foreseen, conflicts soon arose between the opinion he gave the West Cameroon Government and the one he gave the Federal Government as a person charged with directing and controlling the prosecution of criminal offences. At the same time West Cameroon argued that, under the circumstances, there was great need for it to have a Law Officer to advise it in all legal matters.

The first appointee to the post was Mr Emmanuel Kofi Mensah as has been noted. Mr Mensah was among the first West Cameroonians to qualify as a Barrister in England. He was destined to have a distinguished place in the judiciary of the new Republic. So soon after his appointment, he raised a very controversial legal issue. He argued that with the creation of a Federal Department with responsibility for the overall direction and control of criminal prosecution in West Cameroon, the place and role of the Attorney-General from the mere appellation, belonged to the Federated State; in other words, the office of Attorney-General had thus been broken down and the Federal Legal Officer in Buea who had now become the Procurer Général should not be referred to as *Attorney-General*. To him the nomenclature of *Attorney-General* was now reserved to the Law Officer of West Cameroon. Yaounde could not understand the fine point raised by this argument.

Mr Mensah pursued his argument with such vigour that he decided to invoke the procedure of "case stated" by placing the matter before the High Court in Buea for a ruling. The motion and statement were circulated to all members of the Bar including the official Bar to submit on the legal issue raised. It was at this point in time that Mr Mensah expressed his fervent wish to have me join him in the Legal Department of the Federated State. This was given a political interpretation since the Honourable Augustine Ngom Jua was the Prime Minister of West Cameroon.

Somehow, the matter just fizzled out. It raised too much political cloud. Thereafter the Law Officer in the Prime Minister's Office became known as the Legal Adviser to the West Cameroon government. The Federal Law Officer of the State was known as the Procureur Général because the common lawyers in West Cameroon did not find, *from his functions*, an adequate appellation. The Law Officers in the Procureur Général Chambers were called Federal Counsel (F.C).

Mr E. K. Mensah, as a Federal Officer, was appointed to the Bench but because of the political heat generated by the changes among the principal political actors at the time he decided to resign from the Cameroon judiciary. It was generally alleged that Mr E. K. Mensah was an acknowledged friend of the Hon. Augustine N, Jua who in 1968 was replaced as Prime Minister by the Hon. Solomon Tandeng Muna.

Mr E. K. Mensah was born to a Ghanaian father and a Cameroonian mother. In the midst of all this, he seems to have decided to retrace his paternal roots. He left for Ghana where before long he was appointed a Judge of the High Court.

Criminal Prosecution

The common law provides for a system whereby a private citizen may initiate a criminal prosecution because, in any case, the responsibility for commencing any criminal action rests on every citizen. According to Sir Norman Skelhorn in discussing the functions of the Director of Public Prosecutions in England and Wales when addressing the members of Gray's Inn, London, in 1965, he postulated:-

"It has always been a firmly entrenched principle of our constitution that in England and Wales the enforcement of law and order is in the hands of the ordinary citizen, and even today there are, strictly speaking, no public prosecutions".

The principle was applicable to West Cameroon where the common law was *received law including texts of general application before 1900.*

Generally, all prosecutions are commenced by a government or quasi-governmental authority. Nevertheless, minority prosecutions are brought by individuals acting in a purely private capacity.

It was not unusual that trouble between neighbours resulted in both parties cross-summoning each other for assault. An individual may also feel so outraged at the decision of the prosecuting authority not to prosecute that he would take the initiative and commence proceedings himself.

The principle was re-enacted as a law of Anglophone Cameroon in sections 342 and 343 of the Criminal Procedure Code as follows:

"Section 342: The registrar (of the court) shall receive an information from a private person if:

(a) *it has been endorsed thereon a certificate by a law officer to the effect that he has seen such information and declines to prosecute at the public instance the offence therein set forth; and*

(b) *such private person has entered into a recognizance in the sum of (fifty pounds to be converted), together with one surety to be approved by the registrar in the like sum, to prosecute the said information to conclusion at the times at which the accused shall be required to appear and to pay such costs as may be ordered by the court, or, in lieu of entering into recognizance shall have deposited one hundred pounds (to be converted) in court to abide the same conditions".*

Section 343 imposes conditions for the initiation of a private prosecution by stating that:

"Where any private person has complied with the provisions of section 342 the information shall be signed by such person and not by a law officer or other person designated by the Minister as aforesaid and such person shall be entitled to prosecute the information but nothing in this section shall be construed so as to exclude the provision of the constitution".

The problem with a private prosecution is its cost to the individual prosecutor but where the State refuses to cater for the rights of the individual, I think that there should be an opening available for him to right a wrong suffered by him.

In considering this point, the common law practitioner has found solace in what Sir James Stephen said in 1883[4] in Vol. I of his "History of the Criminal Law of England":

> *"The management of a criminal prosecution is so expensive, so unpleasant and so anxious a business, that no one is likely to undertake it without strong reasons. Many such prosecutions, both in our days and in earlier times, have given a legal vent to feelings in every way entitled to respect, and have decidedly peaceably an authentic manner many questions of great constitutional importance".*

Our jurisprudence has not been well developed. The reason, in my opinion, is that when the procedural and evidential laws are considered, the pursuit of such an enterprise would be quite expensive.

To carry out investigation that will lead to the establishment of criminal proceedings to a logical end is a task that only a wealthy citizen can accomplish.

Under the common law as received and practised in Anglophone Cameroon, discretionary powers to prosecute or not to prosecute are exercised at a three-tier level of the Department of Public Prosecutions. The principle being to ensure that an innocent citizen should not be deprived of his liberty for a flimsy reason or reasons.

1. common cause for dropping minor charges is that the citizens cannot cope with the overwhelming number of cases awaiting trial.
2. prosecution may serve no useful purpose, e.g., disorderly conduct and domestic disputes.
3. where criminal prosecution is instigated for ulterior motives i.e. to collect debts or restitution.
4. whether there's sufficient evidence in support of the facts to justify the institution of criminal proceedings.
5. citizens are guided by the rule that prosecutors must use their good sense as regards the application of old regulations which may be out of date and unrelated to modern conditions.

The police or law enforcement agents exercise these powers as soon as a suspect is apprehended. Even then the apprehension must be on reasonable suspicion, not at the whim and caprice of the public official.

---

[4] "History of the Criminal Law of England" Vol. 1.

Where the arrest is reasonable and there is good cause to introduce a criminal charge against the suspect the police may detain such a person and thus set in motion the machinery of justice. In many cases, the investigation may reveal that an offence has been committed.

Nevertheless, to suggest that the police must arrest everyone suspected of committing an offence is unacceptable. There is and there should be no duty imposed upon the police or enforcement agencies to arrest or prosecute every citizen indiscriminately.

In Anglophone Cameroon *in my time* these tenets were scrupulously respected. The sight of a police constable was welcome relief whenever there was a brawl or dispute of any sort between individuals; even in cases where a stranger in strange surroundings could not find his way. The law enforcement agent gave him/her assurance of immediate and willing assistance.

Enter the Gendarmes

On the other hand, after October 1, 1961, Anglophone Cameroonians suffered from a cultural shock. Firstly, a new agent of law enforcement appeared on the scene. The gendarmes are a paramilitary force looked at from any standpoint. They are armed and ruthless in their understanding of keeping the peace. Probably they are taught to be brutal in their manner of apprehending suspects. The use of force and a tendency to detain anyone who questioned their powers of arrest is part of their sub-culture.

Stories abound of the abuse of these powers by the administrative authorities at their various levels. There is the one where the *Prefect* or Senior Divisional Officer is alleged to have been lustful of somebody's wife. He signed, using his powers, an order of detention for the husband and thereafter had his way. The gendarmes will never question a Prefect's order. The most they insist on would be to ensure that it was written and duly signed.

Law No. 90-54 of 19 December 1990 *relating to the maintenance of law and order* enacted as part of what the Cameroonian Legislature described as 'Special Liberties'; which for the sake of clarity, provides in section 2 as follows:

" – *Administrative authorities may, at all times and depending on the circumstances, take the following measurers within the framework of operation for the maintenance;*
– *control the movement of persons and goods;*
– *requisition persons and goods according to the law;*
- *requisition the police and gendarmerie to maintain or restore order;*

— *take measures to detain persons for renewable period of fifteen (15) days in order to fight banditry."*

Preceding this section, there is the provision in section 1 that *"…. the law shall lay down these principles to be observed by administrative authorities and the forces of law and order in time of peace to maintain or restore law and order when it is threatened".*

It is worthy of note that these provisions are intended to be invoked by administrative authorities in time of peace. One then wonders whether they do not run counter to article 16 of Ordinance No. 72/4 of 26 August 1972 which empowers the High Court to hear and determine the immediate release of persons imprisoned or detained illegally. I do not intend to go into the provisions enshrined in the new Criminal Procedure Code which deal with the rights and protection of the rights of the individual. We may well have to wait sometime to see how the courts interpret these provisions over a period of time.

Loh Emmanuel Mufi, Loh Michael Akeh, Ngundu Anthony Abonge, Aghoh Michael and Agiam Ivo Vuzenegho were all natives of the village of Kedjom Ketinguh, otherwise known as Babanki Tungo in the Mezam Division of the North West Province. They are by any standard enlightened people of their community. The first-named was a retired civil servant and at the material time discharging the functions of the Traditional Council of the village and in that capacity represented the chief in all public activities. The second person was an educationist; the third, like the second an educationist, the fourth was a quarter head of the village and the last mentioned was a serving Senior Superintendent of the Central Prison, Bafoussam, in the West Province.

The five persons were on May 9, 1995, summoned at the *gendarmerie company* by one Pagou Philippe who, at the material time, was commanding the company in Bamenda. On arrival at the company, the five were ordered to be detained for no good cause or lawful justification.

When our Firm was consulted by the relatives of the detainees, Counsel wrote to the Commandant to know why these men were detained. The answer was a rebuff. All along the detainees were informed by the commandant that he was acting on the orders of the Prefect of Mezam, an administrative authority.

On May 18, 1995, Counsel applied to the High Court, Mezam, for leave to bring a *habeas corpus* action against the commandant. On May 22, the application was granted. Notwithstanding the order, the detention persisted. Both Counsel and the detainees were informed that their continuous detention was by the administrative authority who, at the material time, was represented by one *Sufo Samuel*, the Prefect of Mezam. Leave is not required under article 16 of Ordinance No. 72/6 of 26 August 1972. This Ordinance was abrogated by Law No. 75/16 of 8 December 1975 in its article 41.

While the detainees remained in detention, they were subjected to penal servitude such as grass cutting and carrying of water.

Having thus been frustrated by the intransigence of the administrative authorities even when the court had ordered the release of the detainees, it was found that a civil suit against the individuals for taking the law into their hands would be appropriate. General and exemplary damages were claimed against the Prefect and the commandant jointly and severally in their personal capacities.

After a hearing lasting over one year, Mr Sufo Samuel and Mr Pagou Philippe were jointly ordered to pay the defendants, namely, the detainees the sum of ten million (10.000.000) francs cfa plus costs of two hundred thousand (200.000) frs cfa.

As of today the detainees have not reaped the fruits of the judgment and every obstruction has been placed in their way of doing so. Mr Sufo Samuel, the Prefect, subsequently died and the estate remains unattached.

The case brings out the nakedness of our justice system today due to the overriding dominance of the administration over the judiciary. Many are not aware of this case because there does not exist any system of law reporting in Cameroon. This renders lawyers and legal scholars ignorant of the development of the law and thus its aberrations are buried in the archives of the court.

This case is important because of the principles of justice invoked in the provisions of Law No. 90-54 of 19 December 1990.

The act of both the Prefect and the company commandant violated the rights of those detained to the extent that the order of the court was of no consequence to them. The damages awarded by the civil court are virtually unclaimable because the State machinery for enforcing such remedies is moribund.

It should be observed that the gendarmerie in Cameroon are a paramilitary force and experience has shown that they are generally high-handed in their brutal treatment of the citizens. Cameroonians are all too familiar with *"operation calé-calé"* usually carried out in big urban centres. This consists of breaking into private homes around 5 a.m. and getting everyone forcefully to the streets or some open space in the quarter where they are systematically searched and beaten. The rationale in these operations is that there are bandits and dangerous elements refuging therein.

In the street or open space, everyone and I mean everyone, man, woman and child, is striped to the pants and forced to sit on the ground. Sadistically, the wet places such as water pools are preferred. Any resistance by anyone is visited by flogging and kicks with military boots.

The result has turned out to be negative in that the gendarmes are among the law enforcement agents who are a hated and detested lot. No citizen is willing to cooperate or collaborate with them in the discharge of their supposed noble task.

Obviously, the law we are dealing with neglects the very concept of human rights; the dignity of the human being is consistently abused. The citizen is denied the *"unalienable rights, ... Life, Liberty, and the Pursuit of Happiness"* an idea bought from the Americans by all civilized and enlightened people of the world. In a word, it dehumanizes the human being. These are instances where the perpetuators of such acts should be brought under the provisions of section 291 of the Penal Code which punishes those *whoever in any manner* deprive another of his liberty. The forces of law and order seem to enjoy an undefined immunity. They are known, where pressure is brought to be bear on them to set criminal process in motions, to frustrate it by putting off the credible and potential witnesses from testifying.

Under these circumstances, not even the Public Prosecutor (*procurer de la Republique*) can do anything. The end result is a trial where either the State Counsel or sitting Magistrate/ Judge is compelled to dismiss the matter for want of evidence.

This state of affairs has led to members of the public taking the law into their hands by summarily killing or maiming anyone they are convinced has committed an offence. The tools used include putting a tyre round the suspect's neck (*called a ring*) or hammering a nail into his head. It has come to be popularly referred to as *jungle justice*.

For those who experienced the working of the machinery of justice in the Federated State of West Cameroon, this is beyond their comprehension. It appears as if the entire world is an Armageddon.

The function of prosecuting in the Federated State of West Cameroon was as exciting as it was challenging.

In the discharge of my functions as prosecuting Counsel, I was guided and inspired by the principle enunciated by Sir Christmas Humphrey in an address to law students on the duties of a prosecuting counsel. On that occasion, he said:

> *"It is not the duty of prosecuting counsel to procure a conviction; nor should any prosecutor ever feel pride or satisfaction in the mere fact of success...*

Always the principle holds that Crown Counsel (State Counsel) is concerned with justice first justice second and conviction a very bad third".

It is sad to note that, today, the discretion to prosecute is an abuse of the cardinal principle of the basic freedoms even where they have been legislated upon. The 1990 Liberty Laws in practice have not worked out as intended by the legislator. Our prisons and detention centers like the police and gendarme lock-ups are still infested with *awaiting trials,* some of whom, if not the majority, are young persons. This is an unacceptable phenomenon at a time when the crusade for the enforcement of human rights has taken first place in the international agenda.

The manner in which some of the cases are handled gives room for wondering whether the prosecuting authorities do not benefit from such acts in one way or the other.

To the West Cameroonian a law enforcement agency appeared on the scene of law maintenance and peace keeping.

Before the union he experienced a force that was committed to protecting the citizen and his property. To control a rowdy crowd of demonstrators, the worst weapon used was the baton. It was carried around the waist. Invariably, it was used as a weapon of defence against an aggressive crowd. Put very simply, the *baton was a shield rather than a sword* employed to ward off an attacking group of rioters.

The gendarmes were another force, not to substitute or replace the existing force but in addition to the one already in place.

They carried lethal weapons, namely, pistols and wore red berets; hence they were generally referred to as the red berets. The sight of a *red beret* invoked in every citizen the use of force and brutality.

They behaved like a force of occupation, striking terror in everyone in the way they discharged their supposed duty as peacekeepers or protectors of the person of the individual or his property.

What the West Cameroonians did not know was that this was a force that had para-military training.

The manner in which gendarmes conducted themselves was so repulsive and repellant to West Cameroonians that people began wondering what action to take to stop such bestial attitude to the citizen.

For example, they allowed themselves to be used as debt collectors. Any creditor who couldn't get the debtor pay up his debt, lodged a complaint with the gendarmerie. The debtor was arrested and detained in a brigade and tortured to the point where he was forced to pay the debt. Naturally, this was done at a price to the creditor. This naturally led to corrupt practices on the part of the gendarmes.

In the State of West Cameroon, the gendarmes were an irrelevant force. In the eyes of the West Cameroonians, they symbolised the force from which its appellation was derived, namely, *gens des armes*, the ordinary French citizens or masses who, in order to storm the bastille (1789), picked up any weapon they could lay their hands on.

The protruding pistols around the waists and red berets did not assure the West Cameroonians that they could be a State apparatus out to protect them or their property.

As often as nearly always happens, there was a listening ear somewhere. Someone who had a better perception of the future of the union came up with a brilliant idea.

Bright ideas are not the monopoly of intellectuals or academicians. In the majority of cases, they are usually from the simple, ordinary and realistic individuals.

Mr Issa Bakari can't be described as being erudite. He was a simple man with common sense which, to many, is uncommon. He held a State position that made him take a common sense decision that went a long way to allay the fears and restless resentment of West Cameroonians. He was charged with responsibility for gendarmerie, *as the Delegate for gendarmerie in the Ministry of Armed Forces* – and was then called upon to make his contribution. He had a bright idea.

He argued that if West Cameroonians recruited as gendarmes had to learn French in order to comply with the procedures applicable in East Cameroon, why shouldn't the French speaking Cameroonians be subjected to the same conditions when posted to serve in West Cameroon.

He went on to propose and it was readily accepted by President Ahmadou Ahidjo that francophones serving in West Cameroon and assigned to investigate cases should be obliged to acquaint themselves with the procedures and mechanics of prosecuting criminal cases applicable in the State of their service.

The outcome of this important policy decision was the establishment of Prosecuting Offices (Bureaux du Procureur in all gendarmerie brigades throughout West Cameroon.

The gendarmes posted to these offices had to undergo at regular intervals courses of training in criminal procedure and the law of evidence. These courses were delivered by members of the Legal Department under the direction and supervision of Mr Rupert Thomas, as he then was, an expatriate from Guyana. His experience and age were determinant. I assisted on several occasions in delivering these lectures.

Just before the abolition of these offices, the gendarmes who had been privileged to benefit from these courses were very appreciative. The courses had helped immensely to sharpen their wits.

The abolition was necessitated by the fact that it was absolutely imperative to decentralise the Legal Department and have it manned by professionals. Maybe, to do away with police or gendarme prosecutors in West Cameroon. This was so soon after the constitutional changes in 1972 that decreed the death of the Federation.

Paucity of trained Lawyers

At the dawn of unification, West Cameroon suffered a paucity of trained professional lawyers. This gap was bridged by a recruitment exercise undertaken by the Hon. Emmanuel Tabe Egbe, then Vice-Minister of Justice. The Hon. Sanda Oumarou was the Minister of Justice.

Mr Egbe was a trained British lawyer. On return home, he had a stint with the Cameroon Development Corporation (CDC) as Legal Adviser. When the KNDP won the 1959 elections, he was made the Speaker and relinquished that post to Hon. Paul M. Kale consequent upon his appointment as the Vice-Minister of Justice.

With his appointment, it was decided that he should undertake a recruitment tour of the West Indies. Why the West Indies? Possibly Mr Egbe during his legal studies in London might have made acquaintances with some brilliant Barristers from that part of the World. In the fifties and sixties, the West Indians constituted a great black population in Great Britain.

I count myself fortunate that for the greater part of my time spent in the Legal Department, many doors were opened to me for continuing legal education which should be encouraged for all legal and judicial officers.

In 1974, I was selected to undertake a six months' course in Legislative and Treaty Drafting – October 1974 – March 1975. This was organized by the Overseas Development Agency of the government of the United Kingdom. During the course, I met interesting colleagues from far away places like Singapore, *Trinidad and Tobago* and Afghanistan. The exception was the guy from Afghanistan who did not speak English well. And yet he was said to be in the Foreign Affairs Ministry of his country. Generally, each participant had no less than seven years experience working with government either as a legal or judicial officer. Because we were from common law jurisdictions, it was an interesting exposure. The drafting exercise was exacting. Each exercise was immediately followed by a practical discussion. For example, an imaginary conference to meet and discuss a treaty either bilateral or multilateral would be preceded by parties discussing a draft that each participant had proposed on an imaginary subject or conference.

Below is a detailed list of those who participated in this important Course:

GOVERNMENT LEGAL OFFICERS FROM OVERSEAS
COURSE 1974 – 175
DIRECTOR OF STUDIES   F C S Bayliss MBE, TD, BA.

MEMBERS OF THE COURSE:

Afghanistan: Mr A Alami   Director, Foreign Relations & Planning Dept, Ministry of Justice.
Bangladesh: Mr A. Hossain   Deputy Secretary, Ministry of Law.
Barbados: Mr E.G Husbands   Senior Crown Counsel
Botswana: Mr E W Legwaila   State Counsel
Cameroon: Mr N Wakai   Procureur General
Gambia: Mr W G Grante   Registrar General
Hong Kong: Mr K W T Y Lee   Crown Counsel
India: Mr M L Gupta   Assistant Legal Adviser
     Mr I S Mathur   Deputy Secretary & Deputy Legal Remembrancer
Malaysia: Mr M. Kamil Awang   Senior Federal Counsel
Nigeria:
- Dr O Aina   Senior State Counsel
- Mr R O Obileye   Senior State Counsel
- Mr S O Ojutalayo   Senior State Counsel
- Mr G I Uloko   Senior State Counsel

Pakistan: Mr M A M Tiwana   Deputy Secretary, Ministry of Law and Parliamentary Affairs
Singapore: Mr P G Lim   State Counsel
Sri Lanka: Mr S Sivarasa   Senior State Counsel (Ceylon)
Sudan:
- Mr A M El-Awad   Senior Legal Counsel
- Mr A E El-Neel   Assistant Legal Counsel
- Mr A M O Yassin   Assistant Legal Counsel

Four years later, in 1978, I was, once again, under a professional exchange program, organized by "Operation Crossroads Africa", to undertake a course in the "American System of Courts and the Legal Process".

I considered this as another door opened to me to share experiences and ideas with fellow Africans. They were from West Africa and

Southern Africa. Discussing with people of the adult world is always enriching. That is what it was.

I have said earlier that I was fortunate to have had these opportunities of furthering my legal education outside the routine work of prosecution. At the time Mr Emmanuel F. Tatabod and I assumed duty in the Attorney-General's Department, Buea, there were already three Cameroonians in place. These were Messrs. Frederick Ngomba Eko, Ekor'h Tarh and Francis Monekosso. Of the three, I had the recognizance of only one, namely, Mr Eko. He preceded me to study law in Britain. When I met him in London, we discovered that we both were enrolled and eventually called to the Bar by the same Inn of Court – Lincoln's.

Mr Tatabod and myself, apart from studying in Britain as contemporaries, knew ourselves well having passed through the Cameroon Protestant College, Bali, and worked in Buea West Cameroon as clerks. He, in the courts and I, in the Ministry. Although he went for legal studies a year before me, we were both called to the English Bar in the term. He by Gray's Inn and I by Lincoln's.

Like Mr Monekosso, I met Mr Hans Ekor'h Tarh for the first time in Buea. He had been a teacher with the Native Administration and taught for several years before going to study Law in Ghana as I was informed. He was the oldest amongst all of us including Fred Eko, the Assistant Attorney-General. Mr Monekosso had a working experience in the Treasury of West Cameroon.

Socially, outside the department, Monekosso, Tatabod and I spent good times. As young bachelors, we were located in the Buea Mountain Hotel chalets

Mr Tarh did not really feature in these revelries as he was already married with a large family.

That's why I count my blessings to have, among my colleagues, been privileged to undertake these courses. They provided me with the exposure that is so essential to professional experience.

There is no doubt that the expatriate professionals, recruited during this time, were of the highest calibre.

In 1960 the Federal Supreme Court Ordinance of Nigeria was enacted and in section 2 (2) its application was extended to the Southern Cameroons which was then deemed to be a region of Nigeria.

By Article 1 of the Federal Constitution of Cameroon, the component parts of the Federation were the "Territory of the Republic of Cameroon" henceforth called East Cameroon, and the Territory of the Southern

Cameroons formerly under United Kingdom administration, henceforth called West Cameroon.

So that before Oct. 1 1961 when the Southern Cameroon united with the Republic of Cameroon which had become independent on January 1, 1960, the Southern Cameroons had a Supreme Court which exercised both original and appellate jurisdiction.

This situation was to remain in force in keeping with the provisions of Article 46 of the Federal Constitution of Cameroon in so far as there was no conflict with the Federal Constitution.

The stage for the administration of justice in the Federated State of West Cameroon was well and truly laid by the necessary constitutional and legal instruments. A brief assessment of the actors might be useful.

Those who constituted the Supreme Court of West Cameroon at the time and assumed duties in the Attorney-General's Department were:

Chief Justice
The Honourable Mr Justice K. L. Gordon

Judges
The Honourable Mr Justice W. K. Fergusson
The Honourable Mr Justice F. O. C Harris
The Honourable Mr Justice J. A Clarence Smith

By 1968 the composition had risen to five Judges inclusive of the Chief Justice and they were:

Chief Justice
The Honourable Mr Justice Michel Cotran. He was later succeeded by Honourable Mr Justice Charles Stewart from Northern Ireland.

Judges
The Honourable Mr Justice S. B. Kesiro
The Honourable Mr Justice S. M. L. Endeley
The Honourable Mr Justice V. R. Devish

(appointed Acting Judge on 17th December, 1967)
(appointed Judge on 12th June, 1968)
The Honourable Mr Justice J. A. O'Brien Quinn
(appointed Judge on 8th October, 1968)

These were men of immense experience and diverse origins. They shared one common trait. Their experience was based on a background overlaid in the common law. One case remained in doubt. This will be considered in its appropriate place in this work.

I consider it useful to briefly treat the contribution some of these learned men of the law made and the lasting impressions and inspirations they had on me and how, in turn, this influenced my outlook subsequently and my attitude and the ethic as concerns the administration of justice.

Mr Emmanuel Tatabod and myself assumed duties in the West Cameroon Attorney-General's Department on the same day. As customary, we had to pay a courtesy visit on the Chief Justice, namely, Hon. Justice Keith Gordon.

We made that visit to his official residence in the afternoon around 4 p.m. when we knew that he would have finished his siesta. It turned out to be an enriching experience. After we had been announced, it did not take long for him to come and meet us. He struck me as a man of good breeding and nobility. I was surprised with the fact that there was no show of officialdom with or about him. We did not have to sit for long waiting for the high priest from the Holy of Holies.

We both stood as a sign of due respect but he quickly motioned us to our seats and did everything to make us feel at ease and relaxed. There was no offer of a drink. We did not even expect it. We introduced ourselves. He then formally welcomed us to the profession. Every word he pronounced was one of encouragement. He told us we would soon find out that the stuff in our heads was different from the reality of practice. That we would suffer from court fright but sooner or later we would get over it. That anyone setting out in the profession needs experience. To him, hard work in studying our case files was the natural solution. He ended by wishing us well.

With the passage of time I found him to be a most admirable person and even as I record these facts, he remains to me as the best man that ever adorned the Cameroonian Bench. It does not matter on which shore of the Mungo you are standing. He was an indefatigable worker. The West Cameroon Law Reports of selected Judgments of the Supreme Court of West Cameroon as compiled, edited and annotated by J. A O'Brien Quinn for the years 1962, 1963 and 1964 and those for 1968 bear witness to this opinion.

He did a great lot to help uphold the common law in Cameroon. As earlier pointed out, the Supreme Court of West Cameroon was established to determine matters at first instance (High Court) and on appeal. Rather than be idle, he sat regularly at first instance. The Law Reports referred herein are testimony of devotion and commitment to his administration of Justice in Cameroon.

The result of the Hon. Emmanuel T. Egbe's expedition was extremely successful in terms of the quality and calibre of the personnel recruited. These consisted of brilliant and eminent men like the Honourable Mr Justice Keith L. Gordon who became the Chief Justice of West Cameroon. The other Justices were Mr Justice W. K. Fergusson, F. O. C. Harris and J. A. Clarence Smith.

Besides there were the magistrates like U. V Campell, Federal Counsel, F.G Smith Assistant Attorney General and on the Legal side were Mr P. L. U. Cross, holder of a *Distinguished Service Order* (DSO) earned as an accomplished Royal Air Force fighter during the second World War.

Barrister Oliver M. Inglis was specially recruited to take charge of the West Cameroon House of Assembly, as its clerk.

Subsequently a crop of English legal professionals began coming like Mr J. A. O'Brien Quinn who assumed functions as the Assistant Attorney–General and subsequently became head of that department. He finally handed over to a Cameroonian, Mr Fred Ngomba Eko whom, I in due time, succeeded.

All these professionals were well grounded in the common law, reason why the common law was sustained for a considerable time in West Cameroon.

Other names in the lower bench quickly come to mind – Mr J. B. Wyatt, P. P. P. Cameron, a tall and huge fellow, Mr Mitchell was subsequently raised to the higher bench. These latter ones were the English professionals recruited directly by the West Cameroon government after due consultation with the Ministry of Justice. The system worked very well because of the understanding and excellent rapport between Hon. Sanda Oumarou the Minister and Emmanuel T. Egbe, his Vice. The recruitment of the professional expatriates was certainly influenced by him. I believe the Minister left everything to him that concerned the Federated State of West Cameroon. In any case, he was a professional in his own right. He did a good job in that, those recruited, were by any standard, of exemplary character and erudition.

CHAPTER III
THE LEGAL PROFESSION

The cult of the robe means 'the concept of the judge as a high priest with special talents for elucidation of the "law" that sacred and mysterious text which is inscrutable even to the educated layman forms a sort of institutional charisma which is bestowed on judges with their oath of office.

I am not sure that our lawyers are aware of the '*Universal Declaration on the Independence of Justice*' adopted at the final plenary session of the First World Conference on the Independence of Justice held at Montreal (Quebec Canada) on June 10th 1983. Many don't read; even material related to the profession. If they did, they would be touched by the provisions on the lawyers' functions.

Under Article 3.27, it is provided:

The functions of a Bar Association in ensuring the independence of the legal profession shall be *inter alia*:

    (a) to promote and uphold the cause of justice, without fear or favour;

    (b) to maintain the honour, dignity, integrity, competence, ethics, standard of conduct and discipline of the profession;

    (c) to defend the role of lawyers in society and preserve the independence of the profession;

    (d) to protect and define the dignity and independence of the judiciary;

    (e) to promote the free and equal access of the public to the system of justice including the provision of legal aid and advice....

The list is quite extensive under the declaration and I may leave it at this point because *prima facie* the functions are lucid.

The decadence in the Cameroon Bar had become so manifest that when Barrister Luke K. Sendze became the President of the Council (or *Batonier as addressed in French*), he inherited a deplorable state in the management of the finances and an absolute breakdown in discipline. He swung into action with all enthusiasm and seriousness.

What emerged from his administration was revealing. What he attempted to do was to bring once more sanity, discipline and honour to the Bar. He paid the price. He served but one term of two years. I understood very well the reason. The Bar was sick. Charlatans had control of the Bar and corruption found its way into its fabric.

Several times I abstained from meetings of the General Assembly of the Association. My reason. The first time I attended a meeting of the Association after enrolment as a private practitioner soon after my retirement from the judiciary, I came away absolutely disillusioned. The conduct of the proceedings was anything but decorous. It looked like a Portuguese Parliament. An occasion to make long and illogical harangues. Speakers were rudely interrupted.

Later, I leant that this was a tactic employed by those who had to account for their stewardship. They and their cohorts *would go on a filibuster* in order to wear out the honest and sincere ones so that after a long time of such diatribes, the majority, being worn out and tired would leave and so leave them to pass such resolutions that favoured them.

Having decided against spending my time in vain at meetings that ended up without any useful accomplishment, I decided to exercise my right of vote or choice by giving proxies to those members of the Bar believed to be beyond reproach. Once again, I was in for a shock. On one occasion, I was informed of the abuse to which these proxies were put, namely, selling them to contestants. My source was so dependable that I no longer bothered to know what goes on in the mad house, excuse me for the language. Nevertheless, I pay my dues to continue to show that I can be relied on to honour my obligations.

These are the times in which we live. Nobody really takes the law seriously. Applying the law is burdensome. It's good for the Statute Book but not for our daily living, at least not when it may be a source of inconvenience to ourselves and friends.

The judicial machine will never cease to function well if the lawyer abdicates from the sublime objectives of his profession. The inspirational words of the English Mr Justice Grampson in laying down the *forensic duty of the Advocate* are relevant and pertinent in this instance. He said:

> *"This court in which we sit is a temple of Justice, and the Advocate at the Bar, as well as the Judge on the Bench, are equally ministers in that temple. The object of all equally, should be the attainment of justice; now justice is only to be reached through the ascertainment of the truth, and the instrument which our law presents to us for the ascertainment of the truth and falsehood of a criminous charge is the trial by jury; the trial is the process by which we endeavour to find out the truth. Slow and laborious, and perplexed and doubtful in its issue that pursuit often proves; but we are all-Judges, Jurors, Advocates and Attorneys-together concerned in this search for the truth; the pursuit is a noble one, and those are honoured who are the instruments engaged in it. The infirmity of human nature, and the strength of human passion, may lead us to take false views, and sometimes to embarrass and*

retard rather than to assist in attaining the great object; the temperament, the imagination and the feelings may all mislead us in the chase but let us never forget our high vocation as ministers of justice and interpreters of the law; let us never forget that the advancement of justice and the ascertainment of truth are higher objects and nobler results than any which in this place we can propose to ourselves. Let us never forget the Christian maxim: 'That we should not be evil that good may come of it'. I would say to the Advocate upon this subject let your zeal be as warm as your heart's blood, but let it be tempered with discretion and with self-respect, let your independence be firm, uncompromising, but let it be chastened by personal humility, let your love for liberty amount to a passion, but let it not appear to be a cloak for maliciousness.".

I have known cases in the Cameroon Bar that all fall short of these precepts. A president of the Bar Council Mr Monthe was alleged to have misappropriated hundreds of millions of client's money. Yet we have a beautiful text that forbids such practices by any lawyer. How did such a character get voted to be head of a professional body like the Bar Association, you may ask! The answer can't be too far to get. The obvious. Undue influence or money. Such cases are legion. If they were to be pursued, the Bar in Cameroon would count in the hundreds and not in the thousands as per the current roll.

Aspirants and pupil lawyers are supposedly trained regularly in the ethics of the profession. The reality in Cameroon is a joke. Their masters themselves are guilty of professional breaches of ethics and one wonders what examples they portray when in most cases the trainees know who and what they are.

How can anyone who to the knowledge of the public, embezzles client's money, notoriously touts and advertises his business, be taken seriously by the public or the community in which he practices. The result will be to transmit his bad ways, habits and practices to his pupils. This is bound to impugn the dignity and honour of the profession.

The outcome of these defaults by lawyers has been a breakdown of discipline in the profession and explains why the likes of Lawyer Luke Sendze of great focus and honour don't last in leadership positions; in their effort to instill discipline in an indiscipline society they are met with great resistance and unpopularity. It is like someone trying to be an angel in hell!

On call day to the English Bar, the newly qualified lawyer is given free a book entitled: *"Conduct and Etiquettes at the Bar"* by W. W. Boulton. From the title, it is clearly intended to be the lawyer's pocket bible.

Two factors in my opinion seem to account for the falling standards:

(a) the type or nature of training that a young aspirant or pupil undergoes. He may be articled with a lawyer who has not acquired enough experience to instruct a newcomer and in the majority of cases lacks a well equipped library which is the key to any learning process and exposure.

(b) the lack of a common training institution with a well planned and laid out programme. Such an institution would certainly be equipped with necessary literary works and follow a uniform scheme of work with tutors who are carefully selected from the world of outstanding practitioners themselves, men and women of probity dignity and who must not be less than five years in regular and active practice.

To achieve all these it is obvious that a legal body should be established to ensure that all the foregoing are in place. The body envisaged could be referred to as the Council for Legal Training. It should enjoy administrative and financial autonomy.

When we speak of the Bar, we mean the Bar Association. There is no Bar in Cameroon *strictu sensu*.

The West Cameron Bar Association was established under a West Cameroon Law of 1963, namely, Federal Law N°. 63-37 of 5 November 1963 to organise practice at the Bar of West Cameroon. The Federated State of East Cameroon had no such organisation because of the differences in and the attitude to the two legal cultures. The legal profession is differently conceived in the system inherited from France by Cameroon of French expression where the Code Napoleon was in vogue. We'll come to this later in this work.

Before 1963, Southern Cameroons was under British Administration as part of the Colony of Nigeria which had the profession structured as in Britain. The only difference in practice between Britain and the colonies to where the system was exported lay in the fact that whereas Britain divided the profession into Barristers (Advocates) and Solicitors, it was fused in the colonies.

The Solicitor trained in the law is legally qualified to act for another in a court of law (especially formerly a court of equity); advises, prepares deeds, manages cases, instructs counsel (barristers) in the higher courts and acts as advocate in the lower courts.

Barristers, on the other hand, are advocates or counselors learned in the law who have been admitted to plead at the bar and who are engaged in conducting trials or arguing causes. Simply put, they are qualified to plead at the bar in a law court.

In a fused system as adapted to the overseas territories one qualified in the law was both a barrister and solicitor, that is to say, instructing the barrister who pleaded before the courts and at the same time pleading before the same courts.

A barrister therefore draws up legal instruments as well as does advocacy. It blends very well and is certainly less expensive to the litigant or potential litigant.

The training of the barrister demanded qualities that were geared towards having them well cultivated in the study of the law.

I know that I may be accused of being nostalgic or for looking back at the good old days or memories.

All I dare say is that comparisons may be repulsive and there's always a tendency to regard the past as the glorious times. But we must agree with he who has said that "…. *history has relevance in so far as it enables us to use our knowledge of the past to tackle the problems of the present and thus fashion the shape of the future*".

When I and some of the older Cameroonian practitioners look back to the sixties and seventies we see in retrospect a very *dignified, respectable and self-respecting profession* – the pride of all lawyers, the ambition of many and an object of reverence by the generality of the people. I must confess that I decided to take to the law when I was doing my high school in Enugu, Nigeria (now the Enugu Campus of the University of Nigeria Nsukka). The event was a commission of inquiry set up to probe into the irregular award of contracts by the Regional Ministry of works. The Commission was headed by an eminent lawyer – Michael Ikpeazou. Both in his dignity, build and conduct, he was the embodiment of respectability and an object of reverence. Added to this, he drove a long American car; it must have been a chevrolet, buick or ford. I was very impressed. So I took my decision which I kept to myself until the opportunity offered itself.

I don't regret and will not regret that decision. I'm concerned with the present situation of the profession. Today, things have fallen apart. The *awe* and *reverence* with which the profession was associated have evaporated. The appellation of *learned and honourable* is now anathaema.

In my opinion, the new comers are not well instructed nor have they imbibed the traditions and conventions of the *great* profession. Traditions and conventions, as we know them, are the unwritten laws that govern any community of people. Even though they are unwritten, they sometimes have greater force than written law. The question we are called upon to answer is what can be done to restore the dignity, splendour and glory that once was the legal profession of yesteryears.

Before 1972 as we know, there was no structure in the Federated State of East Cameroon. In fact there were not more than eight private practitioners, and of this number between were expatriates. The Cameroonian practitioners were not more than four. The first list that was published after the passage of the above-cited law showed that both West Cameroon and East Cameroon did not have more that thirty-two private legal practitioners. West Cameroon had the greater number, namely twenty-two or more. All of them were trained in common law and in Great Britain. The East Cameroonian lawyers were trained in France and accordingly schooled in the Napoleonic Code, the basis of continental European civil law. The paucity of the number of francophone lawyers might have been the reason for the non-existence of a professional body like the Bar Association. That the first President of the Bar, was an Anglophone, in the person of F. Y. Gorji Dinka, was no surprise.

The lack of many practitioners in East Cameroon could not inspire the formation of a viable association.

The Law defined the academic qualifications and conditions of membership to the association, pupilage, that is internship and training for the initiated. It created a Role of Practitioners. The general rules governing practice and discipline were attended to. The Law has undergone several amendments. Each time an effort is made to have the association properly structured has ended in a fiasco.

Experience has taught us that it is not so much the content of the law that matters but those who administer it. It has been said time and again that *it is better to have bad laws and good judges than to have good laws and bad judges.* The same goes in all fields of human endeavour. The administration of the Cameroon Bar Association leaves much to be desired.

How can we be proud of a Bar where its leader misappropriates a huge sum of his client's money? That the elections to membership of the executive organ of the Bar is generally characterized by the selling and buying of votes is a chilling experience with an organization sworn to promote in every way the administration of justice. It doesn't portend well either for the future of the profession nor for our justice system.

In my opinion, Chief Justice Gordon deserves great tribute in that he successfully administered justice in a system that was baffling to many who wanted to see how the two systems would affect each other and at the same time be reconciled. Cameroon is the first country in Africa to attempt a reconciliation of the main legal systems in the world.

Added to this were the local customs recognised by the colonial administration because of the strong force that they exerted in the lives of the colonised peoples. The attitude of the courts to them was of great importance.

In West Cameroon which, before unification, applied three different systems of law, there was obviously an intermingling of the systems. In a Foreword to the first West Cameroon Law Reports (1962, 1963) by the honourable Emmanuel T. Egbe, then Deputy Minister of Justice, this pertinent observation was made:

> *"Such is the peculiar nature of our legal system. Judging from its origins, its principal features and operation in practice, it would hardly be wrong to say that our decided cases would be the most suitable when adopting and applying the doctrine of 'binding force of precedent'. Indeed, in some cases, cases cited under our system may be the only proper authorities to be decided.......This is why our courts owe a special duty of care to our people; care that when the systems in our system affect each other they are carefully reconciled and applied in the best interest of justice and, above all, care that their judgments are clear, precise and fully written. As pioneers in this enterprise, such is the duty they owe to our people and in particular, to the lawyers coming after them[5]"*

A few cases may be cited to show how Chief Justice Gordon tried to blend the three systems that the West Cameroon State attempted to fuse. One of such cases is that of *Njume Ngeh (by his next friend) Plaintiff vs. Gustave Etone Ngome* as defendant and the *Kome Ngeh (by his next friend) vs Gustave Etome Ngome* as defendant. This case was decided on 17th February 1964. To explain away the conundrum in the case, Chief Justice Gordon examined the facts:

> *"Defendant and Paulina Mekong had been married according to native law and custom for 10 years without issue, when in 1952 Paulina Mekong left and eventually went to live with Ngeh in the same year. On 28th January, 1953 Paulina Mekong gave birth to twin sons, the two plaintiffs and she and Ngeh and the twins have lived together ever since. Defendant brought a suit in the Native Court Kumba against Paulina Mekong for a declaration that the twins were his and was successful as Ngeh had not paid the full bride-price. On appeal to the Special Appeals Officer the decision of the Native Court on the paternity of the twins was upheld. This decision is now appealed against under Section 86 of the Southern Cameroons (Constitution) Order in*

---

[5] Reported at page 106 of the University of Yaounde Law Reports – 1968 - 1970

Council 1960. From the facts stated, there is no doubt that the twins were undoubtedly the issue of a union between Paul Ngeh and Paulina Mekong. The children at the time of trial were ten years old and should have been given an opportunity to testify in matters bearing directly on their future. This omission was in flagrant breach of the accepted principles of natural justice and of Section 76 of the Southern Cameroons (Constitution) Order in Council, 1960".

He then proceeded to declare null and void and of no valid effect the Order of the Special Appeals Officer.

In spite of statute law, the honourable Chief Justice took the natural and realistic view in this and similar cases when he said:

"It is in this setting that the Appeals Officer has allowed rules and regulations of native laws and customs to have so enslaved him as to have caused him to close his eyes to biological and other realities."

Another opportunity was offered the honourable Chief Justice when the court had to define the place of the Native Court in the justice system of the State of West Cameroon. This was in the case of: *Jesco Manga Williams vs. The President of Native Court Victoria*. The question before the court was whether or not the Victoria Native Court had full jurisdiction in causes relating to inheritance, testamentary disposition and the Administration of Estates and if so whether any other court can interfere with that jurisdiction. After distinguishing the applicability between the Native Court (Colony and Protectorate) Ordinance cap. 143 which by virtue of Section 1 applied to the "Colony and Protectorate including the Cameroons under British Mandate and the Native Courts Ordinance (Cap 142) which by virtue of Section 1 applied to the Colony and Protectorate (including the Cameroons under British Mandate) he concluded by stating the law on the point as follows:

"By Legal Notice No. 12 of 1962 the Victoria Native Courts are all Grade 'A' Native Courts, and by virtue of Section 8 as amended by Ordinance 8 of 1961 'A' grade courts have, inter alia,, "full jurisdiction in causes relating to inheritance, testamentary disposition, the administration of Estates and in causes in which no claim is made for, and which do not relate to, money or other property....".

It should, however, be noted that the term 'Native Court' was employed before the Adaptation of Existing Laws. As from 1st March 1964, the term 'Customary Court' had substituted it. Even though the decision was handed down on 15th May 1964, the original action had been filed under the old terminology. In fact, the action was commenced in the Native Court Victoria by the senior brother of the appellant, Chief Ferguson Manga Williams on the 19th February 1962.

I have made extensive references to these two cases because of the responsibility imposed on our courts to reconcile the legal systems and still do justice. Secondly, I admired Keith Gordon as a pioneer in laying a sound basis on which the common law flourished as a result of his hard work and devotion. The West Cameroon Law Reports covering the period 1962-1964 contain about 30 reported cases. Of these, the majority opinions were handed down by him, one opinion by W. K Ferguson who acted for him while he was on home leave and two opinions were by a panel that sat on his judgment because he heard it at original instance.

For a man to sit at first instance, hear appeals and effectively administer the department is an accomplishment worth admiration and emulation. I have dwelt on Chief Justice Keith Gordon because I regard him as an *icon* when it comes to honouring that tapestry of those who contributed immensely in laying the foundation of the common law in a Cameroon that was at cross-roads in building what Deputy Minister of Justice, the honourable Emmanuel Tabe Egbe, wished would be a unique system in Africa. We now know that it was nothing but a dream, unrealisable most of the times, like many dreams are; an ideal that is ephemeral.

His departure from Cameroon, even though all the expatriate staff were on contract, is a sad episode. He handed down a decision which a person in a high political position could not swallow. It was a divorce case – *Mensah vs. Mensah*. This embarrassment of the manner of ending his most valuable service in the Cameroon justice system left one with the question as to whither goeth justice.

These were the days of the existence of the West Cameroon Bar with Barrister Fidelis W. Atabong as the President. I was the Secretary. The Bar was regarded as having two branches; viz; the Private Bar and the Official Bar (for qualified barristers working for the state).

The occasion was a reception given by the Bar in the President's Residence at Mutengene – Tiko. An expensive ivory tusk was specially bought as a gift for the departing judicial luminary. After presentation, he turned round and handed it back and thanked the Bar for the gesture but added that he was not the person to have his services terminated by telegram. The party turned sour. In fact, he actually resigned on 30th September 1966.

Thus, we lost a great man of the law with the finest brains that could not be easily replaced. When he presided in the court, the atmosphere was one of awe and the aura around radiated the grandeur of justice. No one could doubt his dignity either in court or out of court. And yet he had a human side in that frame of his. At the club – the Buea Mountain Club – a heritage of British Administration, which he visited every Saturday, he sipped his favourite drink – cognac. He was admired and respected by Club members.

He could not, till he left, reconcile himself with Law No. 62-LF-10 of 9th November, 1962 which punished offenders for life for what is known as misappropriation of public funds. Every time the evidence was overwhelming and he had no choice but to convict, he would produce the text and read it from the first paragraph to the last. He would then end by saying:

"I am here to administer the law as I find it. I am not a law maker."

As was noted earlier, one of the judges that adorned the Supreme Court of the Federated State of West Cameroon during the Federation was the Honourable F. O. C. Harris. To me, he fell in the mould of Chief Justice Keith Gordon. Like Gordon, he was from the West Indies, most precisely from St. Lucia. He was ascetic and assiduous and would have fitted very well in a serious university environment. I did not see him much in the Club in contrast to Gordon. But I must quickly point out that he did not stay for long after I assumed duties. Our offices were all housed in the same building. At the time, the building was popularly referred to as the "West Cameroon Development Agency Building" because it happened to be the Headquarters of the West Cameroon Development Agency. It has two floors. The Agency Headquarters occupied the first floor and the Attorney-General's Chambers was on the ground floor.

I took the initiative to introduce myself to Mr Justice Harris. The niece lived in the same hostel with me during my last year in London. I went to see him to present the greetings from her. He was extremely busy but he gave me sufficient time to counsel me as a beginner. Just like Gordon had done when Tatabod and myself went to introduce ourselves. Each one in each case advised on hard work; preparing a case file well in advance of the trial or hearing.

For the few years that Justice Harris was in Cameroon, he succeeded to collect, edit and compile the 'Laws of the Federated State of West Cameroons' into volumes. These included the relevant Adaptations Orders and Legal Notices. By the time he was leaving, everything was in place except the printing. I believe we could easily have found a Printer specialised in this field had someone followed up this Herculean task done by one man in so short a time for many to benefit from. Unfortunately this great achievement remained in the dusty shelves of the Legal Department in Buea. On proclamation of the United Republic by President Ahmadou Ahidjo, they were carried to the Ministry of Justice. If my mind serves me right, it was Mr Mbella Mbape as either Secretary General or Director of Judicial Affairs who gave the marching orders. And so we have lost a treasure. Our future scholars will find themselves badly starved if and when the time comes to write our legal history.

I later learnt that the Honourable Justice Harris had been given a consultancy through the U.N by the Malawian government to carry out a revision of their laws to meet up with their newly acquired independent status.

In the same line the Honourable Justice Clarence Smith will go down in Cameroon Legal History as one of the architects of our bilingual Penal Code. I do not have much to say about him because the opportunity never offered itself for me to interact with him since he was based and worked mostly in Yaounde. He came to Buea only to complete the panel of the Court in its appellate jurisdiction.

The Honourable Mr Justice Charles Stewart replaced the Honourable Mr Justice Keith Gordon as Chief Justice of the Supreme Court of West Cameroon between 30 September 1966 and 15 September 1967. His recruitment is alleged to have been greatly influenced by Mr Emmanuel K. Mensah, then Legal Adviser to the West Cameroon government. He was attending a training course in legal drafting in Belfast, Northern Ireland, when he met the future Chief Justice.

There is little mentioned of him in the Law Reports published to date because of his short stay in that position and his contract having been terminated after one year because the political actors of the day found him rather controversial. For his one year's stay he never convicted any criminal. One came away with the impression that he was against the prosecution of criminals. I think that he wanted a very high standard of proof. Usually, he would dismiss the prosecution's case with very biting sarcasms and invective and sauciness. I remember well the case of *The People vs Peter Awa Ngwa (No 1)* where he, after listening to a witness, one Aji; he dismissed the Prosecution's case by concluding:

> "... *when it came to lying, this witness was fluent but when it was to tell the truth he stammered. It is on such evidence that the prosecution is asking me to perform the <u>acrobatic trick</u> by jumping to conclusions...*"

My boss, Mr Frederick Ngomba Eko, the Procureur Général who was leading the prosecution's case left the court with his head bursting with rage. It meant our case was so bad that we should never have thought of bringing it for trial.

In *The People vs Patrick Fokum*, the first sentence of his judgment was:
"The effect of this judgment is to discharge and acquit the accused...."

When a judgment is so commenced, is there any reason to bother to follow it to the end? All the beautiful legal reasoning which interests everyone kills interest. Nevertheless, I found the few judgments he delivered during his stay well crafted as far as the use of the English language goes. Sometimes his language was poetic.

His disappearance from the judicial scene in Cameroon was as quiet and unannounced as his appearance had been. *There goes Chief Justice of the Supreme Court of West Cameroon in the person of Charles Stewart.*

The Honourable Mr Justice Charles Stewart was succeeded by the Honourable Mr Justice R. L Mitchell in an acting capacity and soon left due to ill health. He was replaced by Mr Justice Michel Cotran. He was another interesting character study. He was believed to be a Jordanian by nationality. His legal qualifications and judicial experience remained questionable to the end. He had a son, Eugene with a very high academic standing and a lecturer in SOAS, (School of Oriental and African Studies), University of London. He was author of many books on African Law, particularly East African Law. That is that for his son.

The contribution to the development of the law by the Honourable Mr Justice Michel Cotran may be dismissed in a few words. He spent most of his useful time hobnobbing with politicians in Yaounde, the political capital.

A close study of the judicial situation in the West Cameroon Supreme Court discloses an interesting development by the end of 1966. All those Judges who assisted in laying the foundation of the judiciary in West Cameroon had left.

All to a man by resignation. Messrs. Justice W. K Fergusson on 8th February, 1996, F.O.C Harris on 24th June 1966, J.A Clarence Smith in July 1966 and finally Chief Justice K.L Gordon on 30th September, 1966.

It is a bit hard to find the reason for this exodus. Since they were sequential, I would like to hazard one. West Cameroon at unification was truly democratic and unification was fought on multiparty lines. 1964 was crucial for the party that had campaigned for unification, namely, the Kamerun National Democratic Party (KNDP). The party was riddled with internal dissentions and by 1965, there was no doubt that things were drifting towards a one Party system which, at the time, was fashionable. It finally came on September 1, 1966.

By premonition, these learned men of the law must have concluded that the place and role of the justice system would be put in doubt or come under the scrutiny of the political *gurus.*

The 1966/67 judicial year opened with a new panel consisting of the Honourable Mr Justice Michel Cotran Chief Justice, with the Honourable Messrs Justice S. B Kesiro, S. M. L Endeley, V. R. Dervish, and J. A O'Brien Quinn. The Honourable Mr Justice S. M. L Endeley was therefore the first Cameroonian to be appointed to the Supreme Court of West Cameroon.

The public commissions of inquiry provided me with an enriching experience in the dynamics of public prosecutions.

Commissions of inquiry were said to be *fact-finding* bodies which did not pronounce on a penalty or penalties but restricted themselves to making recommendations that could lead to a judicial or administrative sanction.

Nevertheless, the skill and exacting detail required in establishing facts are the same. In a criminal prosecution the prosecutor is concerned with establishing unassailable evidence that must secure a conviction. The high standard of proof decreed by the law, statute or convention hunts throughout the process.

I recall very vividly how I used to spend sleepless nights writing down all the questions I would ask a witness while leading him in chief. That would be followed by the possible questions in cross-examination. What a straight jacket in which I cast my human actors. I never realized that both prosecutor and witness usually come under the spell of the aura of a silent courtroom with anxious eyes watching an unfolding drama.

In the relaxed environment of a Chambers the witness knows that counsel will do everything to assist him to tell his story. The story is their story. He does not, for one moment, think that the story is his and his own only. Counsel is tied down by rules that limit him as to what questions to ask or not to ask. Above all, he can't predict what questions the opposing side may ask; in any case not all questions.

All notwithstanding, I learnt with the passage of time that my initial approach to indulge in the details of imagination in preparation was useful for a beginning. It made me, like it does everyone, to develop the habit of indulging in the minute. There lies the central point in the battle that rages in the courts. The *fine point* that will tilt the scales for or against.

The tribunal is expecting the opposing side to join issue. Come to what is at stake! Once that has been achieved, all the facts fall into place and the work of the court is made easy. There is no time for long speeches or filibustering. An experienced court will easily detect it and rule the faulty party out. You will often hear the court or Judge say: "will counsel get to the point". That is a hint that counsel is talking irrelevant nonsense. If counsel ignores this hint, he could incur the wrath of the presiding judge. 'Patient as a judge', has its limits.

Years of prosecuting earns one an incisive mind. A virtue than a vice! A prosecutor who realizes his role as that of a minister of justice will soon discover that only facts unemotionally presented will achieve the ends of justice. Sir Christmas Humphreys has been quoted in this regard.

His profound statement on the role of the prosecutor remains the beacon that guided me in the years I spent in the Department of Public Prosecutions, both as a junior member or its head. I enjoyed it to the fullest taxing as it was especially with extensive travels to cover assizes spread out in different parts of the Federated State of West Cameroon. Quite often the toll on my health, mostly bouts of malaria fever was heavy.

And when the commissions of inquiry were added to the plate, the strain and stress is best imagined than recounted.

Involvement with commissions had its beneficial aspects. They brought in their wake an awakening that public office is a public trust. The trustee should constantly remind himself or be reminded that the public has and will always have the power and responsibility to demand an account, if deemed necessary to do so publicly.

Personal gain or unlawful enrichment through holding such an office should be probed and where abuse is established such action as is equitable should be put in motion with a view to exacting a sanction in accordance with the principles of fair play.

It is a matter for regret that present day administrations or government are reluctant or find it difficult to invoke these salutary measures which have worked in the past. Certainly these precedents can be followed. Talk of corruption that has eaten into the national fabric (psyche) would not find much of a place in our vocabulary. The lesson that has been taught Cameroonians is that: "if you can't beat them, join them".

Chapter IV
Legal Cultures

Here lies the difference in the legal cultures inherited at the dawn of unification. The Common Law as received in West Cameroon was declared in sections 10 etc; etc; to be:

"10. *The jurisdiction vested in the High Court shall so far as practice and procedure are concerned, be exercised in the manner provided by this law or any other written law, or by such rules and orders of court as may be made pursuant to this law or any other written law, and in the absence thereof in substantial conformity with the practice and procedure for the time being of Her Majesty's High Court of Justice in England.*

11. *Subject to the provisions of any written law and in particular of this section and of sections 10, 15 and 22 of this Law cited as the Southern Cameroons High Court Law 1955.*
    - *(a) the common law,*
    - *(b) the doctrines of equity; and*
    - *(c) the statutes of general application which were in force in England on the 1ˢᵗ day of January, 1900, shall in so far as they relate to any matter with respect to which the Legislature of the Southern Cameroons is for the time being competent to make laws, be in force within the jurisdiction of the court.*

12. *Subject to the express provisions of any written law, every civil cause or matter commenced in the High Court concurrently and in the same manner as they are administered by Her Majesty's High Court of Justice in England.*"

Generally speaking Cameroon law is the product of its heritage. Until harmonisation is achieved, the dichotomy will continue to exist. Harmonisation will codify the laws. Codification has to be brought about through legislation.

The administration of a uniform criminal process will only be achieved by a legislative enactment on procedure. Until that event takes place, the Criminal Procedure Ordinance in use in the common law provinces must persist while the 'Code d'Instruction' used in the civil law jurisdiction (Napoleonic derived) must be invoked in the criminal sphere.

To me the differences found in the two enactments do affect, to a great extent, the end result of the administration of criminal justice. The philosophy behind the very basis of these enactments can be said to be the same.

Then *Mbeng Mbeng vs. The People case* reported in West Cameroons Law Report 1968 page 83 goes to reveal the different views in the two systems of a finding of mitigating facts in a criminal case.

Mbeng Mbeng was the finance clerk in the Federal Inspector's Officer, Buea. He was charged and convicted of misappropriation of public funds. In considering the sentence to be inflicted on him, the trial judge found that there were mitigating factors in his favour. He took account of the fact that the section of the law under which he was convicted expressly provided the minimum that should be imposed under the circumstances. Not being satisfied with the conviction and sentence, he appealed to the Federal Court of Justice. In its reasoned opinion, the Court upheld the conviction but reduced the sentence below the minimum provided by the section of law under which he was convicted and sentenced. It laid down the principle that where mitigating factors are established, the court may impose a sentence below the minimum provided for in the enactment creating the offence.

This concept is new to the Common Law Judge accustomed to a system where no floor is provided for an offence; in which case the trial Judge may, in the circumstance, caution the convict or order the individual to enter into a recognisance to be of good behaviour for a specified length of time.

To the common law lawyer, *prima facie*, there is no "caution and discharge" under the system. Once convicted, a sentence must be imposed even less than the minimum provided by the law where mitigating factors exist. Here, we are, *"having a single Code whose words mean the same thing in the entire country but differently interpreted so long as the methods and sources of interpretation differ".*

This leads me to recall what a lawyer friend of mine once said when we were discussing the awards obtained in accident cases in the different regions where the systems apply. He expressed the opinion that if it had been destined that he should die in an accident, he would wish this to happen where the civil law operates. Experiences had shown that accident cases attracted huger awards there than in the common law jurisdiction. The standard of proof is different in so far as the two jurisdictions are concerned. Whereas the common law jurisdiction has a branch of law known as the *"Law of Evidence"*, the civil law operates on the basis of any means of proof and the judge's conscience. Our conversation took place before the coming into force of Ordinance No.

89/005 of 13 December 1989 to lay down the system of indemnifying victims of road accidents.

Something should be said about a problem posed by the proposed appointment of Mr S. M. L Endeley as a Judge of the West Cameroon Supreme Court. This is one of the first cases that, for the first time, brought to light the difference in the bijurial system as it was in the process of developing in Cameroon. It was noted earlier that Honourable E. T. Egbe, Deputy Minister of Justice, was a trained common lawyer. Members of the Bench in that system are recruited from a wide field. Government legally qualified personnel and those in private practice are put on the same scale and the best is chosen. Not so in the civil law system where the choice is limited to a corps who are products of a school for training legal and judicial personnel. However, common sense and good sense prevailed, it has never been repeated.

In the system practiced in West Cameroon, nobody would have questioned the qualifications, experience and ability of Mr S. M. L. Endeley. He was a successful legal practitioner where integrity and credentials more than qualified him for the Bench in the common system.

The differences in the two systems are clear. One system believes that members of the Bench can be trained in an institution. In Cameroon, the School of Public Administration and Magistracy or Ecole Normale de L'Administration et Magistrature (ENAM) in French, is established for that purpose. One who graduates therefrom is destined as a career civil servant because he has undertaken a specialised career training and not a professional appointed because of his professional experience or competence.

The other system believes in a professional corps that is completely independent of any control by the public administration. It aims at producing persons who are learned and competent in their chosen profession. They have had a common professional training and are governed by common ethics. The difference lies in their choice of service – the State or self-employment. It is generally believed, and I share the view that the system offers a good opportunity for anyone to ascertain and choose between the chaff and substance.

In the area of a justice system, the importance of this consideration of choice cannot be over emphasised. It believes that membership of the bench evolves. A good advocate is not necessarily or generally a good arbiter. They call for differences in attitudes and temperament.

Whereas an advocate's elocution is as spice in enunciating his understanding of a principle of law, the person on the bench struggles all the time to suppress his emotions. The advocate very often plays or at least is tempted to play to the gallery. The judge, on the other hand, restrains himself and his court from being transformed into *a circus or theatre*. He is more concerned with getting at the issue and having it resolved.

This is not to say that one approach is better than the other in the administration of justice. Justice is ephemeral and elusive. It takes persons with guts to administer it.

I have raised this point to show that the Honourable Emmanuel T. Egbe was unusually optimistic when he believed that Cameroon would be a good laboratory for a polygenous legal system.

One would have imagined that looking wider a field had solved the question of appointment to top positions in the legal and judicial service. The matter was, once again, put to the test when Mr Frederick Ngomba Eko, the first Cameroonian Procureur General of West Cameroon went on a training course and it was thought that he would resume duties in a higher position on return.

The set up in the Legal Department was such that I was his natural successor. Mr Eko himself when he was in his good moods usually referred to me as the "dauphin" especially when we went to see him to demand certain rights and privileges, not from him as such, but to push him to put these demands to the authorities in Yaounde.

Discussions over, Mr Eko would turn to me and address me in a solemn and formal way:

"Mr Wakai, there is no trade union in the department, you know.
Besides, you are the dauphin"

I would reply, "no, Fred, but we want but our rights". We got on very well as he respected my age and I his authority as the departmental head.

This interlude arises because I want to make the point that the legal and judicial service limited its choice within the service and also I want to show how it was not a principle of an open choice. It had been put to the test before the situation in the Legal Department arose.

The government in Buea thought that the formula applied in the case of the Honourable Mr Justice Endeley could be invoked on this occasion. Things had changed. There was no longer a deputy Minister of Justice who, during the consideration of Endeley's appointment, was an Anglophone, and a trained lawyer.

In the present instance, the *deputy position* had been scrapped. The incumbent Minister at the time was the Honourable Felix Sabal Leco, an administrator of vast experience. This was unacceptable to the decisions makers in the Ministry who did not find any provision in the rules and regulations governing the legal and judicial service in Cameroon to warrant it. The proposals of the West Cameroon government were unacceptable. The Procureur Général of West Cameroon accumulated his post with that of *'Avocat General de la cour supreme'* (Advocate General of the Supreme Court).

Proof Beyond Reasonable Doubt

What was the common denominator between Marcus Mbome, Victor Motuba and Emmanuel Ebako Bekondo? They were junior civil servants employed in various capacities in the forestry office in Kumba, South West Province. Mbome was the Finance Clerk, Motuba the Head Clerk while Emmanuel Ebako Bekondo was the office messenger responsible for opening and locking the office both at the commencement and end of the working day. The head of department kept a duplicate key.

As always, the unusual happened. It was on the 3rd November 1967. As the staff reported for work it was discovered that the office was broken into and the sum of 293,458 fcfa found to be missing. "Agartha Christie's epic was in the making".

After the preliminary inquiry, I was assigned to conduct the prosecution of the three who were jointly charged with misappropriation. Invoking the evidential principle of the swing of the pendulum, the trial judge, Justice S. M. L. Endeley, as he then was, discharged and acquitted the three accused persons.

It's noteworthy to follow the Judge's analysis of the facts and evidence before the verdict:

> *"On the evidence before me, I have no doubt that in accepting Mbome's, first accused, testimony as truthful and probable and accordingly in finding as a fact that (i) When he received the 350,000 francs from the Sub-Treasury he put the money in the envelope he was seen with, and that the slip Exhibit "A" was also in the said envelope. (ii) The figure 350,000 francs was boldly written on the back of the envelope. (iii) After paying out wages on the 3rd November, 1967, he returned the balance of the unpaid wages into the safe. (iv) When he handed the envelope containing the money and the safe key to Motuba on the 3rd November 1967 after receiving the supposed telephone message (about the father's grave illness), Motuba did not count it to verify whether or not it amounted to 350,000 francs and when Mbome took it back later that afternoon, he too did not count it to verify that it still was 350,000 francs. (v) In the confused state in which the supposed message left him, he inadvertently forgot to ensure that the safe was securely locked on 3rd November, 1967, after he had put the unpaid wages in the envelope back into it. (vi) On the 4th November, 1967, when the Police were called to the office,*

he did tell them that the slip Exhibit "A" was inside the envelope which contained the money.

The evidence surrounding Motuba, the 2nd defendant is a little more difficult to interpret in his favour. The timing of the telephone message which turned out to be as false as it was without foundation, is striking. The suggestion that Mbome proceed on two days' leave and the request that he hand over the safe key along with the money even before the Forest Officer (Mr Maimo) had arrived to be informed, are also very strange aspects of his behaviour in this particular day.

Ebako, the 3rd defendant is a very simple man and appeared rather sincere. He seemed to be pointing the accusing finger for this theft very directly to Motuba. From the nature and tenor of his evidence I find it impossible to infer that there was even the slightest element of concert between him and Motuba. Ebako was the last person to leave the office on the 3rd November. In the evidence he said that in offices where he had previously served as messenger-cleaner, he had on occasions found the safe unlocked and had kept its contents safe and intact until the officer in charge arrived. The significance of this evidence is that, as a messenger-cleaner Ebako must have acquired the habit of testing safe doors before closing the office. On a day like the 3rd November, when he well knew there was a large sum of money in the safe, it will be difficult to assume that he could have left without even casting a casual look at the safe... In fact from his cross-examination of Nyimen (Prosecution Witness1) and the apprentice mechanic, Patrick Wanda, he seemed to suggest that in the circumstances in which he saw them in the main office on 3rd November and 4th November, each of them also had the time and opportunity to have removed the money. The result of this evidence is that despite his apparent sincerity, Ebako does not appear as innocent of the theft as he would want the Court to believe.

The Court is placed in the position where the accusing finger has swung sharply and definitely from Mbome and is pointing strongly at Motuba and rather shakingly on Ebako. There is no evidence of concert between these two defendants. If, therefore, the money was taken by any one of them, he would have done so independently of the other.

The law governing situations of this nature was expounded in a number of celebrated cases... and may be summarized as follows: Where several defendants are charged with a criminal act, but only one unidentified defendant commits it, the jury must, in the absence of proof of a common design, ascertain who was the actual perpetrator, or failing this must acquit all.

In the present case while on the evidence before me I have no hesitation in clearing Mbome absolutely from the offence charged. I am unable to find *evidence of a common design between Motuba and Ebako and unable to identify with certainty which of them actually stole the sum lost.*

In the result, while I find Mbome completely innocent and therefore discharge him with an order of acquittal, I am impelled, even though reluctantly, to apply the law as cited above to Motuba and Ebako who are in effect also acquitted.

As soon as they were charged, they had been suspended from performing their functions. The question arose whether, after their discharge and acquittal, they could resume duty and in the same capacity. Their head of department thought otherwise. The matter was then placed before the West Cameroon Public Civil Service Commission. It would appear that the Commission was unanimous in its opinion and considered that a legal opinion was necessary to clarify the position.

The Secretary to the Commission was my childhood friend, the late Chief Solomon M. Nji III. A very assiduous and hard-working man.

I was then heading the legal department. I gave a written opinion. Simple. The individuals had been cleared by a discharge and acquittal which meant they had been placed in their positions **ante** particularly so in the absence of an appeal by the prosecuting department. Consequently upon this opinion, the three were reinstated in their different service positions.

Personally, the matter was dead and decently buried.

Months after, I returned home to find a big goat tied in the premises.

On inquiry, I was informed by the children it was brought by one Mr Marcus Mbome. I got in touch with Mr Mbome and requested him to see me in the Chambers. He answered my invitation. I asked him why he had to give me a goat. After all, was I not the one who prosecuted you? I asked.

He said: That is correct but you did something which no other prosecutor would do. You reinstated me in my civil service position. I have not only been reinstated but I have received my arrears of pay for the period I was suspected pending the completion of trial. Your opinion to the Public Service Commission changed the stand of my head of department, namely, the Chief Conservator of Forest.

I told him I wrote confidentially. Yes, I know, but my sympathizers on the Commission informed me in confidence. Sir, this is in appreciation of your sense of justice. You did your job without any bitterness. Thank you, Sir. I then dismissed him and convinced my family that we could have the goat. Convinced my family, because I had a standing instruction that no gift brought in my absence should ever be accepted. Mbome became the exception.

While Mbome was a public servant who had a brush with the Law, Paul Senju fell in a different class of persons seeking justice. Outside his reputation as a rich man in the locality, I had never met him until when the event I am about to recount, occurred.

It was a weekend and probably a Saturday afternoon. Christine was away in Nigeria where she was pursuing a degree course in the University of Nigeria, Nsukka.

She left me with the houseboy and our first three boys, namely, Abel, Terrence and Ache.

As we sat there waiting for lunch to be prepared, a vehicle drove in with three women in it. They wanted to know if I was the occupant of the residence. Buea had official and traditional residences for the heads of departments. That for the Attorney – General was by the wayside as you drove into Buea and immediately after the road branching to the Buea production prison as it was known at the time. It was production because there was a farm attached to it which produced food-stuffs for sale to members of the public and for feeding the prison inmates.

The driver of the car bringing the three women began unloading plantains, yams and drinks. Inquiry as to whom these items belonged revealed that the carriers were the wives of one Mr Paul Senju, a businessman in Tiko. By any standard Mr Senju, as I came to know him, was a very successful importer and exported sundry goods and articles.

One of his wives, Emerencia (née Simo) Senju is the elder sister of Miss Pauline Simo a good friend of my wife who was her schoolmate in Q. R. C. Okoyong, Mamfe. I knew Christine's friend because she was working in the Lands and Surveys department in Buea. This made the conversation more relaxed for me. The food they said was for the household since the woman of the home, meaning Christine, was away in Nigeria. The drinks were for me to entertain guests with. I expressed my ignorance of the husband. They told me he was planning to see me in person. He never came to visit me either at home or in the office. Then one afternoon, I went to Tiko for shopping. Both Tiko and Victoria (now Limbe) were the main shopping centers in those days. Apparently Mr Senju knew me but I did not really know him. His office overlooked a petrol station he was running.

As I pulled up to fuel my car someone ran out from the building, came to me and addressed me. He introduced himself as the husband of the women who had visited me with the food and drinks. He wanted me to join him in his office for a minute. I agreed. In his office, he said he was happy to have the opportunity to make my acquaintance, more so because of what I had done for him.

I said I did not know him although one of his wives had introduced herself as my wife's friend's elder sister. That is even better, he said.

He then went on to tell me about his travail with the customs and his imported goods. He told me how my predecessor had advised stringent and hard measures to be taken against him. He realized that I took a different view when, on appeal, the matter was referred to me which had saved him 75,000,000 francs in taxes and customs duties. He said I did so without even knowing him unlike my predecessor who knew him very well. I told him I was merely doing the work to the best of my own sense of justice of the case.

We soon became friendly but I did everything to keep a distance to avoid over familiarity especially with people of that calling who believe that money is everything.

All the same I thanked him for his generosity he and his family had demonstrated in the absence of my wife.

Like Marcus Mbome's case, I treated Mr Senju's and many other cases that can't all be recounted here without any emotion.

The story of unsolicited gifts would not be complete without the mention of one or two cases that I regarded as being Trojan gifts.

SOCOPAO (voyages) was and is a maritime carriage enterprise with headquarters in Douala, the main economic port of Cameroon. It has operated in Cameroon before and since independence. There is some basis to assert that such expatriate enterprises become arrogant with their Cameroonian employees or when dealing with small businesses on a local basis. Occasion arose for SOCOPAO to exhibit this attitude. Eventually it got up one day to find itself in a case of criminal defamation.

At the material time, I was acting Procureur Général in place of Mr Fred. Ngomba Eko who was on a training course in London.

SOCOPAO had obtained the services of no-less a Counsel than the late Mr Paul D. Koti. The latter had in a short time after call to the Bar by Gray's Inn, made a name as a defence lawyer on return to Cameroon.

The day the General Manager and his local representative in Victoria (now Limbe) decided to come and see me their Counsel was not aware.

The local representative introduced his boss to me while adding that they were there to see me in connection with the case against their company. I inquired of them if they were there with their Counsel. They denied. Without any hesitation, I told them I could not receive any of them in the absence of their Counsel. Thereafter I did not want to listen to any further discussion and so they were obliged to leave rather unceremoniously.

The following day, the secret broke. A relation of mine, the late Mr Michael K. Amaazee, a businessman in Victoria / Limbe, turned up in our Buea residence. He was the type of man who cannot keep a secret to himself. He said:

"Yes, I know that you do not take bribes. You refused a big bribe yesterday"

I asked him who told him I was offered a bribe not to talk of my refusing it. I did not know that he knew the local agent of SOCOPAO.

He then went on to narrate the story of my reception of the General Manager of SOCOPAO. They were at a drinking spot when his friend without knowing that he knew me began telling the story of the event the day before. He said there's a *"graffi boy"*[6] who does not know money. He went on to say how he was at the Procureur Général's Office to discuss the case against their company and the man said he would not listen to them unless their Counsel was present. That his boss had a fat envelope for the man. To him the local representation, it is the manner in which they were sent away that shocked him rather than the refusal to listen to their story.

To me, it only went to confirm my opinion that there is nothing hidden under the sun. Bribery or corruption would pass through dark alleys to arrive at its destination but sooner than later it would still be known or found out.

This scenario was repeated some years later when I was President of the Court of Appeal of the North West Province. It concerned a case that was pending on appeal. The parties were far from being equal before the law. A village chief and a big construction international company.

Fon (Chief) G.N. Ndikum II, the village chief of Akum, initiated an action against Groupement d'Enterprises itinera Mondelli Ltd claiming 500.000.000 francs cfa as damages for trespass onto his land, conversion of his property and causing inconvenience. Mr Justice George Mbanda Asu, a member of the Court of Appeal, heard the matter at first instance. He entered judgment in favour of the Chief in the sum of seventy million (70.000.000) francs cfa.

---

[6] A term used by the people of the coastal tribes to describe someone from the grassland region or grass fields.

Dissatisfied with the decision and award of the trial court, the company appealed to the Court of Appeal[7]. The Christmas of the year in which the trial court delivered its judgment, an incident of note took place. On the day in question, I was busy in my Chambers when a small vehicle drove into the premises of the court. Some strange person emerged from it carrying some cartons. He was directed to me after making the necessary inquiries. He said he was sent by his boss to deliver the parcel to me and my colleagues who were specifically mentioned in a note he had on him. My own packet looked bigger than that of any of my colleagues. Conspicuously, there was none for one of the members of the court, that is to say, Mr Justice George M. Asu, as he then was, who had heard the case at first instance. The contents as revealed were bottles of champagne. I invited in my colleagues who were equally the beneficiaries of the largess of Groupement d'Enterprises itinera Mondelli Ltd. All to a man they refused to have anything to do with the gift. The panel was going to be composed of myself, Mr Justice F.A.K. Monekosso (deceased) and Mr Justice S.M.A. Anyangwe (deceased).

I was so furious with this manifestation that I decided to write to the Barmi-Njoh Chambers headed by Barrister Luke K. Sendze registering in the strongest terms my sentiment about a matter pending before us. On his own part, Barrister Sendze wrote to his clients disapproving of their action taken without consulting him and stating that if they persisted in this manner, he would cease to represent their interest. He sent me a copy of his letter to his clients. The matter was then allowed to rest there.

In what follows hereafter are means employed by a government to demonstrate unequivocally that once formed, it remains accountable to its electors while the public officials are obliged to account to the government and the people at large.

A public official or government that has as an article of faith to receive gifts will certainly have its eyes blinded by the gifts. And there lies corruption and undue enrichment.

---

[7] Appeal No. BCA/46/83 of 12th June 1984.

CHAPTER V
GOOD GOVERNMENT AND GOVERNANCE

In defining government it should be generally regarded as an agent of State. It is characterized as embodying a constitution, written or unwritten, which spells out the functional institutions of the State. These are the executive, the legislative and the judiciary. Each in its own scheme of things operates as a machinery of government in ensuring that the public health, safety, morals, general welfare, security, prosperity and contentment of the inhabitants of a given political division is guaranteed.

Looked at from another point of view, government is that body of persons authorized to administer the laws that regulate the lives of the citizenry, in such a way as the Americans, in their *declaration of independence*, unequivocally avowed, namely that:

> *"all men are created equal; that they are endowed by their Creator with certain unalienable rights; that among those, are life, liberty, and the pursuit of happiness. That, to secure these rights, governments are instituted among men, deriving their just powers from the <u>consent</u> of the governed; that, whenever any form of government becomes <u>destructive of those ends</u>, it is that right of the people to alter or to abolish it and institute a new government, laying its foundation on such principles and organizing its powers in such form, as to them shall seem most likely to effect their safety and happiness."*

Good government in my opinion is therefore the structures set up by the State to ensure that they fulfill their missions in that those charged with their operation do so with transparency and are accountable for their public acts. The State would then have fulfilled its contract with the people. Failure by public officials to guarantee the good life, liberty and the pursuit of happiness, the State, through the officials fails in its mission.

The difference I make between good government and governance is that, in governance, the public officials prioritise the interests of the State. They put themselves before the State by exploiting the positions they are responsible for. Examples are numerous, e.g. corruption, bribery, clientelism in the use of the offices entrusted to them.

In order that good governance should be the order of the day, it is absolutely imperative that those who are called upon to serve their fellow citizens do so in transparency, not counting the cost and living lives that are exemplary so that they can be seen as deserving the honour given to them to promote the purposes and objectives propounded as a basis of good government.

Having said this as a prelude, let us now examine in some detail some of such cases that were intended to bring out the point by the institution of public commissions of inquiry in West Cameroon into the management of State enterprises.

There was under the Federated State of West Cameroon legislation on commissions of inquiry that provided that the Prime Minister, following the adaptations of the laws of the Federation of Nigeria, could, whenever he deemed it desirable, issue a commission appointing one or more commissioners, and authorizing such commissioners, or any quorum of them therein mentioned, to hold a commission of inquiry into:

- the conduct of any officer in the public service of the Federated State, or of any chief, or
- the management of any department of the public service, or of any local institution, or
- any matter in which, in his opinion, an inquiry would be for the public welfare. ....a secretary who shall perform such duties as the commissioners shall prescribe shall be appointed....

Each commission specified the subjects of inquiry, in the discretion of the Prime Minister, if there were more than one commissioners, directed which commissioner would be chairman, and directed where and when such inquiry would be made and the report thereof rendered, and prescribed how such commission would be executed.

The legislation in question was the Commissions of Inquiry Ordinance (cap 36). It further provided that such inquiry, subject to the powers of the commissioner provided in the enactment, would be held in public, unless the Prime Minister gave a direction to the contrary, but the commissioners would nevertheless be entitled to exclude any particular person for the preservation of order, for the due conduct of the inquiry, or for any other reason.

Any person whose conduct was the subject of inquiry .... Or who was in anyway implicated or concerned in the matter under inquiry was entitled to be represented by counsel at the whole of the inquiry, and any other person who considered it desirable that he should be so represented could by leave of the commissioners be represented in manner aforesaid.

The enactment finally demanded of the commissioners *"to make and furnish to the Prime Minister a full report in writing of their proceedings, and shall record an opinion and reasons leading to their conclusions. Any commissioner dissenting from conclusions, or any part thereof, shall note the reason for such dissent".*

The commissioners enjoyed immunity in that no commissioner was liable for any action or suit for any matter or thing done by him as such commissioner.

It is from this legal background that the legal department headed then by the late Fredrick Ngomba Eko and I got entangled in the task of probing publicly the lives of public officials.

I would say that 1967 to 1969 may be described more appropriately as the years of the inquiries. An inquiry into the management of the West Cameroon Electricity Corporation (abbreviated POWERCAM). Powercam was headed by a highly qualified Cameroonian with a very wide experience in the field in different parts of the world. He was Mr E. A. Mbiwan. The commission was presided over by Mr Rupert A. Thomas, then a Legal Adviser in the Prime Minister's Office and later to become the first President of the Court of Appeal, Bamenda, North West Province.

An inquiry into the management of the West Cameroon Development Agency, headed at the time by *Mr William P. Lebaga* as an Executive Board Chairman, having taken over from Mr R. J. K. Dibonge in 1960 who had held the position since 1959. The Chairman of the West Cameroon Development Agency's Commission of inquiry was an expatriate Judge, Mr Justice V. R. Dervish, a Turkish Cypriot. I enjoyed his sense of humour. Prior to the 1968/69 inquiries, there had been one commission a year before, in 1967, into the Lands and Surveys Department published as West Cameroon Notice No. 90 in the West Cameroon Gazette No. 13 Vol. 7 of 01 April, 1967.

This particular inquiry was chaired by Mr Oliver M. Inglis, then Clerk of the West Cameroon House of Assembly. He is a lawyer by training and was among those the West Indian governments placed at the disposal of the West Cameroon government for service. He preferred to stay on when his time was over. He is a naturalized Cameroonian and carries on private practice in Buea, the South West Provincial capital.

There is a recurrent decimal when the terns of reference of these inquiries are closely studied.

They dealt with investigating the conduct of public officials in the discharge of their functions either individually or corporately.

The West Cameroon Development Agency's Commission was to inquire into:

- allegations of corrupt practices against the entire management of the Agency, particularly in relation to the diversion of the Agency's property and labour for personal use;

- any other allegations of malpractices within the Agency and its subsidiaries;
- personal assets of past and present members of the Board before, during, and after their tenure of office and, if established or found that they had improperly enriched themselves by virtue of their positions in the Agency to recommend the fate of such ill-gotten property.

The commission had its foundation on allegations. These would obviously be by petition by probably credible members of the public. Then for any person to be penalised such a person should be heard in his defence publicly. Being allegations they had to be proved. An important aspect of these inquiries worth noting was that they were held in public. A classic example of a listening government. A legal requirement was that the report like the hearing should be made accessible and available to members of the public at large.

The *PowerCam* inquiry was very detailed and more specific in its terms almost pointing to particular persons. Like the West Cameroon Development Agency inquiry, it was to inquire into:-
- rampant allegations of tribalism, nepotism and favouritism against management in the employment of Cameroonian executive and senior grades staff and to:
  - ascertain whether promotions, recommendations for scholarship awards and conditions of service were based on tribal considerations than qualifications, experience, and efficiency and to inquire:-
  - whether the dismissal, redundancy, termination of certain employees were justified.

Like the West Cameroon Development Agency inquiry, PowerCam was to:
- investigate allegations of corrupt practices against management particularly in regard to:-
  (a) the diversion of the Corporation's labour, property and funds for personal use by members of the Board and Management.
  (b) any interest of any member of management in any of the electrical or allied undertakings in the territory.
- the expenditure of PowerCam since its inception and to ascertain whether such expenditure was justifiable.
- the assets and liabilities of PowerCam.

Put in the present political and judicial environment, it would be unthinkable and unimaginable that an inquiry on the basis of what has been considered here be set up even with all the legal paraphernalia clothing the system. Could anyone think of subjecting SONEL before privatisation, the Ports Authority, SNEC, Cameroon Airlines, Post Office Savings Bank, SCPD, almighty SONARA and Societé National des Hydrocarbures (SNH) with exactly the same terms of references as were operational in the Federated State of West Cameroon?

The Legal Department was appointed Counsel to all these Commissions. This was added responsibility to the normal work of litigation by the department. In the Inquiry into the Lands and Surveys, Mr George S. Ekema, as he then was, acted as Counsel for the Commission. Contrary to those already named, this inquiry was into a service department of government.

The following year, the Commissions dealt with corporations; in other words, with investments and with more at stake. A Cameroonian, Mr Frederick Ngomba Eko, was then the legal departmental head. We were fewer in the department than ever. Messrs. Hans Ekhor Tarh, Francis Adlof Monekosso, Emmanuel Fonjeh Tatabod as they then were, had moved to the bench.

I must confess (that) it was a trying time for a young couple, to miss the joy of an early consortium. Above all, Christine was expecting our first child. These times are usually moments of anxiety for newly weds. It is to her credit that she pulled it through and finally Abel Pwengong was born without much difficulty. I owe so much to her for the endurance demonstrated during those trying months.

We remained three in the department including the boss, Mr Joseph Patrick Chewang Nganje, as he then was and myself. The burden of appearing before the commissions that sat on a daily basis and still covering the Assizes during term, is best imagined than described. Once the assizes kicked off it entailed handling matters in Buea, followed by a journey to Bamenda, thereafter to Mamfe and ending up with Kumba, the principal towns of the Federated State of West Cameroon.

One remarkable fact which must not go without note is that cases were nearly always ready when the assize was to open in due term. The police investigators usually met Counsel covering the assizes on his arrival and fully briefed him on which cases were ready, which partially ready and which not.

'Call over' day was devoted to hearing dates with the certainty that the case would go on.

It is from this staffing background that the government of West Cameroon solicited from the Federal Government the services of the legal department in Buea. This was bound to be a strain on the department and the individual actors in this drama as we shall see later.

The three of us held a meeting in the boss's office as soon as the announcement was made regarding the appointment of each commission and its membership and officials.

Work was shared out. Mr Eko, the boss, opted to handle the PowerCam Inquiry. Months before the naming of the inquiries, the General Manager of PowerCam, Mr Mbiwan, was having a hard and rough time to contain Mr Eko's brother, George (Eko) a trained electrical engineer from the University of Denver in the United States.

George Eko's profile certainly could not match the accumulated experience of his boss. The argument was put up that George Eko's training was specifically electricity while Mbiwan's wasn't even though his training as an engineer in the United Kingdom wasn't in doubt.

As a matter of fact when Minister E. T. Egbe came to announce the setting up of the West Cameroon Development Agency commission, PowerCam was not included. In a discussion with Mr Eko as to appointing the department as Counsel – from what I overhead – my boss suggested that one should be appointed for PowerCam. His reasoning or argument was convincing on the face of it. He argued that *'everyone in West Cameroon knew that even though you are a Minister in the Federal Government, they equally know that you are the Chief Adviser to the present government in Buea'*. His Excellency was convinced. Eko was allowed to draft the terms of reference. When these terms are closely studied, it is clear that they were drafted with some individuals in view.

West Cameroon Development Agency inquiry was to expose the outgoing government in Buea while PowerCam was to get the General Manager out of the way and pave the way for George Eko. That's how I saw it. I still see it as such. But all these were done within the legal contexts and openly. Interesting events began to surface as soon as the Commissions began sitting.

There was usually drama in the course of the proceedings of each commission. In the case of the Development Agency Chairman, Mr William P. Lebaga, a lot of fuss was made about the fact that he had installed in Santa Coffee Estate a personal chicken incubator for the production of eggs for his personal use. To the government, this amounted to an abuse of office.

The most contentious and controversial inquiry was that of PowerCam. It was obvious that the General Manager was the target.

In dealing with Mr Mbiwan's financial condition at the time of the inquiry, Mr Njoh Litumbe of Akintola Williams's Firm of Accountants of international repute was summoned in to determine the situation.

In his report to the commission, Mr Litumbe stated:

"I have attempted to analyse as fast as I can, within the time available, all Mr Mbiwan's recorded financial transactions with a view to preparing a comprehensive statement of condition. There are still large amounts of expenditure which cannot be explained. To produce an accurate Statement of Condition would involve deducting from the total assets the unpaid liabilities pertaining to those assets.

In order to simplify matters, however, I have concerned myself with cash spent in acquiring various assets. This cash is not spent necessarily by Mr Mbiwan. If, as in the case of Industrial Development Trust, he struck an agreement whereby the cost of construction was depressed for <u>certain reasons</u>, the actual cost figures to him would not be accurate as they would not have included additional expenditure not invoiced to him. Again Mr Neubeck states he has constructed an 18 bedroom block on the site of Miramare. The actual costs are as yet not disclosed. As the property stands on Mr Mbiwan's land, he cannot disclaim ownership, yet from the point of view of cost to him, it is very likely that he has not spent anything.

To overcome this problem, a valuation related to the cost of construction at the time the asset was acquired appears to me to be the answer, except where, as in the case of Buea bungalow the construction appears executed at <u>arms length</u>. In this case I have accepted Mr Mbiwan's figure of cost to date."

Having investigated Mr Mbiwan's financial condition from the accounting material we had collected as exhibits and by investigating other sources of information that were not available to us, and having interviewed Mr Mbiwan privately himself and obtained from him a signed statement of facts related to his assets and resources, Mr Litumbe was able to present to us in his Report a table of Mr Mbiwan's sources of income.

In their report the commission made the following observation which reveals the spirit in which the proceedings were being conducted.

"Before we acted on the Auditor's Report, we had supplied Mr Mbiwan's Counsel (Prince Gorji Fokum Dinka as he then was) with a copy of it and invited him to appear at a special hearing to cross-examine Mr Litumbe. Counsel slighted the invitation and wrote to us as follows:

"I have myself read through Mr Litumbe's report which is by the terms of reference on page 1 supposed to be an expert investigation by an auditor into Mr Mbiwan's financial conditions on 1st October 1962, and at the time of *this Commission of Inquiry, including his earnings and expenditure between these dates.*

From the terms of reference given to Mr Litumbe, he was supposed to investigate and state the facts as simply as possible. Thus a report of this nature would be expected to state, e.g. that the evidence before him is that Mr Mbiwan had A, B assets and C, D liabilities. Between these dates Mr Mbiwan's earnings were L, K from M, N resources and for P, Q earnings Mr Mbiwan does not remember the sources.

As can be seen such a catalogue does not require expertise or special skill not available to the members of the Commission. And while the judgment of an Architect and a Valuation Officer can be regarded as expert opinion admissible in forensic evidence I can scarcely see what role Mr Litumbe was being asked to play which does not constitute a shifting of responsibility entrusted to the commission. It must have been clear even to Mr Litumbe that the part of his report which is a record of facts, i.e. paragraphs 9, 10 (excluding the last phrase) 11, 12, 14, 17, 18 and the tabulation on page 23 does not require an auditor, these facts being already made available in evidence to the Commission.

It is perhaps the frustrating realization of this fact that unmasked Mr Litumbe's own prejudices which has coloured the report with a perplexed saga of unbridled insinuations, innuendoes, sarcasm, opinions and hurried predetermined conclusions, but all horrifying in pursuit of Mr Mbiwan."

That Counsel's virulence in his answer to the commission's invitation goes a long way to show that many known things were unknown to the public. It could well have been a strategy to discredit the findings and recommendations of the Commission should it go against his client or throw doubt as to its credibility as eventually happened when a minority view was expressed by one of its members who was, at the same time, its Secretary, Mr A. C. S Allen.

"Note of Dissent by MR A. C. S. Allen"

I regret that I am unable to agree with my colleagues on their conclusions on the Sixth Term of Reference and, in accordance with the Provisions of Section 19 of the Commission of Inquiry Ordinance, I explain the reasons for my dissent hereunder.

I cannot agree with the estimate of Mr Mbiwan's resources, which is given as 34,512,130 francs. This seems to me to be an understatement by comparison with the figures given by Mr Litumbe. Appendix D to his report (included as an appendix to this Report) shows that he had resources totaling 45,829,995 francs. Without explanation, Mr Litumbe admitted only

37,124,231 francs after deducting 5,830,008 francs expended other than on assets. I am satisfied that Mr Mbiwan had access to at least 40.000.000 francs for the acquisition of assets.

My colleagues treat the *value* of assets based on the 1968 valuation as though it represented the *cost* of acquisition. I cannot accept that view and call attention to Mr Litumbe's remark that: "To overcome this problem a valuation related to the costs of construction at the time asset was acquired appears to be the answer except where, as in the case of the Buea bungalow, a contract appears executed at arm's length". No such value was given in evidence.

Nevertheless, the only contentious item is the Miramare Hotel property valued at 31,700,000 francs. As I understand it, my colleagues reject the evidence that Mr Neubeck contributed to the capital for its development. I do not share that view and prefer to accept that Mr Mbiwan and Mr Neubeck contributed in the proportions given in the valuation report of Messrs. Inglis and Ekaney, namely; 17 million by Mr Mbiwan and 14.7 million by Mr Neubeck, when he wrote his report: in referring to the eighteen-room extension: "That actual costs are not yet disclosed. As the property stands on Mr Mbiwan's land he cannot disclaim ownership, yet from the point of view of cost it is very likely that he has not spent anything". Since Mr Mbiwan's expenditure was incurred some time before the valuation it would not be unreasonable to assume that the cost to him was less than 17 million francs.

For the purposes of comparison with Mr Mbiwan's resources, my colleagues use the figure of 55,883,086 francs in arriving at his unexplained resources. On the basis of the reasoning given in the preceding paragraph I consider that that figure has been overstated by not less than 14.7 million francs and that Mr Mbiwan could have acquired his assets at a cost of not more than 41 million francs. This compares with the estimate of available resources of 40 million francs as shown above. I cannot therefore accept the conclusion reached by my colleagues that Mr Mbiwan has unexplained resources of 21,370,956 francs.

I am prepared to submit a separate report on this Term of Reference with my own conclusions and recommendations if I am invited to do so.

A. C. S. ALLEN
Secretary/Member

BUEA
31st January, 1969

CHAPTER VI
SUPREMACY OF THE LAW

A Commission of Inquiry can, in no way, interfere with the *rights* of an individual to *seek the protection of the court* with a view to indicating his rights. This is illustrated by the case of *E. M. L. ENDELEY (Dr) vs D. M. FRAMBO & J. TALBOT*.[8]

A Commission of Inquiry (appointed by government) takes precedence over a court or that with the appointment of a Commission any matters before a court related to the subject of the inquiry should be stopped.

Dr Endeley, (M.P) was a member of the – Southern Cameroons House of Assembly and Leader of a local political party (Cameroons Peoples National Convention) and had an equal number of elected seats in the House of Assembly as the Kamerun National Democratic Party. He is alleged to have contrived to conclude arrangement with D. M. Frambo, a member of the KNDP in the House. Arrangement was to pay Frambo £2000 said to be debt due by Frambo to his previous party (the KNDP), if Hon. Frambo undertook to resign from his party in the House and join the CPNC. After some negotiations, matters finalized on the night of the 8th May 1960 at about 11 o'clock, at the home of one Mr Bayu in Tali in the Mamfe Division, when Mr Frambo signed 8 copies of a document which purported to be his resignation from the KNDP and received from Dr Endeley and Mr N. N. Mbile the sum of £2000 in cash.

On 9th May – i.e. the following day, Mr Frambo did not travel to Buea in accordance with the arrangement. It was discovered that he had made a report to the police of the district to the effect that he had been forced at gun point by Dr Endeley and Mbile to sign the document purporting to be his resignation from his party, but that he had no intention of doing so. He followed up this report with a letter to the same effect addressed to the Acting Commissioner of the Cameroons.

Dr Endeley sued Messrs. Frambo and J. Talbot for libel. The libel was alleged to be contained in the letter to the Acting Commissioner of the Cameroons. It read as follows:

---

[8] Suit No. WC.SC/1A/1963.

Tali, Mamfe
9/5/60

The Ag. Commissioner of the Cameroons,
Buea.

Sir,

You might have been given a letter of resignation by one of the KNC/KPP Leaders said to have been my resignation from my party the KNDP. I want to inform you that I have no intention to resign from the KNDP but merely signed under force of arms a printed letter presented to me at midnight on Sunday the 8th by Dr E. M. L. Endeley and Mr N. W. Mbile. I have since reported this incident to the Police and statements have been recorded from me about it.

I have the honour to be,
Sir,
Your obedient Servant,
(signed) D. M. Frambo
cc. to: Hon. J. N. Foncha, Premier of the Southern Cameroons,
N.B.C Buea.

On the 15th June, 1960 Dr Endeley filed a writ against Hon. Frambo and J. Talbot, then Secretary of the KNDP, and some time later a Commission of Inquiry was appointed by Government to enquire into the circumstances of the transaction between Dr Endeley and Frambo.

In my opinion, this case is important in two aspects. Administrative authority and judicial supremacy. In setting up the commission of inquiry by government, the politicians believed that this would render the machinery of justice inoperative. In other words the courts would be compelled to halt the proceedings to await the outcome of the inquiry.

A commission of inquiry is undoubtedly a fact finding tribunal. A court of law does not end with a finding of facts but invokes and applies the law in so far as justice is done; namely, it is guided by due process.

A court ends up with inflicting a sanction whether it be a sanction or an award of damages and/or compensation for damages.

The conclusion is irresistable that Dr Endeley did not only want to cleanse his name, not only as a former Premier but also as a political leader and Member of Parliament. Besides, had he kept quiet, he could easily have been charged with bribery and corruption, a crime punishable under the criminal Code as applicable in the Southern Cameroons.

The case was definitely high profile. The personalities involved and the facts were of such a nature that the integrity of the individuals and the system were on trial.

The decision of the court was a triumph on the exercise of legal powers rather than in the interpretation of the law because the Commission of Inquiry had a legal basis [9].

As was held by the Court of Appeal in this:

"The Court cannot agree with the contention implied in the argument that a Commission of Inquiry appointed by Government to inquire into a specific circumstance can in any way arrest the rights of an individual if so minded to pursue an action brought by him in Court, neither can the Court agree that a Commission of Inquiry takes precedence over a Court or that with the appointment of a Commission any matters before a Court related to the subject of the inquiry should be stopped".

Mr N. N. Mbile's account of the facts of this story in his Book, *"Cameroon Political Story – Memories of an Authentic Eye Witness"* Published in 1999 is fairly correct except that he spilled some political beans.

It is necessary at this point in discussing *due process* in the Federated State of West Cameroon to mention the case of Hon. *William Ndep Orock Effiom vs. Mpawe Ashu* [*]

At the time of the case, the Honourable W. N. O Effiom was Secretary of State in the West Cameroon Government holding the portfolio of Minister of Natural Resources while Mpame Ashu was an employee with R. & W. King Limited of Victoria (now Limbe).

This was another case of libel with political over-tones. The circumstances were the campaigns for general elections to the West Cameroon House of Assembly. In the previous election, Mr Effiom had been the elected member for the Mamfe Division and above all held Ministerial Office in the government as earlier noted. In the present election, like in the previous one, he was running on the ticket of the Kamerun National Democratic Party (KNDP).

Mr Mpame Ashu was the Secretary of the Ejagham Block in Victoria which favoured Mr J. O. Takim. Mr Takim eventually withdrew from the election contest before election day. The suit before the court alleged that defamatory material injurious to Effiom was contained in a circular letter dated the 11th November 1961, that bore the name and signature of Mr Ashu as *"Secretary for the Ejagham Block Victoria"*. Mr Effiom in bringing his suit, complained that the publication *contained untruths and allegations*

---

[9] Commissions of Inquiries Ordinance: Cap 36
[*] WC/3/1962 – 1962, 63 and 1964 West Cameroon Reports (1962-64 W.C.L.R 21)

against him which were both false and malicious and thus caused untold damage to his reputation both as a politician and as a private individual.

Among the allegations complained of by Mr Effiom were the following:

" (a) *Has this plan not failed because Minister Effiom was unable to get contractors who would make him a shareholder in the venture? Should he then pretend that he has our interest at heart?*

(b) *We must have foresight as the first time Effiom entered the House, his greatest achievements has been to carry through a law prohibiting women from forming any cultural organization*" [10].

Against these allegations, Mr Effiom defended himself by saying that he was instrumental in initiating an Oil Palm Estate in the constituency, and while there were delays in getting the project going on was because of shortage of personnel in the Cameroon Development Agency, the Authority responsible for the project.

That negated the first allegation against him. As to the 2nd allegation which concerned the Ekpa Society – a Women's Cultural Society – Mr Effiom said that the legal instrument by which the Society was brought into effect by the then Colonial Commissioner for the Southern Cameroons under special enabling powers was not by the Legislature or the Cabinet of West Cameroon and that the ban was as a result of the Commissioner's adaptation of certain laws of Nigeria to West Cameroon. Other legal instruments were cited by Mr Effiom to exonerate himself.

In summary, the decision went in favour of Mr Effiom who was awarded damages assessed at 1.038,000 francs CFA. The two cases, so far considered, have some common features; namely, their genesis were political. The first dealt with political juggling and highlights the ugly aspect of political maneuvering for the sake of power.

The second brings out the expectations of constituents of their political leaders. From a legal perspective, the resort to due process is accepted because the judiciary stood out as a credible institution and absolutely beyond reproach. I wish one could say this of the same institution today. The impression nowadays is one of usurpation of the judicial power by the politician. Both Dr Endeley and Hon. Effiom realised that submission to the jurisdictions was the best way to publicly clear their names and restore their reputations.

---

[10] The facts of this case are reported in the West Cameroon Law Report of 1962, 1963 and 1964 paged 21-23. (Suit No. WC/3/1962 of 30th April 1963).

The commission of inquiry into the Endeley/Frambo saga aroused a lot of public interest because it was conducted in public which gave the right of access to the hearings. I recall very vividly how some of us the young civil servants used to leave or should I say *sneak out* from our offices to go and watch the array of the famous Nigerian lawyers we read of in the press, luminaries like Rotimi Williams and Chief Authur Prest. Mr Burk, the West Indian and Chairman of the Frambo commission was of a commanding personality. At one point in the evidence when someone said they were four men in the small *Beetle VW vehicle car* that was transported *to and fro* Tali from Mamfe, he leaned forward and said something to this effect: *I hope they were not as huge as myself.*

Another case of interest to illustrate the majesty of the law in West Cameroon was that of Augustine N. Jua on the one hand and Fongum Y. Gorji – Dinka and Hope Printing Press and Dynx Press on the other.

The Honourable Augustine N. Jua at the time of the suit was Prime Minister of West Cameroon while Fongum Y. Gorji-Dinka was a legal practitioner based in Victoria. The High Court presided over by Chief Justice, Charles Stewart, had found that the lawyer and the Printing Presses, were liable to the Hon. Jua for libel and damages of 2,500,000 francs CFA and costs of 200.000 francs CFA were awarded against them and each to be liable as follows:

   a) Fongum Y. Gorji-Dinka two thirds and
   b) Hope Printing Press and Dynx Press one-sixth each.

A stay of execution was not granted by Chief Justice, Charles Stewart, who ordered payment into court within seven days, i.e. by 12 o'clock noon on 14th November 1966. Barrister Y. Gorji-Dinka and the others filed notice and grounds of appeal. On that basis they applied for a stay of execution.

To cut a long story short, the substantive appeal was withdrawn, on terms, in open court. It is interesting to note that the matter was withdrawn in open court by the editor of the West Cameroon Law Reports (WCLR22). This, in my opinion, was to bring out in a subtle way the political under-tones which were at work in the whole case.

Here again we are confronted with a high profile case where a head of government confronts at law a legal luminary.

The case of Isidore Boboh, a superior police officer who in execution of a search warrant found some drugs and decided to keep them after endorsing on the warrant that *"nothing incriminating had been found"* is of interest because the law was invoked to affirm the principle of equality before the law.

He then conspired with another police officer to extract 150,000 francs CFA from the person who had been in possession of the drugs.

At the trial he was found *guilty* of conspiracy, official corruption and demanding money with menaces contrary to sections 516, 115(1) and 406 respectively of the Criminal Code and sentenced to seven years' imprisonment on each of the first two counts and eighteen months on the third, the sentences being ordered to run concurrently.

On appeal to the West Cameroon Court of Appeal, the conviction on the first two counts were upheld and the appeal allowed on the third count.

In their judgment, their Lordships concentrated more on the sentence imposed on the appellant than on the facts which they obviously considered overwhelming. They were strongly influenced by appellant's service record as a police officer. They said, inter alia:

> "On the question of sentence of 7 years' imprisonment imposed on the appellant on each of the 1st and 2nd counts to run concurrently, we agree that it was very excessive having regard to the long service and good conduct of the appellant in the police force. We believe that after serving with distinction for 21 years during which he earned 4 commendations for good work and courage, it can reasonably be said that the appellant succumbed to temptation and that he had not previously taken advantage in abusing his position as a member of the police force. These facts are specially applicable to the appellant and not to the offence itself which we consider as very serious and which should ordinarily be punished with severity. For these reasons we reduce the sentence of 7 years' imprisonment on counts 1 and 2 to one of 3 years on each count… and sentences to run concurrently".

This case is mentioned to show the duty and responsibility to curb corruption and excesses amongst public officials. We are aware of similar cases where members of the forces conspire to shield one of their numbers because there is none clean amongst them who would dare throw the first stone. Another point that may be made, is the fact that you need a court without blemish to condemn a corrupt individual.

The court demonstrates its inculpability when it succinctly gives reasons in the judgment that it hands down. The *silent jury* the people, are free to give their verdict as to whether or not they agree with the honourable and learned man of law. Boboh's length of service during which he earned four commendations is certainly a compelling factor to deserve consideration in the severity of the pain to be inflicted on him.[11]

---

[11] Isidore BOBOH vs. The People (WCCA/11C/67.

One may argue that after such a brilliant service record he would not have allowed himself to be tempted. After all everyone is subjected to temptation. In real life, temptation comes to one and sundry. In real life again, not every one is moulded in the like of another. The task of the judge to recognize this ends there. Being human, judges have their own idiosyncrasies. They can be as temperamental as they can be introverted or uncommunicative. Into whatever compartment they are placed, they are part of humanity with feelings. All that can be demanded of them is that they be impartial.

The mitigating factors outlined by their Lordship in the case under review illustrated their good common sense. It would not be in good taste if an apposite situation is analysed here but the fact remains that there are reported cases when the public is stunned by some of the pronouncements that are handed down for the generality of society to swallow. Pronouncements like *"the court's hands are tied"* are not only odium but palpable nonsense.

This unsatisfactory malediction found vent in the 1992 Presidential elections when the Supreme Court, presided over by His Lordship Mouelle Dipanda, after a finding of irregularities and fraud ended by stating that the court found itself unable to give a clear-cut opinion because the court found its hands tied. Everyone then asked: by whom?

We noted earlier in this work that in dealing with the commission of inquiry into *PowerCam* (West Cameroon Electricity Corporation) persons highly placed were mentioned in one way or the other. The Lead Counsel for the General Manager of *PowerCam* was F. Y. Gorji-Dinka and Mr Frederick Ngomba Eko in the opening stages of the inquiry for the West Cameroon Government. In the course of the inquiry, Mr F. Y. Gorji-Dinka delivered to the Chairman of the Inquiry, a document concerning the proceedings of the inquiry as they were ongoing. Mr Rupert Thomas, as he then was, took great objection to the conduct of Counsel. Mr Rupert Thomas, a very austere man, was so provoked that he decided to hand over the document to the Police for investigation.

Barrister F. Y. Gorji-Dinka was eventually charged to court. The charge read:

> *"On or about the 10th day of October 1968 at Buea in the West Cameroon Magisterial District you, F. Y. Gorji-Dinka, made to Rupert Thomas, a person in authority, a false report by submitting memorandum dated 7th October, 1968, accusing Frederick Eko, Procureur Général of West Cameroon of partiality, bias, tribalism and corruption before, during and after the Commission of Inquiry into the West Cameroon Electricity Corporation*

which was liable to lead to the prosecution or disciplinary proceedings against the said Frederick Eko."

Mr Justice V. R. Derrish, J. presided at the trial in the High Court, Buea. The *memo* in question was produced in evidence by Mr Rupert Thomas, the chairman of the said Commission of Inquiry. The Chairman recounted the circumstances in which Barrister Gorji-Dinka handed him a document – *Document A* – which was produced at the trial for purposes of identification only. Nevertheless, objection was taken as to its adminisibility on two grounds:

(a) that it was evidence taken under the circumstances of the Inquiry Ordinance and hence inadmissible in those proceedings by virtue of section 10 of that Ordinance (i.e. Cap. 36)

(b) that the document, being a document made by Counsel in the course of a judicial inquiry, is privileged from production by virtue of the doctrine of absolute privilege.

Before going into any further consideration of the legal issues that bogged down the trial, it is important to refer to the provisions of section 10 of the commissions of Inquiry Ordinance. Section 10 stipulates:

"No evidence taken under this Ordinance shall be admissible against any person in any civil or criminal proceedings whatever, except in the case of a person charged under section 12 of this Ordinance with giving false evidence before the commissioners."

Section 12 deals with cases where the false evidence is given before the Commissioners on oath or declaration or where the Commissioners appoints someone to interpret or translate any document produced before them and the person takes an oath or an affirmation.

A further consideration of the legal tangles of the case may obscure the ultimate objective of this work. Suffice it to say that Gorji-Dinka was discharged and acquitted by the High Court. The prosecution appealed to the West Cameroon Court of Appeal.

The appeal was dismissed by a majority decision of M. Cotran, C. J. and S. B. Kesiro J. with Mr J. A. O Brian Quinn dissenting. The majority held that:

- the word 'evidence' as used in the Commission of Inquiry Ordinance is not to be given its ordinary meaning as when it is used in a court of Law, that is to say, oral evidence given on oath, and that once the document in question has been

accepted by the Chairman of the Commission it becomes evidence in writing under section 7 (a) although not on oath.
- the document in question constituted evidence under the Commission of Inquiry Ordinance and hence inadmissible in these proceedings by virtue of section 10 of that Ordinance.
- it would be strange indeed if the doctrine of absolute privilege should apply to the tort of defamation and not to the criminal offence of defamation and making a false report, and the doctrine does apply even if the statements made by Counsel in the course of a judicial proceedings amount to criminal offences.
- the function of the prosecution acting on behalf of the people in criminal cases is to act fairly and impartially in the interest of justice and that it is[12] not the duty of the prosecution to secure convictions, and especially not to use their official positions for their own personal advantage.

In his dissent, O'Brien Quinn, J. pointed out that he had been informed of the salient points in the majority judgment. By this statement he was insinuating that the majority opinion was neither deliberated upon by the panel nor was it circulated among the panelists for each person to let his opinion be known by the others with a view to effect a change of mind if he was convinced by his colleague's point of view.

Be it as it may, Justice Quinn distanced himself in the conflicting meanings given to 'evidence' in section 10 of the Commissions of Inquiry Ordinance (cap. 36) by both the trial Judge and his two colleagues.

He argued:
a) that the document given by the respondent to the chairman of the Commission at the latter's request only for his personal information could not be said to have been 'evidence' of any kind whatever.
b) that it was information given to the chairman outside the scope of the inquiry which was the substance of the charge against the respondent.
c) that "the absolute privilege which covers proceedings in or before a ourt of justice can be divided into three categories; namely, all matters that are done *coram judice*. This covers everything done in the course of proceedings by judges, parties, counsel and witnesses and includes documents put in as evidence. Secondly, everything done

---

[12] Criminal Appeal No. WCCA/3C/69. (1968-1970) U. Y. L. R. page 112.

from the commencement of proceedings onwards and extends to all pleadings and other documents brought into existence for the purpose of the proceedings beginning from the issue of the writ or other documents which show that the process has taken off. The third is that a privilege attaches to evidence which a witness gives *coram judice* as extending to the precognition or proof of that evidence taken by a solicitor.

Justice Quinn again went on:

"There is no doubt that what the respondent did does not fall within the first category because it was not said by counsel in the course of the proceedings coram judice *nor was it a document put in as evident. There is no doubt that it does not fall within the second category as it was not a document brought into existence for the purpose of the proceedings, since by its very opening words it says. "I prefer to write to you now that the proceedings are over". With regard to the third category it is useful to follow the reasoning of Devlin L. J.... "I have come to the conclusion that the privilege that covers proceedings in a court of Justice ought not to be extended to matters outside those proceedings except it is strictly necessary...."*

The learned Judge questioned: The question before this court is, *is it strictly necessary to extend the privilege to cover a document handed by counsel to the chairman of an Inquiry at his hotel bedroom after the Inquiry had ceased hearing evidence, and before deliberation".*

After an exhaustive review of English case law on all the ramifications of the case before their Lordships, Justice Quinn, nevertheless ended his dissent by dismissing the appeal like the others. The unformed would ask why then disagree from the beginning if the end result would be the same. To the lawyer, there is much to be introduced into the art of legal reasoning and since precedent plays a lot in any legal system and more so in the development of the law and legal thought an issue should be well reasoned out in order to lay down a principle and have it withstand the test of time.

Mr Justice Quinn had a word for the lawyer in circumstances like the one being considered and then concluded by quoting Lord Justice Cockburn, when he said:

[79]

"The Advocate must wield the weapons of a warrior, not those of the hired ruffian. It is his duty to fight for his client per fas, not pernefas, and to reconcile his interests with the eternal interest of truth and justice".

In my opinion, the commissions of inquiry were an absolutely eloquent example of why good government should be instituted. Their just existence is to secure the rights of the people so that they can freely purse their well being and happiness.

Opinions like the one expressed in the Economist Intelligence Unit, of October 2007 leave much to be desired of our country. The report in treating political outlook and the economist policy outlook disparages the country by its analysis as follows:

<u>Political Outlook:</u>

The opposition is no longer a serious contender for power, having lost much of its credibility and public support following its repeated failure to unite against Mr Biya. The main opposition party, the Social Democratic Front, which has in the past rallied most of the Anglophone vote as well as a large proportion of those disenchanted with the old regime, has seen its parliamentary representation dwindle from 22 to 16 seats. As a result, the opposition will continue to have little power to monitor the work of the executive. Voter apathy is on the rise as a result of public disenchantment with the opposition and disappointment over the progress made by the current government. Although organised protests will continue to take place, they will not pose a significant challenge to the regime. Given the personality based nature of the regime, the main risk to political stability remains Mr Biya's sudden departure from the political scene. However, this is unlikely to occur over the forecast period, barring unexpected health problems.

<u>Economic Policy Outlook:</u>

In recent years, Cameroon has carried out several reforms that have helped to maintain macroeconomic stability, improve governance and enhance public financial management. *However, the business environment remains among the most difficult in Sub-Saharan Africa owing to red tape, lack of access to credit and an inefficient court system.* To promote growth in the non-oil sector, the government is expected to pass reforms that will reduce the red tape involved in opening a business and improve access to credit for local businesses. The Economist Intelligence Unit expects that the government will meet most of the quantitative targets under the current poverty reduction and growth facility (PRGF), especially those related to fiscal performance, but some delays are expected in the privatisation programme. The government will continue to make some progress in reducing corruption in the public sector and will continue to fulfill most of the commitments made under the extractive industries transparency initiative (EITI).[13]

---

[13] ·Economist Intelligence Unit, Country Report: CAMEROON   October 2007

[82]

Part Two

Part Two

CHAPTER VII
THE BENCH

Judges should be checked or judged by the informed judgment of history.

As I said from the very beginning, October 1977 was an eventful month in my professional career. That is when I was installed as President of the Court of Appeal, North West Province (Chief Justice of the Province). It happens to be the month in which I was born 42 years before as of that year.

Unlike many of my contemporaries, like the Late Mr Justice George Simon Ekema from whom I was taking over and Mr Justice Emmanuel Fonje Tatabod to whom I handed over, I had not had any experience of presiding in any court as a trial magistrate or judge at any level. I spent all my time after assuming duty in the Attorney-General's Office, Federated State of West Cameroon. As a State Counsel I spent my time discharging the duties of a public prosecutor. Later, I headed the department when I directed public prosecutions in the state.

Again, I observed earlier that I was coming to the bench after eleven years in the prosecuting department where I worked my way to be head. The second republic ushered in 1972, saw the legal department going through a decentralisation process. By 1977 branches of the department were established in Limbe and Tiko in Fako Division, Kumba in Meme Division and Mundemba, in Ndian Division. The legal department had since 1971 been opened in Bamenda with Benjamin Mutanga Itoe as State Counsel. When the Court of Appeal was eventually established in 1972, he was named the interim Procureur Général (Director of Public Prosecutions). The legal department was now well spread out in the Anglophone Provinces of the Republic.

For eight years, I presided over the North West Provincial Court of Appeal (1977-1985), the longest serving president of that court, as at the time of writing this treatise.

I had the collaboration of some nice and easy going professionals. Indeed, during my presidency of the court, I had the unique opportunity to work with some of the finest persons one could ever wish to work with.

There may be one exception, but his problem was domestic which inevitably reflected on his disposition at the workplace.

At various periods, I had Justice Hans Ekor' Tarh, Joseph Patrick Chewang Nganje, Tiku E. Mbuaghaw, Scott Moses Ateba Anyangwe,

Abel Nfor Njamnsi, Florence Rita E. Arrey, George Mbanda Asu, Francis Adolph K. Monekosso, Martin Deba as collaborators.

What I leant from working with fellow professionals is that so long as one doesn't become unnecessarily bossy, one will usually enjoy maximum cooperation from his associates.

It was a team of varied backgrounds. Justice Ekor' Tarh was a trained and professional teacher with many years of teaching experience before he went to study law in Ghana. Justice Anyangwe was a qualified Pharmacist, and like Justice Ekor' Tarh went to study law in Nigeria after working with the government for several years.

The rest or at least the majority had similar working backgrounds either as civil servants or in the private sector. These backgrounds were of immense value and enriching in the adjudicating process in which the court was daily challenged.

My working relationship with these learned colleagues demonstrated a remarkable camaraderie that is rare to come by. For instance, the incident described earlier about my installation, illustrated the degree of support my associates gave me.

Nevertheless, each held an independent opinion that went a long way to enrich our deliberations in Chambers.

Generally speaking, a judge is a public figure appointed to preside and administer the law in a court of law. It entails carrying out such functions. The good training required, like a qualification or qualifications vary from country to country.

Qualification, in my opinion, means being well experimented in matters of the head and the heart acquired over the years. Perhaps the more varied the experience, the better. Of course, this, by no means excludes being well tutored in the law and being able to apply the law with a human face.

Since the judge is vested with authority to decide questions of disputes between parties and to award the proper punishment to offenders in appropriate cases, the experience is an absolute necessity. So that the judge can do this without fear or favour, he or she does enjoy or should enjoy some form of immunity. The statute of magistracy as amended from time to time does provide for some form of immunity. This will be elaborated later in this work.

I consider those who were my associates in the North West Provincial Court of Appeal as examples of an endowed and rich court in so far as some had as an adjunct to their legal qualifications an expertise that became immensely handy and useful when intricate issues required some experience. This turned out to be very useful during deliberations.

Deliberations took the form of each judge giving his opinion on the basis of the facts as recorded during the trial. They ended with an application of the facts to the law as laid down by statute or interpreted by other judges or courts whether in Cameroon or beyond. The first proposition could be binding while the second, non-Cameroonian decisions were cited to persuade the court.

The opinion of the court that was handed down was either unanimous or a majority. A dissenting opinion still had to be written for the record. My memory tells me that we had only one dissenting opinion. It is not in the record because when asked to present his dissenting opinion, the judge concerned was unable to do so and never did to this day.

It is a tedious matter to write out an opinion especially where two brilliant lawyers have argued the pros and cons of a case.

I adopted a practice whereby deliberations took the form of calling upon the most junior associate to express his individual opinion after studying the record of the proceedings. This followed the hierarchical set up of the panel. I expressed my own last. The person who wrote the opinion of the court, if unanimous or a majority, was the one I judged as having had a very clear idea of the facts and the law.

In those cases where I judged that my colleagues were rather nervous to write, I undertook to write the opinion. Sometimes, they would unanimously agree that I write the opinion. In that case, I had no choice. These were usually cases of public interest or that had a political colouring.

I am always being asked if I can remember any case that stands out in my experience as a judge. That is a difficult question to answer. Not all cases are on all fours. The ambition that every judge wants to achieve is that at the end of the day, everyone or the generality of the people should agree that justice has been done or the Judge tells himself: I have done justice today.

The rest is for the silent jury – the general public. The rules, whether statutory or judge-made, are there to guide the adjudicator and they form the anchor on which he can rest his conscience.

I always found consolation in the fact that the parties enjoy a right of an appeal. It's a right no one should deny a litigant in so far as the aggrieved litigant fulfils the provisions of the law.

There are, no doubt, cases where a personality in the community comes face to face with the law or the offence is odious. In these cases the public pass their judgment even before the poor fellow is heard. They approach it with a prejudice and strong belief that in any contest the big flies break through the cobweb of justice while the small ones are easily caught by the web.

I seek the indulgence of Walter F. Murphy to quote from his book "Elements of Judicial Strategy" (1964) page 210 in which he himself refers to the eminent English Judge, Lord Alfred Denning as pronouncing on the role of a judge. According to Lord Denning, the cardinal virtues of a judge are:

- "*Patience* to hear what each side has to say;
- *Ability* to understand the real worth of the argument;
- *Wisdom* to discern where truth and justice lie;
- *Decision* to pronounce the result". To this list one might add:
- *Prudence* to know how much truth and justice and wise policy can be achieved at any time and how they may be most surely and effectively attained;
- *Courage* to pursue such a course even when it means risking some political dangers and enduring bitter criticisms from contemporaries as well as from historians for refusing to risk other dangers.[14]

It is therefore most regrettable that, today in Cameroon, we read disturbing opinions of our judiciary in such *odious* terms as those referred to herein:

> *Cameroon has a long-established reputation for official corruption:*
> Cameroon is in many ways the francophone African equivalent to Kenya and Uganda, with a diverse medium-sized economy *but also a long-established reputation for official corruption and a notoriously weak judiciary.* In recent years several multinationals, including extractive sector specialists with a commitment to ecological and local community ethics, have been dissuaded from investing by risk specialists, because of the rapacious nature of what is known locally as the classe d'état: the bureaucrats. One executive said, "We could have made money; the locals could have made money, but we can't pay bribes in all directions."*

---

[14] Cited by Walter F. Murphy in book "Elemens of Judicial Strategy" (1964) page 210.

* BBC FOCUS ON AFRICA – JULY – SEPTEMBER 2007

CHAPTER VIII
JUSTICE

Justice is generally considered as qualities displayed in a judicial and administrative setting. We acclaim a just judge as one who, in our opinion, declares the law impartially. The unjust judge therefore is one who punishes an offender who is believed to be innocent or undeservedly.

The guilty who is condemned has been justly punished, not the innocent who goes scot free when he has been so proven.

The ancient philosopher, *Plato*, illustrated in the context of conducting an examination of *Michael Foster* on academic examinations, refers to two instances thus:

"In the conduct of an academic examination, the examiners ought to refrain from favouritism and the candidates from cheating. We should call an examiner just who refused to favour but we should probably use some other term, such as 'honest', to describe the candidate who refused to cheat".

Foster postulates that the behaviour of the candidate would be a perfect example of what Plato means by "just". In other words Plato equates justice to 'morality'.

If morality is considered equated to what is right or evil or virtuous, then a moral person may not necessarily do justice or vice-versa because his sense of justice judged by moral values may not necessarily agree.

Moral values are universally accepted while a sense of justice may be determined by an enactment. An enactment may be intended to cure a particular ill at a particular time in society.

Experience has shown that good laws can be enacted but if those who administer these laws lack moral virtue, an injustice may result from their decisions. On the other hand, virtuous or morally experienced judges can administer bad laws in a manner that justice is the ultimate aim. Briefly put the saying that it is better to have good judges and bad laws than to have good laws and bad judges cannot be gainsaid.. In the end a judge arrives at a decision according to his moral values or virtuous nature or when he allows himself to be influenced by extraneous factors or influences.

I hold very strongly that it is the individual judge who takes an independent position than some power outside his conscience and / or training. History is made by those who resist influences intended to buy their consciences than by those who, for cheap and transient considerations, usually struggle to please the powers that be. The Supreme Court of Cameroon made itself a laughing stock during the 1992

Presidential election. In delivering what in judicial parlance is nobly described as a reasoned opinion, the court said that "their hands were tied". In other words, although they held a different opinion based on the facts, invisible hands prevented the court from the exercise of its true and honest opinion. The question had been asked again and again who tied their hands. The Statute of Magistracy, i.e. the 'Rules and Regulations governing the Legal and Judicial Service' provide for the independence of the legal and judicial office in the oath that they take before assuming their functions.

The Constitution of 1996 in its Article 37 (3) provides expressly as follows:

> "*The President of the Republic shall guarantee the independence of judicial power. He shall appoint members of the bench and legal department.*
>
> *He shall be assisted in this task by the Higher Judicial Council which shall give him its opinion on all nominations...................*"

I recall vividly the late President Ahmadou Ahidjo on one of the occasions of the solemn opening of the Supreme Court telling the corps of judicial officers something to this effect:

> "*Yes, I, the President is the guarantor of your independence but that independence belongs to you and not to the President*". Where a judicial officer fails to render justice to anyone without fear or favour or to be impartial he should not place his fear, favour or partiality at the door of some other on the basis of his hands being tied. If, indeed his hands are tied, his judicial conscience should speak out and say who has tied his hands, for the judicial oath states:

> "*I....., swear before God and all men honestly to serve the people of the United Republic of Cameroon in my capacity as a member of the Judicial and Legal Service, to render justice impartially to all in accordance with the laws, regulation and customs of the Cameroonian people, without fear, favour or malice, and in all ways, in all places and at all times to bear myself as a worthy and faithful member of the service.*"

The oath shall not be renewed.

Anyone who has experienced presiding in contentious matter(s), or aspires to preside or may be appointed to preside in any court of law, would soon realize that when all the facts have been exposed and the law married with those facts, he is left only "in the embrace of dear friends and his immediate family members and the unimpeachable resolution of his conscience and conviction.

That, to me, says a lot about those who will not brace up to their responsibility in administering impartial justice.

For, as Marcus Aurelius in "Mediations"; says:

"Once you have done a man a service, what more would you have? It is not enough to have obeyed the laws of your own nature (conscience) without expecting to be paid for it? That is like the eye demanding a reward for seeing, or the feet for walking. It is for that very purpose that they exist; and they have their due in doing what they were created to do. Similarly, man is born for deeds of kindness; and when he has done a kindly action, or otherwise served the common welfare, he has done what he was made for, and received his quittance." *

A lot may depend on how we look at justice. The unfortunate thing that happened to our justice system after unification was that no exercise was ever carried out as regards the adaptation of the laws. This was more so when we were about to embark on an extensive "operation harmonisation" of our laws.

We spent the time adapting the laws received from our colonial master. The new dispensation, a new mentality was buried in the old ways of doing things. Meanwhile, our society was changing but the change was not being reflected in our laws.

The legal history of common law in Cameroon abundantly shows that when Southern Cameroons separated from the Eastern Region of Nigeria and later became a Quasi-Federal Territory, the Nigeria (Constitution) Orders in Council, of 1954 and 1955 undertook an adaptation exercise of the laws that were proclaimed and published in the Official Gazette of the Southern Cameroons.

On unification, the process was to resort to the principles of repugnancy and transitional provisions with very indeterminate dates of entering into force of the envisaged legislative enactment. The exercise depended upon administration of ordinances while *loi* or law that had gone through the legislative process played second fiddle.

We failed the test of enacting laws that reflected our newly achieved sovereignty. Where we dared venture we merely adopted our peculiar heritage. This I believe, made our administration look so different in each component of the union. The same applies to the national constitution that takes so long to put into force all its provisions; sometimes very vital provisions in the life of the body polity.

---

* Book Nine paragraph 42.

Because the administration of justice is indispensable without the existence of law, it is useful to elaborate on the distinction between *adaptation* and *adoption* of laws.

In *adaptation*, we are dealing with an object that has been referred to as having been suitable or to conform, in this case, to the new state of affairs. It has been changed in such a way that it fits the prevailing climate.

Adoption of laws, on the other hand, is to accept as binding a state of affairs that was already existing without changing or altering the original form. In the area of legislation applying laws that were out of date or are out-of-date in a new environment.

Too often our legislation provides clauses that are to become operative by a subsequent enactment which is never known. In many cases that never materialises. Our Constitution of 1996 makes the case most abundantly clear. Promulgated in January 1996, the most important provisions have not and cannot be implemented because these are waiting an enabling enactment. When these will be respected, only the promulgator knows.

Until then, we all wait the high priest to go into the tabernacle and return with the tablets containing the law. The *certainty and stability* which are essential aims of the law are badly lacking. *Dean Roscoe Pound*, like *Austin* before him, is agreed on this jurisprudential thought.

This work is not a general work on jurisprudence of justice or law but the experience of an individual as a lawyer covering his active life as a practitioner, be it in the service of the State as a State Prosecutor or on the Bench. No two experiences are the same. The society and its environment, the people and their interests either individual or collective, their cultures and traditions, all influence experiences. The standard of the people one is called upon to serve as a practitioner expect knowledge of these particularities. Your personal frustration in this so-called service to the people haunts you always. Lawyer here is considered as that professional man who claims to be learned in the law and thereby imbued with a sense of doing justice through the law.

The role of a lawyer in the broadest sense, as I have attempted to point out here, has been the subject of academic debate down the years.

Whether as a lawyer you share the views of the German Jurist *Rudolf Von Thering* who "believed that a lawyer should be an analytical positivist, or one too pre-occupied with the jurisprudence of conceptions, the proper task of the lawyer should be the jurisprudence of interests". To him, law should exist to serve certain social interests and becomes meaningless when taken out of this context.

The American Dean Roscoe Pound who, in a way, followed Austin before on the other hand considered the lawyer as a *social engineer* who should be concerned with what the law is rather than what law is for. In other words what *the law should be for or like*. He saw the law from this point of view:

> *"Looked at functionally, the law is an attempt to satisfy, to reconcile, to harmonise, to adjust the overlapping and often conflicting claims and demands, whether securing them directly and immediately, or through securing certain individual interests, so as to give effect to the greatest total of interests or to the interests that weigh most in (our) civilization with the least sacrifice of the scheme of interest as a whole.*
>
> *Variants of the sociological jurists are the functionalists and the so-called realists., whether of the American or of the Scandinavian type. According to the functionalists, the most important thing for the lawyer is to have regard to the operation of law in human society, what end it serves and whither it is tending."*

A cursory study of the American so-called realists' preoccupation is the nature of the judicial process based on increased attention to the phenomena of the actual administration of justice as contrasted with exclusive attention to the authoritative materials for the guidance of judicial action.

The foregoing discourse has arisen because I felt that we missed an opportunity at the beginning when no thought or consideration was given to having our laws adapted. This would have led to a compiling of our inherited laws from where we could take up the important task of compilation.

Through compilation, a lot could be learnt by our new generation of lawyers. The Cameroonian common lawyer takes time to understand in legislative texts the civil component part of the distinctions between *loi, ordinance, decrête* or / *Arrête*. When dealing with colleagues inspired by the Napoleonic Code, these words may be common place but not so with the common law lawyer.

In Cameroon, use of these terms are legally loaded. Ordinarily, *loi* imports an enactment that has gone through Parliament after the representatives of the people have had a full dress debate on every section presumably before being presented to the Chief Executive for promulgation and proclamation. In so doing the legislature is merely carrying out the responsibilities imposed upon it by the electorate. Should

---

* Introduction to Jurisprudence (with Selected Texts) by Dennis Lloyd 2ⁿᵈ Edition 1969.

it abdicate from that duty or responsibility, then the action should be looked upon as a betrayal of trust of the people.

Ordinance, on the other hand, is the command or act of the Chief Executive invoking his powers under the constitution, the fundamental law of the land. Where, as it has been noted in Cameroon, it should be seen as a usurpation of the power of the other legislative arm of government when that arm has decided to surrender its birth right to the executive arm of government. One can find justification in cases where the legislature by extraneous circumstances has been rendered unworkable; e.g. an imminent threat of war or invasion by a foreign invading army in which case parliament may be suspended or a coup d'etat.

In 1972 when the transition from the Federal Republic to the United Republic took place, it was generally agreed that a peaceful revolution had taken place, more so, when it was preceded by a referendum. Legislative history in Cameroon shows that period to be rich in legislation by Ordinances. Very important subjects of vital interests were surrendered to the Chief Executive. The outcome of this legislation is simply legislation by technocrats through, and by whom the Chief Executive functions. Among those subjects were:

    a. Land Tenure in Cameroon: Ordinance No. 74/01 of 6 July 1974 (Ordonnance No. 74-1 du Juillet 1974 – fixant le regime foncier – and several others on Land Tenure.

    b. The Judicial Organisation of the State: Ordinance No. 72/4 of 26 August 1972.

    c. Ordinance No. 73/9 of 25 April 1973 to further amend Ordinance No. 72/4 of 26 August 1972.

    d. Ordinance No. 72/6 of 26 August 1072 – to fix the organization of the Supreme Court.

    e. Ordinance No. 72/7 of 26 August to orgainse the Court of Impeachment

    f. Ordinance No. 72/8 of 26 August 1972 to fix the composition, functions and procedure of the Higher Judicial Council. (Later repealed by law No. 82-14 of 26 November 1982).

    g. Ordinance No. 72/16 of 28 September 1972 to amend certain provisions of the Penal Code.

    h. Ordinance No. 72/17 of 28 September 1972 to simplify criminal procedure in respect of acts of lawlessness.

    i. Ordinance (Ordonnance) No. 81 – 02 of 29 June 1981 to organize Civil Status Registration.

The list is long and conspectus and makes boring reading. Let's leave it here, suffice it to say that the Cameroon legislature in our democratic process is nothing but a toothless bulldog. It neither barks nor bites. Perhaps it can be described as irrelevant nonsense. No wonder it only sits for at most ninety (90 days) out of three hundred and sixty-five days a year.

Cameroon has not known any political crisis since independence. Not to the degree of suspending any Parliamentary session. The Chief Executive tended to request the legislative arm to surrender to him their powers and they too seem to do so with relish. All this happening in circumstances under a constitution which ordains in its *PART ONE* that:

"2(1) The National sovereignty shall be vested in the people of Cameroon who shall exercise same either through the President of the Republic and Members or Parliament or by way of referendum. No section of the people or any individual shall arrogate to itself or to himself the exercise thereof."

It is rare in the judicial history of Cameroon to find cases where the authority or power of any institution has been challenged. Yet the tapestry of legal history provide rich ground for such challenges. Maybe, our lawyers are not so erudite to venture on an exercise that does not yield financial reward or the profession is still young both in terms of age and experience or not courageous enough to seize the courts with cases that the courts would be too scared to entertain for fear of compromising their echelons with the future of their careers.

It is my view that the Cameroonian lawyer, as against what was considered in dealing with the place of law in the justice system, is like a frightened chick, as soon as a hawk appears in the sky.

If we must agree with Dean Roscoe Pound that the lawyer is *a social engineer* or with Rudolph Von Thering's analytical positivism, and both are correct depending on the legal environment, then we cannot go along with the view that *"the most important thing for the lawyer is to have regard to the operation of law in human society, what end it serves and whither it is tending"*

I hope this is a wake up call to our legislators, lawyers and all those who exercise power or authority to ensuring we direct the law and thereby the administration of justice to where we want the Cameroon society of science and technology to take us, or better still to our place in the global world of tomorrow.

Our justice system was put to the test in the case of *The People versus Peter Ndifor & others*. Mr Peter Ndifor was a Police Inspector in the West Cameroon Police Force and was accused along with two other persons of being in unlawful possession of ammunition. Peter Ndifor and Others fall into the category of *Joseph Adu Ncho's cases* referred to somewhere in this work. There were two facets to the case. On the first, it was heard by Mr J.B. Whyat, then an expatriate magistrate serving in Buea. In discharging and acquitting Mr Ndifor and his co-accused he said, *obiter*:

> "I have no hesitation in acquitting the accused when I recall that they have been tried by a court from which no appeal lies".

Because of the sensitivity of the case for reason of the government's anxiety in controlling the possession of arms of any sort by individuals, such cases were looked upon with suspicion. The run up to independence by the State of East Cameroon was characterised by a war of independence and as such everyone was suspect.

The judgment reproduced hereunder highlights the extent to which the government could go to get a conviction against anyone suspected on reasonable or unreasonable grounds. Peter Ndifor and his cohorts whom I would like to refer to as Peter Ndifor No.2[15] was a retrial by Mr Justice R.L. Mitchell, another expatriate.

The drama leading to the case against Police Inspector, Peter Ndifor, deserves, in my opinion a brief narration. Peter Memba, gives an eye witness account of what he witnessed on that eventful day of Peter Ndifor's arrest. He was the bodyguard to Mr Michael Ntune, Commissioner of Police of West Cameroon – i.e. the Inspector General of Police – so to say. Mr Ntune was known to be a gentleman *par excellence*. Because of his soft spoken nature, some people regarded him as too full of the milk of human kindness. His experience went back to when the Southern Cameroons was part of Nigeria. On unification, he chose to come back to Cameroon unlike other Cameroonians in his position who decided to stay back in Nigeria where they already knew their future.

Mr Memba says when the news of Inspector Ndifor's arrest got to his boss, he saw him put on his combat dress for the first time. He called his two daughters, Joana and Carol, and kissed them. He did so in anticipation of the worst that might happen to him. He instructed Peter to stay with the girls. Peter Memba, registered as *WCPF 499*, disobeyed his boss. He pondered aloud. What if the worst happened to him, he would certainly be subjected to orderly room proceedings. He decided to follow him to the Police barracks in Small Soppo, Buea. On reaching the Ministerial Block Building overlooking the hospital, they found out that the junior officers had stormed the Small Soppo gendarmerie brigade and

---

[15] Case No. 62/MINFA/66 of April 22, 1967

released their colleague. The police had so acted because they learnt that Ndifor was being taken to Yaounde for trial in the Permanent Military Tribunal.

This was the first clash of the Titans between the West Cameroon Police Force (WCPF) and the gendarmes. Inspector Peter Ndifor was successfully released but not assigned any special duties.

It was the non-deployment of Inspector Ndifor that facilitated the second. This incident gave a signal to the authorities in Yaounde that the West Cameroon Police Force was a force to be treated with caution or else nipped in the bud. They had exhibited themselves as a very agile and disciplined force unlike the gendarmes who had force as their only tool. Yaounde reacted swiftly by the issue of the federalisation of the Police service. Decree No. 68/DF/431 of 29 October 1968 was the answer to this incident. With the decree, the idea of police barracks saw its demise. The swift mobilisation of the police demonstrated that in the event of a clash between the federated State Police and a federal force in West Cameroon, the federated state police would be more responsive than even the gendarmes, known to be a paramilitary force.

It is in this context that the Ndifor saga was played out. The judgment by Mr Justice R. L. Mitchell reveals more. Because it makes interesting reading, it is reproduced herein.

Mitchell. J.

It would be idle to deny that this case has been one of exceptional difficulty and complexity. It has occupied the Tribunal some 27 days during which 20 witnesses have been heard and an extensive visit has been made to the locus in quo at Muyuka. The trial has not been made easier by the fact that it is in effect a fresh hearing of certain earlier proceedings before a military Tribunal in July, 1966. Then the first two or the accused, Peter Ndifor and Martin Asah, were charged with offences, whilst the present third accused, David Mbene, was a prosecution witness.

The charge against these three accused concerns the unlawful possession of ammunition. There are three counts, the second and third counts being in the alternative.

The first count alleges that on or about the 5th April, 1966, at Muyuka in the West Cameroon Magisterial District, the three accused conspired together to commit a felony, to wit taking possession without lawful excuse of ammunition, thereby committing an offence punishable under section 516 of the Criminal Code.

The second alleges that sometime in April 1966, at Muyuka, an area subject to a State of Emergency, the three accused without lawful authority had *in their possession 497 rounds of ammunition, thereby committing an offence against Ministerial Order 52/ATF/APA of the 30th June 1962 and punishable under Article 8 of Ordinance 61/OF/5 of the 4th October 1961.*

The third count, being an alternative to the second count, alleges that sometime in April, 1966 at Muyuka in the West Cameroon Magisterial District, the three accused without lawful authority had under their control 497 rounds of ammunition, thereby committing an offence punishable under section 88A of the Criminal Code (Amendment) Law 1961.

The effective difference between counts 2 and 3 is that under count 2 the maximum punishment is five years' imprisonment or a fine of a million francs, or both; whilst under count 3 the maximum punishment is two years' imprisonment.

In view of the time taken, the complexity of the case and its importance it will be of value to set out in brief the lines which have governed this Military Tribunal in the conduct of this trial.

As required by law the Tribunal have acted pursuant to the powers conferred on Magistrate's Court (Ordinance No. 61/OF/4 of the 4th October, 1961, Article 5)

Two over-riding considerations have been perpetually kept in mind, namely, the paramount need to maintain and protect the security of the Federal Republic, and the need to ensure that the accused have, and are seen to have, a fair trial. In this latter connection it should be noted that one only of the accused, namely, Peter Ndifor, was represented by Counsel (Mr P.D. Koti). The other two were unrepresented and conducted their own defence.

The procedure at the trial has been that of the Criminal Procedure Code (C.43) and the evidence Ordinance (C.62) supplemented as and where necessary by the rules governing the admissibility of evidence as these operate in an English Court of Law. This has on occasion led to the exclusion of evidence which might have been admissible elsewhere.

Finally, the basic principle of English Criminal Law has been maintained, namely, that it is for the prosecution to prove the guilt of the accused 'beyond reasonable doubt', and, subject to the provision stated below, not for an accused man to have to prove his innocence. If there is reasonable doubt as to the guilt of an accused man he must be acquitted. It is not enough that the balance of probabilities weigh against a man, but there must be a certainty that convinces the understanding, stifles the reason and directs the judgment. To arrive at a conclusion the evidence must be carefully considered. It would be entirely wrong and improper to convict a man merely on the strength of a general feeling or impression of guilty. The evidence must be there to substantiate it.

The provision above referred to which has governed this trial is to be seen in the way Ministerial Order 51/ATF/APA of the 30th June 1962 as cited in count 2, and section 88A of the Criminal Code (Amendment) Law 1961 as cited in alternative count 3 have been drawn. The Ministerial Order by implication and section 88A expressly make the possession of ammunition unlawful in itself, and the onus of proving lawful excuse is immediately placed on the person so found in possession. Of course prosecution of ammunition by lawful authority, and if so there is an end to the matter.

To come now to the facts of this case:

Of the three accused two, namely, Peter Ndifor and Martin Asah, are member of the police force stationed at Muyuka. Martin Asah was a Constable under Ndifor. The third accused, David Mbene, was employed by Ndifor as his servant to look after his house at Muyuka.

The prosecution have led evidence to show that Ndifor was in physical possession of ammunition in his house. To do this they have produced a witness, Manfred Ikome, who lives in a single-roomed dwelling behind and slightly to one side of Ndifor's house, and within 11 feet of it.

Manfred has sworn that sometime in the middle of March 1966 he, Ndifor and a third man named Udoh (who was since escaped from custody) attended an oath-taking ceremony in Ndifor's house, and that thereafter, Ndifor produced ammunition and invited Manfred and Udoh to help him to sell it.

Manfred would have the Tribunal believe that he did not accept any ammunition.

Subsequently on 1st April 1966 Manfred informed Corporal Abane, a security detective attached to the Federal Surety at Buea but stationed in Muyuka, that there was ammunition in the town. Corporal Abane sent him to the corporal's house in the police lines near the Muyuka Police Station. Corporal Abane told Ndifor this and together they interviewed Manfred in his house. Ndifor apparently started off by asking Corporal Abane to fetch Asah who was in his own house also in the police lines and nearby, and who was off duty. The prosecution allege that this was a subterfuge on Ndifor's part to get Corporal Abane out of the way while he settled some plan with Manfred.

Corporal Abane's return some five to ten minutes later with Asah, Ndifor told Asah to go outside and stay around.

Manfred then told a story of how he with a friend Moritz Otte had been in Victoria on 29th March. Moritz had asked a police constable, Augustine Taka, for a lift in his Land Rover, and Moritz and he, Manfred, and others, including other constables, were taken to the road junction at Mutengene. Moritz and Manfred then alighted and Taka who had been sitting in front handed Moritz a bag. Moritz and Manfred then made their way on to

Muyuka. On the way Moritz confided to Manfred that the bag contained ammunition. The story of the lift back to Mutengene junction is true, but Manfred now says that the rest is pure fabrication and that he told this on Ndifor's instructions. From then for some six or seven weeks at least Manfred stuck to this story through thick and thin, and he stuck to it even though he was beaten on or about 18th April for refusing to change it. Manfred's reason for this steadfastness was, according to him, that Ndifor had promised to find him a job.

However, Manfred began to see the error of his ways. He says that on 18th May he was brought before the Government Commissioner, Captain Mbu. Captain Mbu told him that he had nothing to be frightened about, so he told captain Mbu the truth of the matter.

This, it would have been thought, must have been a very revealing statement. However, Captain Mbu's evidence of this is no more than that Manfred made a verbal statement which was not recorded. It is thus most difficult to believe that Manfred made any such statement on that day as alleged by him. But there is no other evidence of how and when Manfred told what, according to him, are the true facts.

Manfred, on his own showing, put about a false story, and was very determined about it. The circumstances of his 'confession' are shadowy in the extreme. His story of the oath-taking ceremony in Ndifor's house, which included the drinking of each other's blood in whisky, is highly coloured. The date he gives for this; about the middle of March, are controverted by Ndifor who says that in any event he did not take up residence until the 21st March. The prosecution did not cross-examine Ndifor, on this point so must be taken to accept the 21st March.

It was ironic that before ever putting Manfred in the witness box the prosecution felt it incumbent on them to put forward four witnesses to prove that Manfred's story to Taka handing him a bag at Mutengene junction was a lie.

In view of all the above circumstances I am bound to hold as a matter of law that no reasonable man could accept Manfred's evidence unless there is adequate corroborative evidence to support it.

It will be convenient now to describe how the ammunition, 497 rounds of 30-06 calibre, was actually caught. Two traps were set, one on the 4th and the second on the 5th April 1966, and they were set on the footing that Moritz Otte or his wife Regina Dibaya Otte were in possession of it. Moritz was already in trouble. He was employed according to his own description as an assistant at the Rainbow Chemists at Muyuka, and on the 1st April had been found by the director to be 63.000 francs short. On the 4th April he was placed under arrest at Muyuka Police station and needed money to be released on bail.

The first trap, on the 4th April, was arranged by Inspector Njike of the Federal Security. With Ndifor who was investigating the whole matter, he went with Corporal Abane and one James Ndutu from the Federal Security at Buea, to Ndifor's house. Manfred was brought in and Ndutu was told to pretend to be a would-be-purchaser of ammunition. For this purpose Inspector Njike gave him his pistol after extracting the magazine. Ndifor supplied sample ammunition. Manfred was told to go some way ahead of Ndutu and lead him to the scene of operations. It may be worthy of comment that Ndutu neither knew the identity of the person (Moritz) from whom he was supposed to buy ammunition nor where he lived. However, the plan proved abortive. Moritz had already been placed under arrest.

The next day, the 5th April, Ndifor, according to Corporal Abane, suggested to him that a similar trap should be set, this time to catch Mrs Otte – hereinafter referred to as Regina. This was on the footing that Regina would be willing to sell ammunition to get money to bail her husband. Corporal Abane was put in charge of the operation, and he of his own volition decided that Mbene, Ndifor's houseboy and now the third accused, should take the part of the would-be-purchaser.

Much of this operation is shrouded in doubt. Corporal Abane went to Ndifor's house and used this as his base – without, according to Ndifor, ever obtaining the latter's permission. Corporal Abane found Mbene in the parlour, and told him that he wanted his, Mbene's help. Mbene replied that Manfred had already told him what was to happen. Corporal Abane had never seen Manfred that morning and never checked up on this item when he did see .him. Corporal Abane told Mbene to dress up as a trader and to get a bag and to pretend to be a purchaser of ammunition. Corporal Abane then sent Mbane with a note to Ndifor asking for the assistance of a constable, and as a result Asah arrived in uniform about 9.15 a.m. Asah was told to hide in Ndifor's house.

Meanwhile Regina had twice been to Manfred's house, the second time being a about 9. a.m. and was then in the house.

Mbene went into Manfred's house and about half-an-hour later returned to Corporal Abane to say that the lady wanted money – '150.000'. There appears to have been considerable going to and fro in which Manfred took part.

Ndifor also arrived on the scene at about 9 a.m. for his break. Corporal Abane asked Ndifor for money, and Ndifor said he would try to get some. Later some money, 10.000 francs, did arrive after Corporal Abane had left the scene of operations to find out why the money was so long in coming.

Corporal Abane met Ndifor who then had the money, and Corporal Abane returned with it, and gave it in a purse to Mbene, the money was wrapped with so as to make it appear more.

It would seem that in the course of the morning Regina was in and out of Manfred's house several times.

There is dispute between Corporal Abane and Mbene as to Ndifor's pistol kept in Ndifor's house. Mbene says that on Corporal Abane's instructions he used this as part of a pretence that he was a terrorist. Corporal Abane denies any such instructions.

Corporal Abane says that he told Asah to secrete himself in Ndifor's bathroom. This is a corner room and nearest to Manfred's house. Asah was to wait until he heard a cough – from Manfred. This was to be a signal to Asah to make an entry into Manfred's house. There was apparently no intention on Corporal Abane's part that Asah should use his eyes by way of detection. Corporal Abane said in his evidence: "I did not know whether Asah could have seen out of the room through the walls. He might have been able to". The house is in fact constructed of wood.

Corporal Abane then left. This was about 12 noon. He knew nothing further of what subsequently happened till he got back to the Police Station at 1.30 p.m.

Meanwhile Mbene and Manfred were back in Manfred's house. According to Mbene, Regina and Manfred left the house, and later with Manfred brought the ammunition in question in Mbene's bag, already handed to her, into Manfred's house. Mbene showed the Tribunal a "private road" at the back along which he says Regina and Manfred came.

Asah in a recorded statement made by him and put in by the prosecution says that he saw Regina pass with a bag. He says that the bag was on her head; Mbene says that she carried it in her right hand. Be that as it may, Regina and Manfred with Mbene were quickly in Manfred's house, with doors and widows at once secured. Asah came out of his hiding place, and knocked on the door, announcing that he was a policeman. The door was opened. The ammunition was there on the table. Asah asked who had brought it. Mbene, so he says, replied that it was Regina. Asah then repacked the ammunition in the bag and escorted them all with the ammunition to Muyuka police station.

Needless to say Regina denies all knowledge of the contents of the bag. She says that much earlier that morning whilst she was in Manfred's house she saw Manfred go up to Mbene at Mbene's (that is Ndifor's) back door. Mbene then gave Manfred a bag which Manfred then brought into his house.

Manfred says that Mbene brought the bag in from Ndifor's house. Manfred makes out the operation was on Ndifor's instructions and carried out entirely by Mbene and himself without Corporal Abane ever appearing on the scene; nor Asah until he knocked on the door.

Subsequent to the 5th April Ndifor continued his investigations as the Chief Investigator, and apparently continued his duties until about the 3rd of June when Captain Mbu laid certain charges against him.

Let us now turn to another important prosecution witness, Patrick Obenson.

Obenson is a journalist and was the editor of the "Cameroon Star". Since the 31st August 1966 he has been under arrest on an administrative matter in Buea prison. He says that he met Manfred in the prison. He also says that when Ndifor was admitted to Buea prison on the 21st September (that is on Ndifor's re-arrest after the previous proceedings), that night he and Ndifor slept on the same bed. Ndifor denies this. Obenson says that he and Ndifor struck up an acquaintanceship. Ndifor denies this. Obenson says that ultimately Ndifor told him the whole story. This evidence is so remarkable that it is worth quoting in full:

"Ndifor told me that he had got 500 rounds of ammunition from Mutengene

He said that he had used one, Udo, to help him to sell the ammunition. But Udoh had brought back the ammunition because the person whom it was thought would buy it had gone home to Nigeria. Ndifor was faced with the problem of re-paying Udoh and disposing of the ammunition. Udoh had another charge of money-doubling against him. He had therefore arranged for Udoh to be tried on that charge, and had later arranged for Udoh to escape. This was because it then became unnecessary for him to re-pay Udoh the 50,000 francs he had received from him. Ndifor said that he arranged as if he had trapped ammunition, and he said that this would boost his promotion in the Force. He said that one Moritz Otte, was detained by the police at Muyuka, and that they had arranged for Moritz's wife to meet Manfred in Manfred's house Ndifor's house-boy had brought the ammunition from Ndifor's house. This was so that it should appear that Moritz's wife had brought in the ammunition. Since Moritz was already detained for embezzling money from his employer, it would appear that Moritz was selling ammunition so as to be able to repay his employer.

To do this Ndifor had enlisted the help of the District Officer at Muyuka - unknowingly to the District Officer. He also used Asah and Mbene as tools to obtain his objective".

A further comment as to Udoh will be made later in this judgment.

Obenson told the tribunal that whilst it was contrary to the code of conduct of his profession as a journalist to disclose the source of information given to him, he was departing from this as this was a case of public security. He said that his union, the African Union of Journalists, permitted this.

It can well be imagined that this evidence came to the prosecution as a god-send. It summed up the prosecution's case with masterly precision. In the whole of my own professional experience, which is not inconsiderable, I have never heard a piece of evidence come out as this did. Needless to say it is condemned by Ndifor as a complete fabrication.

However, not all Obenson's evidence is of this quality.

His sleeping in the same bed as Ndifor on the night of the 21st is considered most unlikely by Mr Martin Kange, the superintendent in charge of Buea Prison who gave evidence for Ndifor. For one thing it is against prison regulations, and should it happen that there are insufficient beds for prisoners additional blankets are supplied. Furthermore beds are no more than about two feet wide. Ndifor is broadly built, whilst Obenson is broad and stout, so that it is difficult to envisage these two men sharing the same bed.

However, what is more important is evidence given by Obenson that Mbene told him why he had "changed his statement" to the Government Commissioner. No evidence has ever been given that Mbene ever did change his statement.

Obenson also testified: "Mbene said that he had been induced by his master to change his statement". This is very hard to believe.

Obenson also said that on the 9th October, 1966, Ndifor told him that if he could get Manfred to change his story he would give Manfred 50.000 francs and get the charges against him withdrawn. Obenson said that he discussed this with Manfred. It is curious, however, that in his own evidence which took more than five days Manfred never mentioned this at all.

Having set out this evidence, I am not going to say that as a matter of law it cannot be accepted in so far as it implicates Ndifor, but it should certainly be received with reserve.

Except as appears briefly hereafter no further comment will be made on prosecution witnesses, but there is a further piece of evidence against Ndifor. This takes the form of a Police Report prepared by Ndifor on this case as a result of his investigations. This bears two dates, the 11th and 17th April, 1966. The first date was said by Ndifor to be a typist's error.

The prosecution put this document in as evidence, and it was accepted as such as part of prosecution's case when Ndifor was being cross-examined. The prosecution put great stress on this Report.

It must be admitted that in it there are some curious uses of the pronoun "I". For example, Ndifor wrote: "The clerk Otte, after the master had left, he went to Tombel on 3/4/66 to look for somebody who could purchase the ammunition to make good the 63.000 francs. I placed his movements on this day under close observation, but nothing was fruitful on this day". Ndifor admits that he did nothing to the sort, but says it was done on his behalf. There is no evidence of this.

Later in the Report he says that he "lectured" Mbene as to the part he had to take in the trapping operation on the 5th April. He says now that he never "lectured" Mbene. This was done for him.

The prosecution invited the Tribunal to regard the Report as very bogus.

Finally prosecution submitted Decree No. 65/DF/432 of the 12th October, 1965, and Decree No. 66/DF/133 of the 17th March, 1966, which together extended the State of Emergency over (inter alia) the Department de Kumba for two periods of six months running respectively from the 14th October, 1965, and the 12th April, 1966.

At the close of the prosecution's case the Tribunal were satisfied that a prima facie had been made out against Ndifor and Mbene, but not against Asah, and Asah was discharged. To avoid interrupting this narrative Asah's case will be dealt with later.

For the defence Ndifor gave evidence on his own behalf, and, in essence, it consisted of a simple and complete denial of the allegations against him, whilst at the same time raising doubt against Taka, it is unnecessary and it would be tedious to go into all the matters covered on the merits and as to credibility. Material points have already been dealt with earlier in this judgment.

He was cross-examined against his evidence in the previous case, and the Tribunal was supplied with a transcript of the whole of the evidence then given by him. Nothing really vital emerged from this piece of cross-examination.

Ndifor called four witnesses of whom Mr Kange has already been referred to. The Tribunal gave them all a very careful hearing but it is not necessary to comment further.

Mbene also gave lengthy sworn testimony on his own behalf. He maintained his complete innocence, and complained that after being asked to help Corporal Abane and his country he was now being made to suffer. His part in the operation of the 5th April and his own account of what took place have already been referred to earlier in this judgment. When giving evidence he went into great details as to his negotiations with Regina, and the Tribunal found it difficult to accept much of this as fact. However, his cross-examination by the prosecution against his evidence in the previous case, when it will be remembered he was a prosecution witness, was minimal, so it is fair to assume that his evidence on this occasion as far as relevant was substantially the same as in the previous proceedings.

He made adverse statement about Captain Mbu. But these were not substantiated.

The least satisfactory part of the prosecution's case against him arose out of a statement made by him to an officer who does not usually investigate security cases, but as President of the Tribunal I came to the view that the case against him could be left to stand without his statement. I advised the Assessors accordingly.

The upshot of the matter for this part of the case is that the Tribunal are unable to accept Mbene's account of how the ammunition got into Manfred's house on the 5th April, but take the view that there can be no reasonable doubt that Mbene himself took it in from Ndifor's house after Corporal Abane had left, and whilst Asah as still hiding in Ndifor's bathroom the Tribunal consider that with Mbene taking the part of a trader he would have had little difficulty in returning to Ndifor's house with the bag, filling it and making his way back to Manfred's house without raising Asah's suspicion.

It follows from this that Ndifor must already have had possession of the ammunition.

It now falls to me as President to decide as a matter of law how these findings fit in to the charge. The only difficulty arises in respect of the first count for conspiracy. The facts as found are that Ndifor was in unlawful possession of ammunition. There is no evidence as to how he came into possession, and there is no evidence that Mbene assisted him in any way in acquiring possession. For the offence of Conspiracy to be committed two requirements are (inter alia): two or more persons, and an agreement for an unlawful purpose. In the absence of any evidence linking Mbene with the acquisition, the charge of Conspiracy must therefore fall to the ground.

In this connection the prosecution have referred me to R.V. Churchill and Others (No. 2) 1966 2 ALL E.R. 215. That was a case of a criminal conspiracy to commit a statutory offence which was an absolute offence, as here in the second and third counts. The appellant was convicted of joining in agreeing to the use of untaxed fuel for road vehicles though he did not know that it had not been fully taxed. The distinction between that case and this is that in that case the offence lay in agreeing to <u>use</u> untaxed fuel, whilst here there is no evidence of any agreement to take possession of ammunition. It would appear that Ndifor was already in possession of the ammunition before Mbene knew anything about it.

Both Ndifor and Mbene are therefore acquitted under Count 1.

Coming now to the second count, it is obvious from what has already been said that Ndifor must be convicted. He has been shown beyond reasonable doubt to have been in possession of *ammunition*, and circumstances of the case show that this was without lawful authority.

As to Mbene, it is equally clear that he is guilty of aiding Ndifor within Sections 7(b) and (c) of the Criminal Code. The prosecution have also referred to R.V. McCarthy 1964 1 ALL E.R. 95, and this authority is also in point.

Mbene is therefore also convicted as stated.

In view of the above the alternative third count does not arise.

Before leaving this part of the judgment I would record this addendum relating to Udoh. The prosecution led some evidence aimed at showing, or at least suggesting, that Ndifor was responsible for this man's escape from custody. This was an ancillary point and latitude allowed in following up such issues must be limited. I was therefore compelled to rule that such line of evidence must stop. If it is desired to pin responsibility for facilitating Udoh's escape onto Ndifor then he must be appropriately charged. Any such accusation cannot be followed up or linked up with a charge, such as this, relating to the unlawful possession of ammunition.

It only remains now to deal with the case of Asah.

From the evidence adduced it was not easy to see why this man was charged, and the tribunal had little difficulty in deciding that he had no case to answer.

An attempt was made to discredit him arising out of a statement made by him to the officer earlier mentioned in this judgment. Apparently about the 27th October 1966 the officer made a visit to Muyuka with Asah and, inter alia, conducted an examination of Ndifor's house. Unfortunately he could not get into the house, but he arrived at a firm conclusion that there was no aperture in the bathroom outside walls through which one could see from the house to the outside. This was an unwise assumption having in mind that, as already stated, the walls are of timber construction. The Tribunal found itself unable to accept the assumption, and no their visit to Muyuka were able to confirm, if confirmation had been necessary, that several cracks and other apertures made it easy to peer from the interior to the outside and to see anyone approaching Manfred's house.

Martin Asah's discharge pursuant to Section 286 of the Criminal Procedure Ordinance is now hereby recorded and confirmed.

To conclude, it is perhaps superfluous to state that at no time have the Tribunal had recourse to the record of the previous proceedings except in so far as their attention has been directed thereto by the prosecution.

The Tribunal would wish to express their thanks to Mr Eko and Mr Koti for their help throughout the trial.

CHAPTER IX
THE CONSTITUTION

The February 11, 1961 Plebiscite did not decide on the constitutional structure of the Federal Republic of Cameroon but merely decided on a Federal Republic of Cameroon to come into existence. The discussions that later ensued were about the detailed constitutional arrangements that arose after the vote. Whereas in Nigeria any constitutional jettisoning was preceded by a debate on the forms, structure and powers of the future State, their independence fitted into a constitutional outfit already in place.

The Southern Cameroons administered by Great Britain under a UN Trusteeship voted to join a new country without knowing of any structure; either political or constitutional.

The debates on the form of the state were a consequence of a *fait accompli*. The so-called Foumban rendez-vous was far from being the result of any debate as to matters of detail. It was an exercise in trying to accommodate the new entities. The outsiders were to realize that it was a matter of the two strange bedfellows trying to accommodate each other.

To President Ahmadou Ahidjo, the question was as he explained as posed and answered in the Congress of his Party in Maroua in an attempt to resolve once and for all the constitutional issue vis-a-vis the Foumban rendez-vous.

Referring to the Congress of his party that held in Maroua he said it was an unforgettable date in that, in September 1960, Cameroon was only nine months old in the concert of nations. The same September the Cameroon Republic was seven months old as a sovereign state while the first Government had been in office for only five months. He went on:

> *"Thus it was that the activities of the Party blossomed with the institutions of the State merged into them. In other words, in September 1960, the Party closed a page in the history of the conquest of independence, in the history of the putting into place of the Cameroon institutions, and opened another page, that of the consolidation of institutions and of national construction.*
>
> *Evidently, ours was not a road without hurdles, difficulties, problems and events arose, and the solutions found for those problems and our reactions to those events were dictated by the pace we had to give to the evolution of the nation.*
>
> *After Maroua, the people, in the Northern and the Southern sections of Western Cameroon had to decide for or against the recovery by Cameroon (his Cameroon) of the territorial dimensions that were hers before July 1919. The*

Foumban Conference elaborated a constitution which gave a federal form to the Republic."[16]

President Ahmadou Ahidjo's argument in his address raised issues which tickle the mind of any constitutional lawyer and political scientist in all its ramifications of what was a build up to what we came to know and accept as the Federal Republic of Cameroon which was welcomed with fanfare in October 1961.

To President Ahidjo, the Republic of Cameroon was the *mother* Nation to which the Southern Cameroons under British Trusteeship was eager to rejoin. Reunification, as he understood it, was to provide a framework within which the differences of language and culture could be accommodated. He regarded the Southern Cameroons as a territory that was previously under British trusteeship and was, by the outcome of the Plebiscite, to join *an independent sovereign state possessing an international, legal personality.* The Southern Cameroons was a territory without a political, international status.

Following this logic, the President of the Republic of Cameroon continued:

"It being unthinkable to tamper with the republican form of the regime, it was the Republic which had to transform itself into a federation, taking into account the return to it of a part of its territory, a part possessing certain special characteristics. The question therefore was not that of the birth of a new republic with a federal form.

Bowing to this logic we decided therefore, to amend the Constitution of the 21st of February 1960, since language and cultural differences needed to be given legal consideration. Thus it was that, at the historic Foumban Conference, after a couple of days of work in an atmosphere marked on either side by cordiality, we announced the main outlines of the modifications by which the constitution of the 21st February 1960 should become the Constitution of the Federal Republic of Cameroon that they can co-operate with the President of the Federal Republic of Cameroon.

As regards the National Federal Assembly, the two Assemblies, of the federated States have, according to the constitutional provisions, elected Federal Members of Parliament in the proportion of the forty members from the State of West Cameroon."

It is not my intention to revisit the Constitution of the Federal Republic of Cameroon except to say that President Ahidjo's

---

[16] AHMADOU AHIDJO: CONTRIBUTION TO NATIONAL CONSTRUCTION : Presence Africaine 1964

pronouncement on this issue in Ebolowa clearly shows that there didn't seem to have been an agreement of minds between the parties. While Ahidjo had in mind a territory voting to join a sovereign and legal nation, the West Cameroonians thought that their vote would lead the parties to negotiate for a nation that would be federal in character with all the trappings of federalism. President Ahidjo further argues or implies that the new territory was not bringing any constitution. Foumban, to him, was a meeting to jettison the sovereign nation to accommodate the new territory - an adjunct. Call the new territory 'West Cameroon' and the existing independent 'East Cameroon' and then you have your Federation; with the President of the existing State as Head of State of the Federation and the Prime Minister of West Cameroon, whoever he may be, the Vice-President.

It is noteworthy that President Ahidjo hardly referred to the name of Southern Cameroons. True to his concept, Southern Cameroons was a *territory* to be acquired by the new sovereign State over which he was presiding at the material time. This ran counter to the assurance he's reported to have given the U.N.; namely, that *la Republique du Cameroun* was not annexationist in its policy towards the British Southern Cameroons under the United Nations Trusteeship system. It is unfortunate that neither the U.N. nor the British government actively participated in the Foumban rendez-vous.

Nevertheless, state status was given to each component of the two territories that formed the Federal Republic of Cameroon. The set up allowed the Federated States to manage their in a manner they were accustomed to. This was true to a certain degree in so far as the Federated State of West Cameroon was concerned. Before long, tensions began to manifest themselves. The introduction of a paramilitary force like the gendarmerie threw West Cameroonians into confusion because they did know where the difference was between the West Cameroon Police Force and the new force which assumed functions in all the domains of the society. They engaged themselves in criminal investigations, traffic control etc; and were generally hostile and brutal to members of the public. Travelers were stopped and asked to produce identification papers, a phenomenon very alien to the peoples of West Cameroon. These were people who could travel all over the territory without anyone stopping them to question their movement except where a crime had been committed.

In public administration, similar tensions raised their ugly heads. Who was senior, the federal or the federated head where services or responsibilities overlapped. There was an overall Head of Administration appointed by the President of the Republic with residence in the federated state capital. Alongside him was the federated state Prime Minister who was an elected representative of the people.

On many occasions, the Federal Inspector claimed to be above the Prime Minister because of his position as a Federal Officer, an entity far larger in concept than the federated officer. No one ever thought of having resort to the constitution for an interpretation. Everything, it seems had only a political solution; no one was willing to upset the apple cart. The *laiser faire* attitude to use the judiciary to resolve any constitution or legal issue(s) is our legacy. We have wallowed in it for so long that the tenacity of our justice system remains doubtful and conveys the impression that our judiciary is weak or lacks the clout.

At the time of writing this piece, the Social Democratic Front (SDF) party is in court over the interpretation of its own constitution. What has astonished me is the fact that reasonable persons including our legal men don't see the sense in this test of our law(s). It is being passed off as an abomination intended to destabilize or attack and ridicule the party's hierarchy. It follows as day follows night that if anyone were to try it with the national constitution, he could be easily indicted for treason.

The basic case of the various anglophone groups is a resort to re-interpreting article 76 (b) of the U.N. Charter and article 47 of the constitution of the Federal Republic of Cameroon vis-à-vis the referendum of May 20, 1972. I will return to this soon.

The anglophone problem means the barring of a people of a common culture and heritage in a union where they are distinct from asserting their distinctiveness and the refusal of their rightful due in the national resources of the patrimony.

It is generally believed that Great Britain only partially fulfilled its obligations under the Trust given her over the Southern Cameroons. She did lead the territory to self-government by the secession from her colony and protectorate in Nigeria. She is blamed for not having guided her to full independence as provided for under the famous article 76(b) of the Charter. The status of Southern Cameroons at the time of the Foumban Talks, the Southern Cameroonians were obliged to talk to the party that claimed it was a senior in the discussions because it already was enjoying sovereignty and a place in the comity of nations while the so-called brothers were fighting to join in order to benefit from the status of sovereignty. To my mind, that is the inference that can be drawn from President Ahmadou Ahidjo's address which I have elaborately quoted herein.

Foumban produced the instrument that became the Constitution of the Federal Republic of Cameroon. In the Southern Cameroons which had now been transformed into the Federated State of West Cameroon, most people, including the elites, were satisfied with the nomenclature, a federation was in existence. Nobody questioned the distribution of powers to the components of this *being*. Essentially, all powers belonged to the central authority in Yaounde. I will leave the set up at this point. My concern is the failure of our lawyers in 1972 to challenge President Ahidjo when he unilaterally carried out a *constitutional coup* in dissolving the federation and replacing it with a centralized state. This was done in the face of Article 47 of the Constitution of 1961.

It is pertinent to study the provisions of the much talked of article under Part X, namely, *Amendment of the Constitution*.

"*47 (1) No bill to amend the Constitution may be introduced if it tends to impair the unity and integrity of the Federation.*

(2) Bills to amend the Constitution may be introduced either by the President of the Federal Republic after consultation with the Prime Ministers of the Federated Sates, or by any member of the Federal Assembly:

Provided that any bill introduced by a member of the Assembly shall bear the signatures of at least one third of its membership.

(3) The amendment may be passed by a simple majority of the membership of the Federal Assembly:

Provided that such majority included a majority of the membership elected from each Federated State.

(4) The President of the Federal Republic may request a second reading of a bill to amend the Constitution as of any other federal bill, and in like manner."

Bearing these constitutional provisions in mind, the question that may be asked is why did Ahidjo choose a referendum. It was done in a hurry. He addressed the Federal Assembly on May, 6 1972 while at the same time announcing the referendum for May 20, exactly two weeks or fourteen days to a day.

Was it right to introduce a bill that impaired "the integrity of the Federation? Was it right where the Constitution laid down specific procedural modalities as to how the federal nature of the Federation could be altered to introduce a procedure alien to that expressly mandated by those who believed that it was the best way for bringing into existence a new State in its diversity in culture, language and heritage in that manner. I am sure that those who participated in the Foumban talks were aware

CHAPTER X
LAW REPORTING

A veritable and credible justice system should be certain and predictable considering the fact that the law is very much influenced by a rapidly evolving society. The law in its content may mean different things to different peoples and even at different times or ages.

Modern society no longer believes in history handed down by oral tradition. That worked when there was a paucity of recorded human events or a total lack of them. Since the invention of printing, things have never been the same and now in a fast changing world of information technology, recorded events will multiply. Nobody can say for certain how far the information technology will take us. In these circumstances, Cameroon should not lag behind or be seen to be oblivious of the changes in the new world order.

If we are to be counted among those who assisted in developing the world in its global form, a record of our own contribution should take pride of place. Our cherished independence will soon clock half a century. In human terms, it is indeed a long time.

It is a sad recollection that, in this time space, there is no consistent record to which one can turn to for an appraisal of which direction our justice system is taking. Outside the enactments of the legislative bodies whose works are not so accessible, no record exists by way of publicising the said enactments nor commentaries or the interpretations given them by our courts.

This raises the question of Law Reports and Law Reporting. In Cameroon, law reporting is a hazardous affair whether we are considering the civil or common law jurisdictions. The past has witnessed a sporadic law reporting in both systems. A close study gives the impression that it lasted for a few years and depended very much on the concern of an individual or a group of individuals and the period covered is short, namely, the late sixties to the late seventies. The reason for this may be attributed to a lack of a steady flow of funds and perhaps lack of knowledge of the importance of this item of expenditure by sponsors. Worst still, is the lack of compilation of the enactments of our legislatures or law making bodies. And yet there is so much work in this area.

Law Reports are of equal importance to everyone concerned in one way or the other in the administration of justice. The judges, the legal practitioners, the common man and law students are equally concerned.

that a referendum was an alternative procedure for achieving the same results. But not in the manner Ahmadou Ahidjo got about it.

It is my view that the meeting in Foumban can in no way be described as a Constitutional Conference when this is compared to the Lancaster House Conference in London and the Lagos Conference that followed so soon thereafter. These were meetings in which the status of the Southern Cameroons had to be decided in the Federal Republic of Nigeria on the latter's attainment of independence.

President Ahidjo saw Foumban in a different light. He saw the exercise to accommodate a new component into an existing body because as he argues in his Ebolowa speech.

"The question therefore was not that of the birth
of a new republic with a federal form"

This reasoning vindicates the warming of the Nigerian Prime Minister, the Rt. Honourable Abubakar Tafawa Balewa when, on the eve of the Plebiscite Vote, addressing the people of the Southern Cameroon, assured them of their constitutional position in an independent Federal Republic of Nigeria following the constitutional arrangement in London and Lagos. He ended by saying that the people of the Southern Cameroons were taking a leap in the dark:

"If I may speak for a moment direct to the people of the Southern Cameroons, I ask you to examine very carefully the issues which are at stake. On the one hand you can choose certainty and security an honourable status as an integral part of a big nation in Africa with your future assured. With Nigeria you can look forward to sharing in the tremendous economic development of our country, to sharing in the massive schemes for expanding education to an extent hitherto beyond our dreams, and to the social benefits which we are now beginning to enjoy. Above all you can be assured of the security of the rule of law, the protection of your lives and houses and farms, and to the guarantee of your human rights. All this is waiting for you if you choose to come back to Nigeria. And now ask yourselves what is the alternative. You would throw in your lot with a country whose government has made no firm promises to you and has given no undertakings, a country which unfortunately has been torn in recent years by civil wars.

It pains me to mention these things and believe me I take no joy in the misfortunes of our neighbours, but it is my duty to warn you of the dangers which lie ahead of you if you go down that road. If you do so then you cannot expect as of right to live in peace, to cultivate your farms in peace, or to receive the same justice which has been provided for you until now. Instead of peace and prosperity, instead of more schools and hospitals and improved communications which you may genuinely expect from reunion with Nigeria, you will risk losing everything. If you vote against Nigeria I cannot control. You will be putting yourselves under a country which has different laws and a completely different attitude towards life. Just think carefully of all this. I do most sincerely ask you because it is not only your own immediate future which will be affected but the very survival of your families.

I shall now give you an outline of the economic and financial benefits conferred on the Trust Territory by the Nigerian Government during recent years. I must do this, not to boast of our generosity, but to refute the shameful lies which have been circulated in order to deceive the people who are going to vote on their future next month".

On a strict construction, Ahidjo's resort to a referendum was deliberate and politically astute. He realized that those in control in the Federated State of West Cameroon as of that date could influence the vote against the restructuring of the State as was being proposed. A majority were die-hard federalists and some, after an experience of just two years, were beginning to wonder whether the experiment would succeed.

Besides, the plebiscite vote for union had been limited to the Southern Cameroons. Now, it was going to be open to all and sundry in which the combined majority owed allegiance to him. The constitution could be put aside while he went on to consolidate his power base.

Very sadly for Cameroonians no challenge was filed and today we find ourselves unable to challenge any law or act perpetrated by public authorities whether for arbitrariness or *ultra vires*.

Our constitutions have become the floor mats of the executive arm of government. Right now we are under the non-implementation of very vital provisions of the Constitution of 1996. Today, we talk of two constitutions in use, the one of 1972 as amended by that of 1996. No individual, not even those who have sworn to uphold and abide by the constitution have dared to challenge it.

As our State has grown older we have departed further and further from the grandeur of a justice system and virtually lost faith in our own constitution. The reason, I think, is that the people never participated in the making of the constitution. It is the product of a few technocrats who surrounded the executive to the exclusion of the *people*. It came to the people like the tablet Moses brought down from the mountain on which were written the ten commandments.

An attempt was made in 1993 after the *Tripartite Talks* to draw up a constitution that would truly reflect the aspirations of Cameroonians with due regard given to their heritage, cultures and thus move Cameroon forward so as to render it modern and democratic. This effort seems to have been doomed to failure. After a few days of its establishment, the preliminary drafting committee failed to agree on the methodology and worse still the disagreement was based on cultural lines, namely, anglophones vis-à-vis francophones. Embittered by utterances made by francophones members, the anglophones withdrew their further participation in the committee. The fall out effect was the calling of an All Anglophone Conference to find if there was an alternative to the impasse. Nevertheless, the francophone-dominated committee went full steam ahead and eventually handed down the 1996 constitution whose structures and institutions have not been implemented up to this moment of writing.

It is clear on a cursory look at the so-called basic law that it installs a dictatorship rather than promote, democracy. So long as this situation persists, the earth underneath will continue to rumble and tremble.

Each, in his position, wants to be enlightened of the current trends of the law.

The judge, because he wants to be satisfied that his opinion is in agreement with that of his colleagues and theirs with his. If the judge is sitting at first instance, he would be happy to know that a higher jurisdiction has upheld his point of view not only on a question of interpretation of the law but also in his sense of justice and in the justness of his judicial intuition.

The legal practitioner, after a studious indulgence in the law reports goes before the court confident that he would not only win his case but would live up to the tenets of his profession in assisting the court in doing justice, an important element in the profession which is intended to ensure that justice is done to all manner of persons. The lawyer does this by citing recent authorities that he knows and may not be known to the court because they may not yet have been widely canvassed.

It is foolhardy for any student to imagine that he can depend on the textbooks to learn the law. Worst still to do so by summarized copies of textbooks (polycopies). The reasoning of the judge in a written judgment opens the mind to the legal principle invoked. The two should go together. The textbook arrives at a principle of law after a study of several decisions. He cites them to justify the principle enunciated.

The student reads the textbook because it is more expansive in scope than a few reported cases. Therefore, a combination of the opinion of the text writer and the logical reasoning of a sitting judge go a long way to fortify the intellect of the would-be lawyer. A summary of textbooks should be absolutely abhorred. They encourage the student to succumb to learning by rote or heart or by cramming.

Law reports are thus a most valuable source of acquisition of a deeper knowledge of the law as it has been interpreted down the years by men of great erudition. To achieve this objective, a system of closely following up the decisions handed down by different jurisdictions of the court hierarchy should be put in place. A good documentation or compilation is not only necessary but important because when these are studied side by side with the bare legislative enactments, they provide the practitioner of the judicial system with an indefinable source of knowledge. Cameroon, at this moment, is in dire need of the machinery for attaining this desired objective. What is to be done?

In old England, judicial decisions were treated as authoritative pronouncements of the law. And so Chief Justice *Priscot* could as far back as 1454 say:

> *"And moreover if this plea were now adjudged bad, as you maintain, it would assuredly be a bad example to young apprentices who study by the year Books, for they would never have confidence in their books if now we were to adjudge in the contrary of what has so often been adjudged in the Books."*

Another chronicler of English law, Black, believed that the use of law reports was "an established rule to follow previous that are cases flatly absurd or unjust.

The law report is the place where you can find the fine point of law that forms the very basis of a decision or judgment. Therefore, it acts as a guide for future decisions where the facts are the same or very near the same, or as one would say on *all fours*. Any system of justice that does not maintain records of its proceedings leaves a lacuna on the record.

In common law Cameroon, an effort was made by Mr J. A O'Brien Quinn, as he was then, to compile selected judgments of the Supreme Court of West Cameroon. The reports were issued under the title of "West Cameroon Law Reports" (to be cited as WCLR) on behalf of the West Cameroon Bar Association. The first volume covered the 1962, 1963 and 1964. The second series covered the years 1965, 1966 and 1967. The last covered selected judgments in 1968. That year Quinnn was transferred from Buea where he had been the Procureur Général for West Cameroon to the Ministry of Justice as Technical Adviser cumulating that position with Judge of the Federal Court of Justice.

The point must be made that Mr Justice J. A O'Brien Quinn was an expatriate from the Republic of Ireland whose departure saw the demise of law reporting in Common Law Cameroon. At least for some time. The departure of Justice Quinn signaled the demise of the reports.

By the early seventies, a good crop of Anglophone legal scholars were employed in the State University of Yaounde. Fully aware of the importance and necessity of recorded judicial opinions they awakened to the unfinished task of Justice O'Brien Quinn.

They produced two sets of reports under the title "The University of Yaounde Law Reports (to be cited as U.Y.L.R. They were edited by the English Law Department Faculty of Laws – U.Y Cameroon, with Prof. P.Y Ntamark and Drs. C. E Anyangwe, C. N. Ngwasiri, E. N. Ngwafor, S. A. Fonkam, S. A. Munsu and J. N. Dion making up the Editorial Board.

Two volumes are available. One covering the years 1968 – 1970 and the other 1971 – 1973 and like the first to be cited as (1971 – 1973). They were patterned on those of J. A. O'Brien Quinn. Once again, their existence was as brief as those of Quinn.

The absence of any law reports henceforth left lawyers in particular depending upon photocopies of judgments they could lay their hands upon in the various registries of the courts.

Not until after over twenty years did Barrister Innocent Bonnu surface with the "Cameroon Common Law Reports" in 1997. The first part appeared and was to be cited as (1997) 1 CCLR and published by the *Liberty Law Firm House* based on Tiko –Mutengene Road, Tiko, in the South West Province.

Justice Florence Rita Arrey as President of the South West Court of Appeal was pertinent in the forward she made introducing Part 1 of the Report when she said:

> *"For those of us trained in the Common Law, the absence of Cameroon Law Reports has created a big void in our Judicial Process. That is why I laud the initiative of the publishers of this Law Report. I hope that it will fill the lacuna which has existed in our courts and that it will be a companion both for the Legal Practitioner in preparing his brief and the Judge in writing his judgment.*
>
> *We hope that this initial publication will be followed by others periodically. I have no hesitation in recommending this Law Report to Judges, Legal Practitioners, Students and their Professors."*

In the first part the authors stated that it would be a quarterly publication. At the time of making this record, we are in possession of Part 11 of 2005 currently in circulation. My concern is that our young practitioners don't seem to be aware of the existence of the reports not to talk of referring to them as sources. I consider it an aberration for a law student not to realise that law reports are an encyclopaedia of knowledge; worse still for the common law practitioner who does not realise that a decided case could be a turning point when a relevant case is cited of which the court was not aware and the opposing party is taken aback. For the judge, it is useful because it leads him to distinguish and reconcile with previous decisions known to him.

If the publishers of this marvelous effort have not respected their article of faith, they should be excused but given honour because of what it takes to keep up a specialised publication like the one that is being considered. The financial outlay is enormous and the reporters to be attached to each jurisdiction are a rare commodity. Such should be of the first class who can very quickly analyse a decided case and see how far such decision help to develop the law.

These joint tasks are financially demanding and I don't know how *Liberty Publications* has managed so far and for how long they can continue if their dream has to be realised.

Besides, for how long shall we continue to speak only in terms of common law application in Cameroon when international law, conventions and covenants are now influencing domestic law to a degree that was unimaginable a few decades ago.

To my mind, the solution seems to lie in setting up a National Law Reporting Council or whatever name may be given to it in so far as it will cover decisions handed down by our domestic courts. It would be of immense interest to know how the Court of Appeal in Bertoua interprets some controversial sections of the OHADA treaty when compared to an interpretation by the jurisdiction in Buea of similar status. The same goes for the new *Criminal Procedure Code*.

The accomplishment of the task of law reporting has to be left to private initiative. A Non-Governmental Organisation would be in a better position to realise the desired results than an officially controlled body. Such a body would be in dire need of funds. It could appeal to government for funding; as well as international funding bodies and Foundations. It should be neutral in its performance especially in its selection of the decisions to be reported. This rules out any sitting Judge or Magistrate from being a member. The structure should be such that there should be trained law reporters at each Court of Appeal jurisdiction and a team of reporters at the Supreme Court.

The worrying problem with law reports is its marketability because of its limited targeted population. One can only count on the legal profession and universities. In Cameroon, Cameroonians who should benefit from the West Cameroon Law Reports by Mr J. A. O'Brien Quinn as he then was and the current Cameroon Common Law Reports by *Liberty Publications,* don't seem to be much enthusiastic. It should be interesting to know Liberty Publication's secret for surviving up to now. Both the West Cameroon Law Reports and the University of Yaounde Law Reports benefited from official funding. Nevertheless, we need the reports in order to build up our own jurisprudence.

The position is more complicated if the reports are to be produced in the bi-jural system that we practise. In the one system law reports are intended to infuse into the mind of the user logical reasoning that goes a long way to make the reader follow what propelled the judge to arrive at his decision.

On the other hand, the other system is so brief that the layman can't say how the court arrived at the final verdict.

As H. C. Gutteridge asserts in his book – 'Comparative Law' 2nd Edition:[17]

> *"The character feature of a continental law report, when compared with its English equivalent, is its brevity. The facts are not reported and the conclusion arrived at by the court are sometimes stated in a few sentences. A continental judgment is purely impersonal; and the decision of the court as a whole, and the voice of the dissenting judge is never heard. Precedents are very rarely referred to in the judgment and, in any event, they are not cited as precedents but are only mentioned as supporting or illustrating the line of reasoning adopted by the court*" and [18]J. G. Wetter makes the point more poignant when he says:
>
> *"A vital and characteristic distinction between the common law and the civil law approach to judicial opinions is that whereas the opinions of common law judges are highly individualised and tend to be personal expression of a particular judge expressed in his characteristic style, the judicial utterances of civil law courts as an institution rather than of the actual personnel who constitute that court. By contrast, when an English court gives an opinion, it is always apparent that "men, not courts are at work."*

As I have pointed out, I assumed judicial duties as President of the North West Provincial Court of Appeal in August and was officially installed in October 1977. I was taking over from my good old time friend, the Late Mr Justice George Simon Ekema.

Heading the Legal Department at the time was Mr Benjamin Mutanga Itoe. The first time I knew Mr Itoe was in the late sixties after his graduation from the University of Lagos, Nigeria. The same goes for the late Mr Justice Hans Kome Ngalame. He, on the other hand, graduated from the University of Ife, Nigeria. Mr Abel Nfor Njamnsi was well known to me from Bali College and in Buea where we worked as young clerks after leaving Secondary School before going our different ways for legal studies. Mr Justice Njamnsi of late like Mr Itoe was a graduate of Lagos University.

The specific mention of these individuals is because of the role they played in the saga that will soon unfold in this part of this work. They formed the new crop of the Anglophone common lawyers who underwent training in ENAM before their integration into the Legal and Judicial Service.

---

[17] H.C. Gutteridge on "Comparative Law" (2nd Edition).

[18] In his "The Styles of Appellate Judicial Opinions (1960) p. 32 quoted by Dennis Lloyd in "Introduction to Jurisprudence with Selected Texts" (2nd Edition p. 392).

After graduating from ENAM, they were posted to the Legal Department Buea headed at the time by the late Mr Frederick Ngomba Eko with me as his assistant. Mr Eko and I had a good working relationship and I think I enjoyed and merited his confidence. Many persons in the profession, especially those in the private Bar, found him un-co-operative and unnecessarily difficult to deal with. Where the issue was controversial, he made it a duty to have my opinion before he acted. Members of the private Bar were surprised that I tolerated his tantrums and idiosyncrasies. Nevertheless, I attest to the fact that he was a very meticulous and hard working person. I think his problem was public relations. He handled the transition from the expatriates to the Cameroonians well.

By 1970, the volume of work in criminal matters was mounting and demanded expeditious treatment. It was considered necessary to decentralize the work of the Procureur General's department by opening up a branch in Bamenda. The decision having been taken, the question arose as to who should fill the position. Mr Eko called me to his office to have the issue resolved. It was his habit to pose the problem and then seek my view.

I told him that I considered that since the work of the department was essentially that of public prosecutions, we needed someone who was "smart" and able to face the very experienced lawyers that we had at the time. Persons like Alakija, Adesanya, David Ogwo, J. O. Otu, Theophilus Anomnachi, Kubeinje the Nigerian lot and Cameroonians like Gorji Dinka, Henry Enochong, Luke Sendze, Godfrey Layu, and A.T. Enow. My idea of "smart" was someone who would not be frightened by the legal juggernauts. In all these considerations, two persons were actually in our minds, namely; Itoe and Ngalame. In the meantime, rumours were reaching me that the Itoe sympathizers were saying that Mr Ngalame, as he then was, would be selected in preference to Itoe because he was a product of Cameroon Protestant College, Bali, as myself. This was far-fetched. I did not have the consideration of the 'old boy's tie' in my mind at all. The professional interest was my pre-occupation. I believed Ngalame, from his composure and disposition would be more suited for the bench than an aggressive prosecutor. I proposed Itoe whom Mr Eko accepted after hearing the reasons I advanced. And so Mr Itoe became the first legal officer to open the branch of the department in Bamenda. By the time he was being installed in 1971 by Mr Justice S. M. L Endeley, Chief Justice of West Cameroon, I was the Procureur General and his head of department. Mr Eko had then been transferred to the Ministry of Justice after a study course.

1972 was a year that experienced constitutional and administrative changes. It witnessed the abolition of the Federal structure which was replaced by an over-centralised State, thenceforth to be known as the United Republic of Cameroon. The Federated State of West Cameroon underwent a mutation that brought into existence the North West and South West Provinces to be headed by Governors appointed by the President of the Republic. Provincial Courts of Appeal were established with headquarters in the Principal cities of the Provinces.

Ordinance No. 72/4 of 26 August 1972 laid down the judicial organization and was amended from time to time. As far as the hierarchy of the courts were concerned, it provided as follows:

"Article 1 (new) Justice shall be administered by:
- The Courts of First Instance
- The High Courts
- The Military Courts
- The Supreme Court

The restructuring naturally led to the creation of posts to be filled. In the Province, a President headed the judicial service while a Procureur Général headed the legal service. Two vacancies became available for the North West jurisdiction, that is to say, the President of the Court of Appeal and the Procureur Général at the said Court. For the President, Mr Justice Ekema who had presided over the High Court in Buea easily emerged as a natural choice. The choice of a Procureur Général posed a few problems. The Minister of Justice at the time was the Honourable Simon Achiri Achu. He was very concerned about the profile of the individual to fill the position. He called me to seek my opinion. We were both agreed that in terms of profile, Mr Oliver M. Inglis, as he then was, most fitted the position. He was an expatriate from the West Indies and was among the first batch of expatriates when on unification, the Federated State of West Cameroon very much needed qualified legal and judicial personnel in the common law. He had been clerk of the West Cameroon Federated State Assembly and the House of Chiefs. He served in the Prime Minister's Office as Legal Adviser. Besides, he had the longest standing in the Bar having been called to the English Bar in 1955 at a very young age. Despite his long stay in Cameroon from 1962 to when this problem arose, he remained an expatriate. He became a naturalised Cameroonian many years later. I pointed out to the honourable Minister that with the appointments of Cameroonians to high posts of responsibility in the Legal and Judicial Service, it appeared it was government's policy to Cameroonise the judiciary. He agreed. I reminded him of Mr Itoe having been running the State Counsel's office since 1970. From the reports he was sending to me as his boss, we could try him even though he was still in the first grade of the judicial scale. Again the Minister agreed. And so Mr Benjamin Mutanga Itoe was named the first Procureur Général in the North West Province in 1972. The appointment was an acting position (par interim) because of his grade.

Our Francophone colleagues were furious. I remember people like Remy-Jean Mbaya, Legal Adviser in the Presidency and Gabriel Djeundjang in the Supreme Court were all mad. They considered it an abuse of the hierarchical considerations in judicial appointments. As soon as the appointment was announced, I got a phone call from Mrs Itoe, Mispa (neé Ntuba) who said:

"*Sir, thank you. We know you are the one who has done it.*" I replied.
'*Let Benji acquit himself well.*'

Contrary to what most people thought or must have imagined, my posting to Bamenda as President of the North West Court of Appeal was not so much *the return of the native to his home land.*

Since my graduation from Cameroon Protestant College Bali (BMC) the North Wes Province to me faded into oblivion. I was first employed by the Cameroon Development Corporation. I think I have already mentioned this fact somewhere in this work. Service took me to Tiko and later to Buea where I began my civil service career. The contact I had with the Nigerians who controlled the Southern Cameroons Civil Service from top to bottom unconsciously kindled my interest or better put inspired me to start the search for the *golden fleece.*

I found the opportunity in the Nigerian College of Arts, Science and Technology, (Nigercol) Enugu, Eastern Nigeria. There were two other branches, namely, in Ibandan, Western Region and in Zaria in the Northern Region. The Nigercol was not a High School. It graduated professionals in the areas of surveys, estate management and other areas of studies intended to prepare qualified personnel for an independent Nigeria.

I traveled to Enugu twice. First, to write the entrance examination, and secondly to attend the interview after my success in the written exam. Suffice it to say that I entered Nigercol in 1957 graduating in 1959. I resumed service in the Southern Cameroons Civil Service after Enugu.

By 1961 I was among the few who won the Southern Cameroons Scholarship to study law in London – Inns of Court School of Law and was called to the Bar by Lincoln's Inn in the Michaelmas Term, 1965.

On return to Cameroon in late 1965, I was appointed Federal Counsel and posted to the Attorney General's Chambers Buea where I began work on January 11, 1966.

Henceforth, I remained in that department till 1977, when I was named President of the Court of Appeal, Bamenda; in a sense I was returning in a responsible capacity after twenty-one years' absence from the Province.

Socially I was better known in the South West Province than in my native Province. The comings and goings to cover the assizes of the High Courts and other court engagements were more officious than social. In Buea both official and private functions offered me an opportunity for lasting relationships.

The very name *Wakai* was considered not native to the North West Province but to the coastal region of Victoria, today's Limbe.

It was alleged that taking over from Mr Justice Ekema a native of the South West, one South Westerner was replacing another. Not until my bio-data was read out in the installation speech did some people take a breath of relief. Since assuming duty in 1966 I knew no transfer. This appointment caused me to experience a transfer. My contemporaries and colleagues had worked in several stations in the Federated State of West Cameroon. My immediate predecessor had served in most of the Divisional capitals in West Cameroon.

As far as I was concerned, I felt comfortable because I was beginning my career on the bench without any prejudice.

My first experience with the Bar was that many lawyers did not put in much time in the preparation of their briefs. As such, many litigants suffered because at nearly every court session, Counsel applied for adjournment manufacturing one excuse or another. Then there was general lateness in appearances in court, without reasons but excuses.

In response to this, I adopted a strategy whereby the sessions began at 09h00; if Counsel was late I told his client to brief a more hard working Counsel. The court would then give the matter one more chance.

In starting sessions at 09h00 in the forenoon or so soon thereafter as required by the service process and embarrassing Counsel before their clients to look for a hard working Counsel, courts sessions and their starting times were respected.

For my eight years as President of the Court of Appeal, the court handled not less than *223* serious cases with judgments delivered on time. Of these, I wrote *140* judgments including rulings. I have compiled in 13 volumes these judgments of the North West Court of Appeal from 1978 – 1985.

As so often happens with contested issues, vested interests are nearly always revealed or manifest themselves. I shall briefly treat one or two hereunder.

In the *People vs. Joseph Dim*[19] the tenacity of our sense of justice was put to the test. Mr Joseph Dim was a Nigerian businessman based in Bamenda with a shopping shed in Bamenda Central Market. Apparently the nature of his business required him to get his supplies presumably from his native country. He was in this particular instance charged with no offence; nevertheless, he was detained in Batibo by the Police. Soon after his arrest, he was searched and the sum of three million one hundred and fifty-seven thousand, one hundred and ninety (3.157.190) francs cfa found on him. This, no doubt, was the money with which he intended to buy goods from Nigeria for his shop in Bamenda. To justify their act, the police alleged that he was attempting to take the money out of the country. Batibo, as anyone who knows Cameroon, knows is the Chief Town of the Batibo Sub Division in Momo Division of the North West Province. Poor Joseph Dim pleaded with the Police that he was a businessman carrying on business in the United Republic of Cameroon. This plea fell on deaf ears. He was subsequently transferred to Police custody in Bamenda, the seat of the Court of Appeal.

Efforts to have him released on bail were frustrated by the prosecuting authorities. The Procureur Général[20] indicated to Counsel for Dim that he was free to apply to the High Court, Mezam Judicial Division, for bail for his client. On December 28, 1979, the High Court presided over by His Lord, Mr Justice J. P. C Nganje, granted the prayer and then proceeded to make the following order:

> *"That the money confiscated from the suspect in the absence of any accusation of theft against him be paid into B.I.A.O. (Bank) Bamenda with instructions for the Police to the Bank that they shall have no access to the money until they were instructed to the contrary by the said Police."*

The reaction of the Procureur Général's Office was one of defiance and arrogance to say the least. They showed their dissatisfaction with the ruling by lodging an appeal. This, of course, was their right in a contentions matter. Something happened that discredited it as a department that is committed to ensure that justice is done to all manner of persons.

---

[19] Appeal No. BCA/3c/80 of 27 Feb. 1980
[20] Mr Benjamin Itoe was the incumbent.

It was both curious and interesting that at the hearing in the Court of Appeal the Advocate General[21] assistant to the Procureur Général conceded that no offence had been committed although, according to him, he imagined or had a suspicion that there could be an offence under the Exchange Control Regulations. As a matter of fact, the department did not possess the alleged regulations.

Once again, the Legal Department per the Advocate General submitted in writing what I consider were sweeping statements when, for instance, he urged the court to hold that in so far as there is an indication from the department that investigations are still going on or in progress, the release on bail is likely to prejudice the course of investigations; the court must, on these indications exercise its discretionary powers in favour of the prosecuting department.

If this argument is tenable, then, the adjudicating role of the courts in criminal matters for that matter, must come to naught. This argument was so naïve that were it to be accepted as a general principle in criminal matters, the courts would cease to be neutral and free arbiters in all contentious matters. It would amount to one party being able to claim victory from the very start. This is what, by necessary implication the court was being called upon to uphold as a sound principle of law.

In writing the unanimous opinion of the court, I found the exhibition of a strong feeling so poorly and puerily presented by a department that acts or should act as a minister of justice. I said, *inter alia*:

> *"We refuse to be taken in by such a dangerous development in a branch of law where the liberty of the citizen is in issue. Again it was submitted by the Advocate General that the evidence showed that if released on bail, the Respondent was likely to escape and thereby prejudice the investigations. The evidence on record is all affidavit evidence, viz, the affidavit of Mr Sendze and the counter affidavit of the Advocate General himself. We have examined this evidence and in particular that in the counter affidavit. We fail to find such evidence. The nearest thing to support this submission is what appears in paragraphs 6,7, and 8 which reads:*
> - *6. That the applicant is a Nigerian doing business in Bamenda.*
> - *7. That there have been several cases where Nigerians released on bail escaped to their country.*
> - *8. That if released, applicant may escape to Nigeria."*

I continued my trend of thought as shared by my colleagues in saying:

> *"We do not see where in these statements it has been shown that the respondent attempted to escape or did such acts as would have compelled any responsible man to conclude that he was attempting to escape. By this*

---

[21] Mr George Mbanda Asu was the Advocate General.

submission, we understand the learned Attorney General as wanting us to presume against the respondent that being a Nigerian businessman in this country, he must escape from justice as soon as an allegation (criminal) is made against him. In this case, there was no offence alleged against the respondent, not even at the time of this appeal as was pointed out by Counsel for respondent and conceded to by the Attorney General.

Another presumptuous submission was that because the respondent is alleged to have admitted that he was going to Otu in the Manyu Division of the South West Province and that Otu being a border Town, that must be taken by itself to be "enough to show that he was not merely traveling with money within the country but raised a strong suspicion that there was an attempt to export the money to Nigeria which attempt was only arrested at Batibo", to use the language of the Attorney General. It would be a sad day for Cameroonian justice when the courts will only act on suspicion and not on solid facts. Once more, we refuse to be party to such a distortion of a fundamental principle of criminal justice".

We concluded our opinion by varying the Judge's order and substituted same with the following:

"- a) that the sum of 3.157.190 francs cfa the subject matter of the proceedings in the Mezam High Court presided over by Mr Justice Nganje (Suit No. 52m/79 be removed from S.C.B Bamenda Branch and paid to Joseph Dim, the Respondent, in cash within twenty four hours from the date of this Orders.

b) that this Order be served immediately on the Procureur General of the North West Province, the Provincial Chief of Judicial Police or by whatever name the person for the time being discharging those functions is called and finally

c) the Manager, S.C.B Bamenda or any person acting in such a post. That these Orders be carried out."

Chapter XI
The Broken Scales of Justice

It has always been a mystery to me how men can feel themselves honoured by the humiliation of their fellow beings. (Mahatma Gandi)

Ncho No. 1

Suit No. HCB/21/79 was heard at first instance in the Mezam Judicial Division of the High Court by his Lordship Mr Justice Scott Moses Ataba Anyangwe (deceased).

The parties were Mr Joseph Ncho, a businessman in Bamenda in his capacity as an applicant with the Commissioner of Police, Bamenda and the Procureur Général for the North West Province as respondents.[*]

The action before the court was by way of motion duly supported by applicant's wife.

The facts deposed to were that the applicant was detained by the first respondent on the instruction of the 2nd respondent on the 27 June 1979.

The next day the 2nd respondent personally interrogated the applicant. By evening of the same day the 1st respondent positively promised to have applicant released on bail if he produced three sureties. When the 3 sureties turned up he changed his mind and refused to grant applicant bail.

It was revealed that applicant's petrol tanker registered as NW 966C was also being detained by the police for allegedly containing ordinary petrol and not supper petrol.

Experts from AGIP, the head quarters of the suppliers to the applicant had, on a previous visit, found no truth in the allegation against the applicant. The AGIP experts issued a written report to support their findings.

Despite these well established facts, both the applicant and tanker remained detained notwithstanding the expert reports from AGIP and neither the applicant nor the fuel tanker was released.

On these facts, Counsel for applicant in his affidavit, deposed to the effect that even if what applicant had done amounted to an offence, such could not be compared to offences under section 276, murder or section 320 which are of a class where bail would not normally be granted because of their gravity.

The counter-affidavit did not suggest that the applicant would jump bail if that was granted. The first respondent deposed. The

---

[22*] Suit No. HCB/21M/79

Commissioner of Public Security filed no counter-affidavit but during the hearing he testified *viva voce*. He acted the way he did on the orders of the second respondent, namely, the Procureur Général.

The learned Procureur Général deposed to a counter-affidavit in addition to oral evidence given before the Presiding Judge.

He tried to justify the continuous detention of the applicant and tanker on the basis that investigations in respect of the allegations were still continuing.

As for the tanker he was not too fussy on its continuous detention because, for him, there must be an alternative reservoir in which the fuel that was suspected to be a mixture – *super and ordinary petrol*, could be stored. In justifying his point of view the Procureur Général alluded to the provisions of the section 118 (2) of the Criminal Procedure Ordinance.

The trial judge held the view that the section applies to cases where the suspect has actually been charged to court and is standing trial. To further expatiate, the judge stated:

> "*It is patently inapplicable in the instant case since on the affidavit evidence no charge has so far been proffered against the applicant.*
>
> *It seems to me that in the instant case the appropriate Law is to be found in section 125 of the Criminal Procedure Ordinance. This section. provides:*
>
> *Notwithstanding the provisions of section 119 and 120 a judge of the High Court may in any case direct that any person in custody in the Region be admitted to bail or that the bail required by a Magistrate's court or Police Officer be reduced.*"

In the face of all these the learned Judge proceeded to pronounce on the law as he understood it. He was convinced that so long as the applicant had not been charged to court, he was empowered to exercise his power under the circumstances judiciously. He agreed with the case of *Re Whitehouse*[23] where the power was refused because the suspect had a criminal record.

To further strengthen the investigative authorities' claim to continue to detain the applicant, the judge resorted to the notorious case of Mamuda Dantata vs. Inspector General of Police where the court held that if there is a deliberate attempt by the suspect to interfere with the course of justice or where the accused person who has been granted bail has clearly indicated his readiness to commit other offences in order to suppress evidence. The judge reasoned that, although in the *Dantata case* the accused had already been charged to court and the principles

---

[23] Re Whitehouse (1951) IKB, 672   2. Mamuda Dantata (1958) N.R.N.L.R.3

enunciated therein as to whether bail should or should not be granted held even better than for cases such as this instant case where no charge had been proffered against the suspect and investigations into the allegations against him were still continuing. The High Courts have consistently refused to grant bail for such grave offences such as murder under section 276 of the Penal Code and aggravated theft under section 320 of the said Code. Once again, the learned trial Judge found himself fortifying his conviction by citing another English case, namely, *Re Robinson 23 L. J. Q. B. 286* [24], which to him, was relevant:

> *"I consider to be of considerable persuasive authority. In the case it was held that the proper test of whether bail should or should not be refused is whether it is probable that the defendant will appear to take his trial and that the test should be applied with reference to the following consideration:*
> 1. *The nature of the accusation*
> 2. *The nature of the evidence in support of the accusation.*
> 3. *The severity of the punishment which conviction would entail.*
> 4. *Whether the sureties are independent or indemnified by the accused person."*

There is no doubt that after applying the principles immediately quoted, the judge came to the conclusion that none of them was applicable to the case under consideration. In the final result, he found thus:

> *"For the foregoing reasons, I find that there are no reasons, real or apparent or circumstances, for supposing that the applicant will interfere with the course of justice or frustrate the investigations which are continuing against him if he is released on bail. Consequently I find that his continued detention is as unjustifiable as it is unwarranted. Therefore by virtue of section 125 of the Criminal Procedure Ordinance the application in respect of bail is hereby granted."*

After a review of the evidence as regards the tanker, the court ordered its release within 48 (forty-eight) hours from the moment the ruling and order were pronounced. That is by noon on 13th July 1979. Suffice it to say that both the ruling on the release and order as regards the tanker were blatantly disobeyed.

Ncho No. 2
This conduct of the Procureur Général opened up further proceedings I would like to be referred to as *Ncho No. 2*.

---

[24] Re Robinson 23 L. J. Q. B. 286

On August 5, 1979, the learned Mr Justice Hans Ekor' Tarh heard in Chambers Suit No. *HCB/23M/79* which I have chosen to refer to as Ncho No. 2 because it was a direct consequence of the ruling and order in Suit No. *HCB/21M/79*. The ruling was delivered in Chambers. The parties were *Joseph Adu Ncho vs. The Procureur Général and The Commissioner of Police*. In his ruling, the judge made a review of the suit whose facts had led to the ones he was now invited to determine. The facts of that case have been dealt with in detail when Mr Justice Anyangwe heard *Ncho No. 1* for the first time.

Mr Justice Hans Ekor' Tarh reviewed both facts and law as was presented before him on the basis of the other aspect that Mr Justice Anyangwe had based his ruling. The original cause of action dealt with granting bail to a person whose offence was under investigation and his tanker unduly detained because it was allegedly used in the commission of an offence.

The first judge having held that the whole process, that is to say, the unlawful detention of the suspect and non-release of the tanker could not be justified in law. *Ncho No. 2,* through his person or action brought by him sought the court to pronounce on his unlawful detention and the impoundment of his petrol tanker.

Mr Justice Ekor' Tarh in reviewing the facts that had brought the case before him made quite profound statements which did not give the matter finality. Instead, his ruling gave room to Mr Ncho to exploit the law following his ruling.

He said, *inter alia:*

> "This court can only comment that considering the oath of office taken by respondents who are officers of the court and very close collaboration in the task of administration of justice in the country in the name of the President, and who are so expressly enjoined by the first Magistrate of the realm, would not be heard to disobey to carry out a legitimate judicial order. As the order of the court which I read in the manuscript was absolute and unconditional, the applicant was perfectly entitled to take possession of his tanker NW966 exactly 48 hours of the order and would not wait for the 1st or 2nd respondent to invite him to take or issue further orders of releasing the object. It seems obvious therefore that unless the applicant will not mitigate his own losses a further detention of the tanker NW966C after 48 hours is not the official responsibility of the office of the Procureur Général and that of the Commissioner of National Security but that of individuals and personal responsibility of any persons who hides under official nomenclature to cause damage to the applicant by not releasing the keys and the particulars of the said tanker as ordered. It is none of the applicant's business as to the content

of the tanker for the order touched and concerned the tanker and not the petrol herein. The respondents cannot even be heard to say they are hiring the tanker without the prior consent of the owner to preserve the suspected petrol for it is their duty to find space for the safe custody of their exhibits. It is most inconsistent with the office of the Procureur Général *and the Commissioner of National Security to defy a court order because it is their respective duties and obligations to carry out such orders without conditions as stipulated in the final statement enjoined in all court orders, rulings and judgments. An appeal does not work as a stay of execution so the point that the* Procureur Général *is appealing against the entire order of the court is not sufficient in the circumstances of this motion."*

Ncho No. 3

Ncho No. 3 was the outcome of Ncho No. 1 in that it was an appeal from Ncho No. 1. the panel comprised Merrs. Justice J.P.C. Nganje, M.A. Deba and T.E. Mbuagbaw.

The appellants were *the Commissioner, National Security Bamenda and Joseph Adu Ncho as respondent.*

The ground of appeal as filed was that:
a) The decision granting bail is unreasonable and cannot be supported having regard to the evidence
b) Other grounds to be filed on receipt of the records.

Before arguing the appeal the Procureur Général filed two additional grounds. In the first additional ground, the trial Judge was accused of making an error of law in granting bail to the respondent in the course of the investigations when there was evidence that the transactions for which he was held in custody were complex and still under verification. The second additional ground accused the Judge of erring in law in failing to order the respondent to surrender his passport to the police in the interest of the investigations that were being carried out against him.

In addition to his written submissions the Procureur Général supplemented them with oral arguments. They were all replied to by F. Gorji Dinka, learned Counsel for the respondent. The Court does not seem to have found much of the arguments for the appellant material and of much help. It took the position as expressed in these words:

"The appellant's contention in this regards is that the court's failure to make the order is such as to justify this court setting aside the judgment of the court below. In view of the divergence of the both Counsel in this respect, we shall examine the records to determine the issue which was before the court in this material particular. It is evident that save in the appellants' oral

arguments in court, the appellants' counter affidavit did not contain anything in this connection. This being so, it will be useful to reproduce in full all that transpired in the court in this regard. At page 10 lines 18-32 of the records the following information is apparent:

<u>Mr B.M. Itoe: Procureur Général</u>: *In objection to this application at least for the time being we would be relying on our own sworn and filed affidavit dated 9th July 1979. As the first respondent has pointed out reports were made to me disclosing offences outlined in paragraph 3 of the counter affidavit. When the agents of the applicant were detained on my instructions by the first on the first respondent of 7th June 1979, the applicant was out of Bamenda.*

It is alleged that he traveled to Europe and from 7th June 1979 to 27th June 1979 the applicant "was a wanted man." Other information which slipped in was that applicant did not go to Europe but was within the country. Up to date and since applicant was detained on 27/6/79 he has not produced his passport to first respondent. So I am unable to satisfy myself that he left the country within this period."

In its opinion expressed unambiguously, the court considered this supposedly oral arguments as a *narration* by the Procureur Général of his experiences to the court and not an application which required the court to make an order.

Like the immediate foregoing ground of appeal, I share again the opinion of the court when it dismissed the second ground of appeal as not being a ground known to the law as it was applicable then or even now.

The Ncho cases have a close resemblance to that of *The people vs. Joseph Dim*. The State in each case was determined to deprive each of his liberty even in the light of the provisions of 17 - 20 of the Criminal Procedure Ordinance (CPO) which have now become a cardinal principle in our new Criminal Procedure Code (CPC)[25] In so determined to undermine the law, the Procureur General was no longer playing the role of a minister of justice but exposing himself as a hardcore persecutor. For what other reason could there be for the court to order that money seized from a suspect (Dim) and ordered to be put in a particular bank is deposited in a bank different from that so ordered? Again what reason could justify the arrant refusal to release the suspect (Ncho) and tanker in the face of the express order of the court?

Ncho No. 4

---

[25] 1 Sections 17 - 20 of the CPO and Section 222 - 235 of the CPC

Prima facie, the treatment meted out to Mr Joseph Adu Ncho by the State officials exhibit a prejudice of a sort that anyone would have been compelled to believe that there was more to the saga than the discharge of official judicial duties. In the end, being so battered by the conduct of the cases against him, Joseph Ncho certainly saw the action of the two officials as going beyond their legal obligations.

His reaction that emerged from such conduct was a personal action between him and Benjamin Itoe and Emmanuel Sancho as defendant.[26] The judgment in this particular matter is extremely brief. The reason. Having filed the *writ*, the defendants refused, perhaps deliberately to enter appearance, i.e. by putting up a defence.

On the 14th May 1980 when the matter was called up for hearing, Counsel for the plaintiff, that is to say for Ncho applied to the court to enter judgment for his client. Counsel cited Appeal case No. BCA/7/79[27] where judgment in default of defence was entered in favour of the applicant/plaintiff. After a review of several English and Cameroonian decided cases, the presiding judge, in entering judgment and making his award, directed himself that he was guided by the law and reasoning. The following awards were accordingly made:

- 1st Defendant:-
  a) Special and general damages claimed .. .. .. 3,000,000 fr
  b) Costs .. .. 120,000 frs
  Total .. .. **3,120,000 frs**
- 2nd Defendant:-
  a) Special and general damages claimed .. .. 5 frs
  b) Costs.. .. .. …….. .. .. .. 5 frs
  Total .. .. …………….. .. .. **10 frs**

The trial judge concluded by taking into account the second defendants' liabilities. This court, he remarked has taken into consideration the fact that he is a subordinate to the first defendant and that he acted though, thoughtlessly, on the formers' instructions.

Ncho No. 5

Ncho No. 5 was the direct fall out of Ncho No.1 where the court had decided that Mr Joseph Adu Ncho and his petrol tanker that had been detained on the orders of the Procureur Général be released and the tanker handed over to the owner, Mr Ncho. The Procureur Général, for reasons best known to him defied these orders of the court. Under the

---

[26] Suit No. HCB/19/79 of 16 May 1980 presided over by J.P.C. Nganje
[27] Bamango C.P.M.S vs. Nji Alassa

circumstances, Mr Ncho decided to move the court to commit Mr Itoe, Procureur Général, as being in contempt of the court. The hearing was before His Lordship, Mr Justice Hans Ekor' Tarh. The action was first commenced by way of *Motion ex-parte* but later converted to motion on notice.[28] The action became No. 5 as an appeal because the learned judge held that he could not grant the prayer of Mr Ncho. In the Appeal Court[29] I headed the panel and was assisted by Messrs. Justices M.A. Deba and T.M. Mbuagbaw.

After a review of the facts which had now become notorious to both the public as well as the professional circles, I wrote the opinion based on *corporation sole* as enunciated by Prof. Salmond in his book on "Jurisprudence" page 362. Prof. Salmond has aptly put it:

> *"The living official comes and goes but this offspring of the law remains the same for ever."*

The court invoked the provisions of Article 9 (1) of Ordinance No. 72/4 of 26 August 1972 as subsequently amended.

Bearing in mind the language of the judge when he ruled in the matter, we found ourselves in a dilemma to reconcile the two views. He said earlier:

> *"This court can only comment that considering the oath of office taken by respondents who are officers of the court and very close collaborators in the administration of justice in this country in the name of the President, and who are so expressly enjoined by the said First Magistrate of the realm, would not be heard to disobey to carry out a legitimate judicial order."*

Having thus recognized the legal obligation of the respondents, we failed to see how the learned trial judge could decisively pronounce as he did justifying his reasoning. On our part, we, *in the final result, reversed the decision of the lower court and declared that the respondents who are, by law, required to execute all court decisions and orders, etc; failed to do so and were thus liable to be called upon to show cause why they should not have been committed for contempt.*

Ncho No. 6

In Ncho No. 6[30] the court of Appeal was called upon to rule on the rightness or otherwise whether the ruling of Mr M.A Deba sitting in the High Court, Bamenda, could be sustained in law when he held that Merrs. Joseph Adu Ncho and *Nasse Guillaume* had no case to answer.

---

[28] Suit No. HCB/23M/79: Delivered on 5th August, 1979.
[29] Appeal No. BCA/43C/79 delivered on 3rd July 1980.
[30] Motion No. BCA/13M/80 of 23rd April 1980.

I presided over the hearing which was *the People vs. Joseph A. Ncho and 1 other*. I was assisted on the panel by Merrs. Justices J.P.C Nganje and T.E. Mbuagbaw. I wrote and delivered the ruling of the court. Because of its brevity, it is advisable to have it reproduced herein.

"On the 11*th* April, 1980 the learned Mr Justice Deba presiding in the High Court of the Mezam Judicial Division, in a reasoned ruling held that the respondents who were accused persons in Suit No. HCB/31C/79 had no case to answer against the indictment proffered against them. On the same date, the Procureur Général, being dissatisfied with the said ruling gave notice of appeal and filed a sole ground of appeal, that is to say the general ground which challenges the decision on the basis of the evidence or what has come to be known as the omnibus ground.

On the 18*th* April, 1980, he filed a motion in the Registry of this court. The motion was supported by an affidavit deposed to by the Procureur Général himself. By the motion, the Procureur Général prays this court to grant him leave to file additional grounds of appeal to be argued if and when the appeal in Suit No. HCB/31C/79 does come up for hearing and determination. The said additional grounds of appeal are expressly stated in the body of the motion. He further prays the court not only to argue the original ground herein already referred to but the additional nine grounds which are the subject of the present suit. We do not see any reason for this further prayer because, once leave is granted for additional grounds to be argued, this by itself, means that these will be argued in addition to any other ground or grounds already filed within the time limit. The learned Procureur Général, when his attention was drawn to this point by the court, conceded that this prayer was superfluous and we so hold it to be.

Finally, the Procureur Général prayed that the appeal for which he had given notice be given an accelerated hearing. The court noted that no special reason had been advanced to convince it to grant the prayer. Besides the Judicial Calendar is such that the grant of this prayer would be futile. The Procureur Général indicated that, in the light of the court's inclination, he would not press the issue.

Counsel for the respondents did not oppose the motion in its general terms. We are rather taken aback by his position because there is no appeal before us properly so called. Nevertheless, we are compelled by the attitude of the respondents' to grant the first prayer. The nine additional grounds of appeal incorporated in the motion before us are hereby ordered to be included with the original ground of appeal filed on the 11*th* April, 1980."

Then followed the Executive Formula.

Ncho No. 7

At the end of Ncho No. 7 the drama of these cases with the Procureur Général will begin to raise many questions about the sense of our justice system. In the end I began to wonder what the role of the State as clearly shown by the persistence of its officials intended to accomplish. Justice or the liquidation of a citizen. *The people vs. Joseph Adu Ncho and Nanse Guillaume*[31] had been indicted on counts charges of aggravated misappropriation, forgery, abetting a forgery, stopping the payment of a cheque, abetting and stopping the payment of a cheque and attempt to destroy physical evidence.[32] The matter was heard in the Bamenda High Court presided over by the Honourable Mr Justice M. A. Deba as he then was. After hearing evidence in the case, the learned trial judge consequently discharged the two defendants on the merits under section 286 of the Criminal Procedure Ordinance on all the counts of the indictment.

On the 11th April 1980, the Learned Procureur Général, being dissatisfied with the decision of the trial judge gave notice and filed grounds of appeal. In all, nine grounds of appeal were filed. *Prima facie*, the grounds indicted the learned Procureur Général in every aspect of his knowledge of the law. Some of these grounds, if put to strict scrutiny fall short of how grounds of appeal should be framed especially where they are based on legal grounds.

Nevertheless, the Court of Appeal was now confronted with examining and pronouncing on the merits and demerits of the entire appeal. The panel consisted of my humble self, Messrs. Justice A. N. Njamnsi and S. M. A. Anyangwe.

The unanimous opinion of the court was written and delivered by the learned Mr Justice Njamnsi.[33] Mr Justice A. N. Njamnsi was a man of detail and erudite and when it came to legal research, he was superb. He began to exhibit these traits when he joined me in the Legal Department, Buea, after his University studies in Lagos and *ENAM*[34], Yaounde. The judgment is detailed in its examination and analysis of the evidence and very rich in its legal research and application.

The long and short of it was that the appeal was dismissed and the decision of the court below was affirmed.

Later in this work, another facet, more murky, will resurface.

---

[31] Appeal No. BCA/24C/80 of 23/02/81
[32] Suit No. HCB/31C/79 of 2nd April, 1980
[33] Both he and S.M.A Anyangwe are deceased.
[34] Ecole Nationale d'Administration & Magistracy (Fr. Acronym for National School of Administration and Magistracy)

Ncho No. 8
The Civil Appeal No. BCA/12M/81 which came to the court of appeal and was ruled upon on 29th April 1981 was brought by *Benjamin Mutanga Itoe vs. Joseph Adu Ncho* by way of motion whereby the appellant prayed the court to:

1. Order the Registrar-in-Chief of the Bamenda High Court or whoever may be keeping them, to produce and tender the original High Court file or files relating to Suits No. HCB/19/79 and also to Motion No. HCB/33M/80 containing the filed originals of the said Motion and its Annextures, the Application for Writ of Summons, the Statement of Claim, and the joint Statement of Defence filed by the Procureur Général for Mr Itoe and Mr Sancho.
2. Order the Registrar-in-Chief of the Bamenda High Court or whoever may be keeping them, to produce and tender the High Court Civil Record Book containing the recorded proceedings and judgment in Motion No. HCB/33M/80 or a certified true copy of the said proceedings and the said judgment, which was disposed of by Mr Justice Anyangwe on the 21st of February, 1981.
3. Order that the applicant/appellant be allowed to adduce evidence on the fact that the Motion No. HCB/33M/80 was filed and paid for on the morning of the 14th May, 1980 before an application for it to be heard was made later hat same morning in open court to the learned trial Judge for the said Motion to be heard.
4. Order that the evidence so adduced and the documents, records and their Annextures so produced including the Motion and affidavit in the present Motion shall constitute part of the Record of proceedings for use in determining Appeal No. BCA/1/1981.

AND *for such further Order or Orders as the Honourable Court may deem fit and necessary in the circumstances to make."*

I headed the panel in the hearing and determination of the appeal and was ably assisted by Messrs Justice A. N. Njamnsi and S. M. A. Anyangwe. Eventually, I wrote and delivered the opinion.

In the course of examining the appeal in its details we noted that the motion was supported by an affidavit of 47 paragraphs and a further affidavit of 10 paragraphs with two annextures appended thereto and respectively marked Annextures 'C' and 'D'. There is no Annextures 'A' and 'B'. to the affidavit and the further affidavit is a counter-affidavit deposed to by Barrister Fon Ade Moma, Counsel for the respondent. The counter-affidavit contains 32 paragraphs. This matter related to Suit No. HCB/19/79. The facts that were, as pointed out by the trial Judge, when the provisions of Section 73(1)(m) of the Evidence Ordinance are invoked, the applicant would observe that his prayers numbered one and two touched and concerned matters upon which the courts take judicial notice. The applicant/appellant agreed and added that in such an instance, he would not insist on them including prayer four.

All these affidavit evidence relate to Suit No. HCB/19/79. At the hearing, the court, conscious of the provisions of Section 73(1)(m) of the Evidence Ordinance drew the attention of the appellant/applicant that the prayers one and two were normally judicially noticed. The appellant/applicant agreed with the court and stated that he was not going to insist on them and would do same as far as prayer four was concerned.

Arguments were now to be heard only on prayer three. Both sides agreed that oral testimony would be heard from Messrs Edmund Kidzeru and Edward Nforsam respectively the Registrar of the Legal Department and the Registrar-in-Chief of the High Court, Mezam Judicial Division, presided over by Mr Justice J.P.C Nganje as he then was. He had been assigned Motion No. HCB/33M/80. His attitude, it was imputed, in hearing the motion was inclined to refuse to entertain the Motion No. HCB/33M/80 and thus prejudicial to the position of appellant/applicant in Suit No. HCB/19/79.

In the end, we came to the conclusion that the altercations that ensued between the Registrar of the Legal Department and the Registrar-in-Chief of the court was the cause of the misunderstanding and certainly no blame could be attributed to the Registrar-in-Chief of the Court in order to frustrate the cause of justice.

Our final ruling was brief. *Inter alia*, we found from the analysis of the evidence that whoever was responsible for the motion not being assigned early enough to enable the Judge, i.e. Mr Justice J.P.C Nganje to deal with the case on the 14th May 1980, caused the motion not to be dealt with on the said date.

We therefore hold that the Motion No. HCB/33M/80 was not before the trial Judge when the trial in Suit No.HCB/19/79 opened in the morning of 14th May 1980 at 09H05, notwithstanding the statutory provisions of 48 hours notice, to be served on the other party. Accordingly, the trial Judge could not have determined a cause which was not before him.

We found ourselves unable to take account of applicants/appellants' evidence that acting as Counsel for the defence, he brandished his own copy of the motion papers to the court as evidence because Counsel's statement from the Bar did not constitute evidence in a court of law. Both on principle and the evidence adduced, the application to the extent that the trial Judge had the Motion No. HCB/33M/80 before him is not granted and so we proceeded to examine the submissions on the substantive appeal.

No order as to costs in this Motion.

Ncho No. 9

The natural outcome of Ncho No. 4 was what we shall now proceed to examine as Ncho No.9.[35] We may propound, without much contradiction, that the Ncho/Itoe saga was directed towards establishing the justice in Ncho No. 4 [36] which has already been referred to and discussed.

The panel comprised this writer, Messrs Justice A.N. Njamnsi and S.M.A. Anyangwe. Mr Itoe appealed against the damages and costs awarded against him while Mr Ncho cross-appealed against the inadequacy of the damages and costs awarded in his favour and thus prayed the Court of Appeal, to vary the said damages to reflect the actual or realistic damages that should have been his just due considering the business he lost as a result of the injustice he suffered all along.

At this stage, one imagines that the entire case had taken up a different colour and it was time to end it, at least, at the level of the highest court in the province. No useful purpose will be served to review the facts here. The court's opinion was unanimous and was written and read by Mr Justice A.N. Njamnsi. It was a well-researched opinion in so far as the evidence and law were concerned and considerable time was given to applying the law to the facts.

In delivering his judgment at the lower court, the trial Judge had exhibited extraneous considerations in awarding damages against the appellant/co-respondent when he said:

> "This court is however satisfied that the fears of the learned Procureur Général is unfounded as records will show that this court has been very lenient with him to the point of twisting procedure to the detriment of the plaintiff and entertaining arguments from the 1ˢᵗ defendant which ought not to be entertained."

---

[35] Civil Appeal No. BCA/1/81 delivered on 13th July 1981
[36] Suit No. HCB/19/79 delivered on 16th May 1980.

The Court of Appeal felt very concerned by the pronouncement of the trial Judge and thought a comment should be made as concerned it. Accordingly, we expressed our views:

> "*We feel greatly concerned and perturbed about the above quoted sentence (statement) from the ruling of the trial Judge, which in our view, is derogatory of the trial Judge as a member of the High Bench of (this) Republic. We are rather shocked by the written confession of the learned trial Judge of perverting the course of justice in favour of the appellant which confession is not only very derogatory but cuts across the oath of office of a Judicial Officer as well as tends to undermined the very existence of the court as the fountain of justice. We frown seriously at the above statement of the learned trial Judge*".

We do not find the awards of damages by the learned trial Judge inconsistent and disproportionate to the reasoning in his judgment but we are at sea as to why damages awarded should be indicated as damages "claimed" which are not equitable and why the awards against the joint tort feasors should be several only instead if jointly and severally.

For the reasons which have been given in this judgment, we hold that the appeal partly fails in respect of special damages and partly succeeds in respect of general damages only on the additional ground four, and the cross-appeal succeeds.

We accordingly allow the partial success of the additional ground four of the appeal and the cross-appeal, but set aside the awards of the court below and make the following awards in favour of the respondent/cross-appellant and against the two cross-respondents jointly and severally.

Special Damages:
- a) Jewelry .. .. 175,000 francs
- (b) Wrist Watch .. .. 150,000 francs
- (c) Cash .. .. 750,000 francs
- (d) Tankers earning at 400.000 francs per week from 6th June 1979 to the 16th May 1980 .. .. 18,000,000 francs
- (e) Repairs on the Tank .. .. .. 4,500,000 francs

General Damages (nominal .. .. 01 francs

23,575,001 francs

No order as to costs because the appeal has partly succeeded.

Justice Martin A. Deba (dec'd)

Mr Jutice Deba was a personality that I met in my legal and judicial service. He was gentle and soft-spoken, full of the milk of human kindness, so humble and simple that he couldn't hurt a fly and exhibited a ready friendship to the point of naivety.

His sympathetic nature gave a wrong impression because somebody passed it for weakness of character and that he could easily be subjected to pressure. Nevertheless he did everything to avoid controversy of any sort. Somebody would interpret it as an inherent fear to take a position.

His written personal depositions that follow are part of his role in the Ncho saga that considerable time has been spent treating in all its facets in this work. They form a case study of the man and his commitment to the administration of justice. In them one can easily spot out one or several of his character traits and I came to understand them for the time that I knew and worked with him. He was outspoken. He didn't hold back any information that was intended to clear his reputation. In his *confidential and private* letter to Mr B.M. Itoe (Procureur General), he says:

> "On the day when we were distributing cases the criminal matter of <u>The people vs. Adu Ncho</u> and one other fell before Scott Anyangwe and he passed it to me to hear because I was completely a new man in Bamenda."

This disclosure as to how and why this particular file was assigned to him by his colleague can be interpreted as an assurance that he would do his best to ensure that justice is done in the end. Forget all what has gone before now. Trust me when it comes to dishing out justice I'm equal to the task.

Having said that about the man, it now behooves us to have a close study of his depositions earlier referred to so that, as usual, individually we, as the silent jury can return our own verdict on the man.

My Lord,
Speak.

PRIVATE AND CONFIDENTIAL:

Martin A. Deba (Magistrat)
Vice President of the Court of Appeal, Bamenda.
2nd August, 1980.

Dear Mr B. M. Itoe,
(Procureur Général),
Bamenda.

I arrived Bamenda on transfer from the Buea Court of Appeal in January this year. Soon afterwards we began the Mezam Assizes. On the day when we were distributing cases the criminal matter of The People vs. Adu Ncho and One other fell before Scott Anyangwe and he passed it to me to hear because I was completely a new man in Bamenda.

When you came from the Heads of Courts Conference which was held in Yaounde, you came to my house and indicated to me your interest in the matter and that you were being sued civilly for doing your work. I promised to cooperate. You said hello to my wife and went away. As a friend you kept on telling me your experience with the other Judges of the court.

When the matter was ripe for hearing you were one of those who testified at length for the prosecution. After the close of the case for the prosecution, Fon Gorji Dinka, Counsel for the defence, made a no-case submission. The matter was adjourned to a later date for a ruling on the no-case submission. I dismissed Fon Dinka's no –case submission and ruled that the accused persons had a case to answer.

Before the date of delivering the ruling, you and your wife came to my house at about 7.30 p.m. on 17/2/80, and in my house was Mr Nkongho Takor of Linguistic Centre in Yaounde and Magistrate Bawak. Your wife passed to greet my wife in the kitchen while you sat with us. Having known why you came, I took you to my writing room and told you that I had dismissed the no-case submission of learned Counsel for the defence. Because of some conversation in which we were engaged prior to my taking you to my reading room, I was told later on by the person concerned that you took both Mr Nkongho Takor and Bawak to your house that night; your wife there and then cooked food and you entertained them with the food and drinks.

The following morning Monday 18th February you came again to my house and collected the office keys which you had forgotten in my room the previous day.

After dismissing the no-case submission, I proceeded to hear the case for the defence. Within this time you came and collected me again to your office and showed me all the other matters pending against Adu Ncho the accused. I still gave you the impression that I was going to cooperate. Before judgment in this matter was delivered, I was made to understand from somebody that you Mr Itoe had gone and told Mr Dibanjo, Chief of National Security in Bamenda that you had seen me in this matter and had convinced me to find Ncho guilty and that Mr Dibanjo had told Mr Nganje what you told him and that Mr Nganje had since related the matter to Mr Wakai, our President. It appears that Mr Dibanjo and others were now just waiting to hear the outcome of the case.

Mr Itoe, having now betrayed me what did you think I should have done? I just had to consider the matter on its merits. I discharged the two accused persons and as usual, having been aggrieved by my decision, you went on appeal according to the procedure.

On Saturday 26th July 1980, there was a decree transferring all of us of the Bamenda High Court. It was yesterday 1st of August that I tried to telephone somebody in Yaounde to find out what happened and the person told me that you had said to him that all of us had gone against your way and that you were going to transfer all of us. Before that it had been rumoured that you had petitioned to the Ministry of Justice that all of us were corrupt.

Mr Itoe, even without having approached me concerning the Ncho's case I would have still helped you taking account of the fact that the very Ncho was claiming you civilly but having seen me as you did, why did you not keep quiet but go to talk to a security man? After the verdict, Mr Nganje himself, with the President, Mr Anyangwe, Mr Mbuagbaw and I were taking tea in the President's Chambers, told me in their presence what Mr Dibanjo had told him about your having seen me in my house about the case. I had nothing but to say that it was true.

I know certainly that it is the Ncho's case which is sending us on transfer. There is no doubt that with your connections in the Ministry you have certainly gossiped us, and therefore my informant was certainly not telling me a lie by saying we have gone against your way and you were going to transfer all of us.

I have written to you as a friend or as a master whatever you may think so that since it appears Mr Dibanjo has also been transferred to Douala, you may contact either of the people I have mentioned here if you feel that Mr Nganje's information is false. Well, you have chosen that I go to Douala and there I can very well read the state of your mind. Mr Itoe, not all birds will reach the Heavens. "We are going as thou sayeth".

I am particularly very happy that you should cause my transfer after six months stay in Bamenda for delivering a judgment which is already on appeal. Long live Justice in Cameroon. This is purely confidential and do not think I will tell any person. I shall suffer in silence and posterity will tell, Amen.

Yours,
<u>*M. A. Deba*</u>

Reading through the justice's letter, you easily find in it a man imbued with a sense of justice so much that he has to go all out of his way and off the bench to let the world know why he took a particular position in an issue that was a subject of popular comment.

Mr Justice Deba's account once again raises the question of the learned Procureur General's hot pursuit of an individual who, in the eyes of the law up to that point, was presumed innocent. What the learned

Judge says next is scandalous for our justice system for one trained in the common law to conduct himself in search of how to nail an innocent citizen in such a cavalier manner. The Director of Public Prosecutions basically as a minister of justice is to ensure that justice is done. His dastardly behaviour in pressurising the learned Judge to convict against his conscience and not allow him to do what he considered to be right and just. He reminds his colleague:

> "The following morning Monday 18*th* February you came again to my house and collected the office keys which you had forgotten in my room the previous day."

After dismissing the no-case submission, I proceeded to hear the case for the defence. Within this time you came and collected me again to your office and showed me all the other matters pending against Adu Ncho the accused. I still gave you the impression that I was going to co-operate. Before judgment in this matter was delivered, I was made to understand from somebody that you, Mr Itoe, had gone and told Mr Dibanjo, Chief of National Security (Provincial) in Bamenda that you had seen me in this matter and had convinced me to find Ncho guilty and that Mr Dibanjo had told Mr Nganje what you told him and that Mr Nganje had since related the matter to Mr Wakai, our President. It appears that Mr Dibanjo and others were now just waiting to hear the outcome of the case.

I have decided to further extract this part of what I termed *deposition* to justify my judgment of Mr Justice Deba. His sympathetic character, giving so much time to listen to Mr Itoe in his private room in the absence of the opposing Counsel as demanded by the judicial ethics, accepting to be taken to the Procureur General's Chambers to convince him that Mr Ncho was a criminal and thereby prejudice his judgment with regards to a pending matter. His patience to listen to such stuff is admirable. Only the simplicity of a Mr Justice Deba would accept such humility from a person who has an interest in a matter. I did say in judging the learned Justice one could pass him as being weak and therefore could easily be subjected to pressure. Ncho No. 6 proves the contrary.

An Inquisition and the guillotine

He who reads the account of the Ncho cases would by now realize that by 1982, the judicial climate that prevailed in the North West Province was far from one to be desired. It was murky. The centre of it all being one person, Mr Benjamin Mutanga Itoe, the Procureur Général. All these tantrums in managing that very important department were destined to land the entire service into a hell of trouble.

1982 saw Mr Itoe transferred to the Ministry of Justice as Deputy Director of Judicial Control. At the same time, unknown to any person, Mr Itoe following a report and recommendation of His Excellency, the Minister of Justice and Keeper of the Seals, was disciplined by the infliction on him of a sanction of a warning by a decree dated 6th October, 1982.

In hindsight, the transfer and the infliction of the sanction gave Mr Itoe more nerve to build the *network* which he surely used to its maximum. Subsequently events establish this fact beyond any doubt.

Perhaps, it would be useful to review Mr Justice Deba's parting words as he concludes his letter to his learned colleague.

> *"I have written to you as a friend or as a master whatever you may think so that since it appears Mr Dibanjo has also been transferred to Douala, you may contact either of the people, I have mentioned here if you feel that Mr Nganje's information is false. Well, you have chosen that I go to Douala and there I can well read the state of your mind. Mr Itoe, not all birds will reach the Heavens. "We are going as thou sayeth"*[37]
>
> *I am particularly very happy that you should cause my transfer after six months stay in Bamenda for delivering a judgment which is already on appeal. Long live Justice in Cameroon. This is purely confidential and do not think I will tell any person. I shall suffer in silence and posterity will tell. Amen"*

Before arriving at this time of Mr Justice Deba's letter, I had, as a consequence of what I considered to be a judicial vendetta between the Procueur Général and members of the Bench with regards to the enforcement of court judgments, contacted the Honourable Ministers to alert him of the crisis that was looming ahead. This was by telegram. When no satisfactory response was forthcoming from Yaounde and the situation was aggravating, I decided, once more, to warn the Honourable Minister. So, I sent off a letter in the following terms:

1. I have the honour to refer to my (earlier) telegram and to say that it is with the greatest reluctance that I transmit herewith the petition of the Vice-Presidents of this court. I have, for a long time, tried to convince my colleagues to bear with me whenever this matter has been brought to my attention. I have also done everything to avoid a clash with my colleague of the Legal

---

[37] In March 2000, April 29 Justice Deba died in his car by a tree falling above it as he and his driver drove. The driver survived. Mr Itoe is presently Deputy Prosecutor in the International Criminal Court, Freetown, Sierra Leone.

Department because I believed all along that this would not be in the interest of the service and also because the image of the judiciary in this Province would be irreparably damaged by squabbles. But I have now concluded that either my desire for co-operation is being interpreted as a sign of weakness or the learned Procureur Général has embarked on a collision course with the courts; perhaps in an effort to demonstrate in positive terms to the public at large his almightiness or to parade the influence he is alleged to wield in the Ministry.

2. I have now decided to accept the challenge and forward the petition because of the case of *Joseph Dim vs. The People*, suit No. BCA/3c/80 in which I personally presided and participated in drawing up the *order* which the learned Procueur Général has violated and persists in violating up to this moment of writing with unbridled arrogance. He is reported as saying that he would have the Judges of the court of Appeal transferred as he did with my predecessor[38] whenever he had cause to disagree with any of them because I know and believe that those who run the affairs in the chancellery are not so naïve to be pushed around without hearing the other side. Perhaps I would not have been so shocked if I had not been a Procueur Général myself. I know of no law which gives the Procureur Général the power to flout the law. On the contrary, the law commands him to ensure that all court decisions, orders, etc; are enforced and the forces of law are placed at his disposal to give him all necessary assistance.

3. Mr Minister, I would not bore you with the goings on here. I can only say that it is not possible to put down everything in writing. An open discussion will reveal more, hence my plea in the telegram. As far as I know, none of my collaborators fear any transfer; the record shows that they are among those who have been subjected to frequent movements more than the Procureur

---

[38] My wife graduated from the University of Nigeria, Nsukka, in June 1977 and it was our wish that I should be transferred to Yaounde so as to enable her obtain admission into the Higher Teacher Training College (ENS – french acronym). I requested my closest friend, then a Member of Government to see my Minister the Hon. Joseph Charles Doumba. When I was posted to Bamenda mid that year. I queried my Minister friend. He informed me that when he spoke to his colleague, he told him that my posting to Bamenda was to come and save a situation. On arrival in Bamenda, I got information from sundry sources to the effect that our young colleague was in the habit of allegedly writing reports about my immediate predecessor that the latter was a habitual drunk and spent most of his time in the Club House discussing judgments. I had nothing else to say.

General. Even now, they are ready to move if and when the exigency of the service so necessitate and not by the whims and caprices of Mr Procureur Général.
4. Assuring you of my highest esteem.

Contrary to what everyone expected, the entire North West Provincial magisterial district had a jolt. Instead of responding to the problems raised in the letter by the Vice-Presidents of the Court, someone somewhere initiated a report that the latter had refused to hold court sessions because the Procureur General of that court had not executed certain judgments delivered by them. Any serious and unbiased mind would have been put on inquiry to ascertain whether the cases of Joseph Dim, *Ncho 1-9* were true or false. Secondly, all statutory courts are courts of record. A cursory look at the records of the different tier of courts, i.e. the High Courts which were assize courts and the Court of Appeal would have revealed the truth or otherwise of the report. From all the surrounding circumstances there is no doubt that some evil hand was lurking in the background. No evidence can speak louder than the following report compiled and edited by the late Mr Justice George S. Ekema who reported as the Rapporteur of the Rogatory Commission to inquire into the allegations. From the instant report, the reader will note that there had been an earlier two-man commission headed by Francois Xavier Mbouyom, a high placed *magistrat* and the late Mr Justice H.K Ngalame.

<u>Report of the Disciplinary Committee appointed by the Head of State to investigate the allegations of suspension of court sessions levied against Mr N. Wakai President of the North West Provincial Court of Appeal, Bamenda and Messrs. S. M. A. Anyangwe, M. A. Deba and J. P.C. Nganje, Vice Presidents of that court at the time.</u>

A perusal of the file in the Presidency of the Republic relating to this matter reveals that by letter No. U/L No. 356/CAB dated 6th October, 1982, His Excellency the President of the Republic drew the attention of the Minister of Justice & Keeper of the seals to the fact that following the report of an Inquiry, it was established that as a result of some incidents in the Bamenda Court of Appeal, certain Magistrates of the Bench, with the connivance of the President of the Court, refused to hold certain Court sessions because the Procureur Général of that Court had not executed judgments delivered by them. His Excellency the President of the Republic therefore wanted to know what disciplinary measures had been taken against these *magistrates who had violated the Oath of office they took when they were assuming office as Magistrates.*

In his letter dated 18th March, 1983, which was addressed to His Excellency the President of the Republic, the minister of Justice & Keeper of the Seals informed His Excellency the President of the Republic that following the incidents at the Bamenda Court of Appeal, he the Minister of Justice & Keeper of the seals had summoned the two Heads of Courts and admonished them to carry out their duties diligently and that on their return, the Courts resumed normal functioning. He further informed His Excellency, the President of the Republic, that the Procureur – General at the time, in the person of Mr ITOE Benjamin who was responsible for this situation, had been appointed Deputy Director of Judicial Control in the Chancellery and that Mr ITOE had been disciplined by the infliction on him of the sanction of a warning by a decree dated 6th October, 1982. As regards the President of the North West Provincial Court of Appeal, Mr Nyo WAKAI, the Minister of Justice & Keeper of the Seals informed the President of the Republic that he did not find it necessary to bring any disciplinary sanction against him and his colleagues – Messrs. DEBA and NGANJE who had been transferred outside the Jurisdiction of the Bamenda Court of Appeal. As regards Mr NGANJE, he further informed the President of the Republic that by a Decree dated 16th July, 1982, Mr NGANJE had been disciplined by being reduced in rank for some other matter.

The Minister of Justice & Keeper of the Seals did not stop at that. On the 6th May, 1983, he issued queries to Mr Nyo WAKAI, the President of the North West Provincial Court of Appeal, Bamenda and to Messrs. Scott ANYANGWE, NGANJE Joseph Patrick & DEBA Martin, Vice Presidents respectively. A similar query was also issued to MBUAGBAW, Tiku Eyong. The query was to the effect that following incidents which occurred at the Bamenda Court of Appeal in February and March, 1980, investigations carried out by the Chancellery revealed that the Vice-Presidents names above suspended the Sessions of the High Courts and the Court of Appeal for the North West Province on the ground that the Procureur-General was not executing their Judgments. This attitude of these Vice-Presidents not only violated their oath of office but also led to the disruption of the normal functioning of the Judicial Services of the North West Province.

These Judicial Officers answered the Minister's queries and in their defence, they maintained that they never suspended any Sessions of the High Courts and the Court of Appeal in the North West Province. They maintained that despite their differences with the Procureur Général over Procurer Général's refusal to execute Court judgments, they held Court Sessions at the High Court and Court of Appeal throughout the Judicial

Year and that the Records of these Courts are there to confirm the fact that Judicial work went on undisturbed throughout the Judicial Year.

Following these explanations, the Minister of Justice & Keeper of the Seals sent Messrs. MBOUYOM Francois-Xavier and NGALAME Hans Kome Director of Legislation & Deputy Director of Legislation respectively, to Bamenda to carry out an on-the-spot investigation to find out whether the Vice Presidents of that Court actually suspended Court Sessions as threatened in their joint letter dated 5th March, 1980. The result of this investigation was that Mr ITOE was largely responsible for the tension that had taken place in Bamenda. The Minister of Justice & Keeper of the Seals informed the Head of State that a perusal of the Court Record Books produced by Mr Nyo WAKAI revealed that Court Sessions were never suspended and consequently, he did not think it necessary to bring disciplinary proceedings against the President of the Court and the other Magistrates of the bench. These facts are contained in letter No. 110/DAG/SPM/MJ of the 15th June, 1983 addressed to the Head of State by the Minister of Justice & Keeper of the Seals. In a subsequent letter No. 059/DAG/SPM/MJ of the 21st June, 1983, the Minister of Justice & Keeper of the Seals addressed another letter to the Head of State enclosing the explanations of Mr NGANJE on the issue of suspension of Court Sessions at Bamenda. In the second paragraph of this letter, the Minister of Justice again re-iterated his stand that he did not find it necessary to bring disciplinary proceedings against the President of the Court and the other Magistrates of the bench in that Court of Appeal.

Despite the Minister's stand that he did not find it necessary to bring disciplinary proceedings against these Judicial Officers, the Head of State, probably taking into account the gravity of the allegations, appointed this Disciplinary Committee to investigate these allegations. Members of the Committee proceeded to Bamenda and on the 11th October, 1984, commenced their work. All the Magistrates concerned stood by their former Statements to the Minister of Justice & Keeper of the Seals. They maintained that the High Courts and the Court of Appeal functioned throughout the Judicial Year and that the Records Books of the various Courts were there to speak for themselves.

The Committee thus commenced its work. Since the allegations were that the High Courts and the Court of Appeal were suspended in the months of February and March, 1980, we confined ourselves to this period. Our task was made easier by the system obtainable in the South West and North West Provinces where the Presiding Magistrate himself takes down the notes of Proceedings in the Court. So if there is an allegation that he did not work for a certain period, who ever is investigating the allegation only has to open the

Record Book and refer to it. The President of the Court of Appeal, Mr Nyo WAKAI produced the Record Book of the Court of Appeal which showed that the second sessions of the North West Provincial Court of Appeal commenced on the 26th February, 1980, and continued to sometime in April, 1980. The Panel was composed of Mr Nyo WAKAI President and Messrs. Scott ANYANGWE & DEBA Martin as Vice-Presidents. The Committee checked the allegations that the Court of Appeal adjourned a case sine die on the 3rd March, 1980, to support the strike of the Vice-Presidents of the Court of Appeal. A perusal of the Record Book of the Court of Appeal revealed that the Court of Appeal did not sit on this day and therefore no case could have been adjourned sine die.

As regards Vice-President NGANJE, the Records show that he proceeded to Mbengwi to hold the Sessions of the High Court of Mbengwi which commenced on the 3rd March, 1980 and ended on the 25th March, 1980. We checked on the allegation that Mr NGANJE adjourned 10 cases sine die because of the strike the Vice-Presidents had organised. Records of the Mbengwi High Court revealed that Mr NGANJE sat in Court on this day but did not adjourn any case sine die. The Record Book shows that the Criminal cases which were on the Courts Cause List on that day were adjourned to the 17th March, 1980, at the instance of the Prosecution and that Mr NGANJE sat in Court on the 17th March, 1980, to hear the cases which were adjourned to that day. Mr NGANJE heard both Criminal and Civil cases during this Session of the Mbengwi High Court.

As regards Vice-President Scott ANYANGWE, the Record Book of the Bamenda Court of Appeal shows that he sat in the Court of Appeal between 26th February, 1980 to the 2nd April, 1980. He also sat in the Mezam High Court on the 3rd March, 1980, on which date he delivered judgment in the case of <u>Regina Asengwe and the Mankon Urban Council.</u>

As regards Vice President DEBA Martin, he sat in the Court of Appeal and also sat in the High Court between 6th February, 1980 to the 20th February, 1980 on Criminal matters.

The result of our findings is that the High Courts and the Court of Appeal of the North West Province never at any time suspended their sessions. The allegation that these Courts suspended their sessions is a complete hoax. We therefore share the views of the Minister of Justice & Keeper of the Seals that it was unnecessary to bring disciplinary proceedings against these Judicial Officers.

Sgd. <u>G. S. EKEMA</u>
<u>RAPPORTEUR</u>

The report is so clearly written and explicit in its language that the reader is at liberty to draw his conclusions. On my part I can only make a footnote, namely, that both Messrs Benjamin M. Itoe and Hans K. Ngalame had both served under me as State Counsel and each paired me in the Legal Department as Procureur General in the North West Province. Mr Ngalame, as he then was succeeded Mr Itoe as he then was. It is but a footnote and should be so regarded.

Sanctions under the Statute of Magistracy
The Presidential Decree No. 82-467 of 4 October 1982 laid down the rules and regulations governing the judicial and legal service. In 1984, by another Presidential Decree No. 84/623 of 29 June 1984 the earlier one was rectified by correction of substantive errors in the Provisions of Decree No. 82/467 of 4 October 1982.

These correction affected articles 5(2) and 76.

Discipline is dealt with under chapter viii, that is articles 46 to 64. on a finding that a judicial or legal officer has breached any of the offences spelt out in article 46, namely, is guilty of:
- action which violates the oath taken by the magistrate;
- impropriety, breach of honor and dignity;
- failure to fulfill the duties and obligations attached to his rank;
- error resulting from professional incompetence.

The measures that visit a victim of any of the above are in an ascending order of gravity – (a) warning (b) reprimand (c) cancellation from the promotion list and finally – the severest, dismissal with suspection or loss of pension rights. Sub paragraph 2 article 47 specifically states that sanctions (a) and (b) shall be pronounced by an order of the President of the Republic or of the Minister of Justice as the case may be; while 47(3) empowers the President to pronounce the next following more severe sanctions[39] by Decree. According to the report Mr Itoe was caught by (c)[40] while Justice J.P.C Nganje was penalised under subsection (e). The consequence of this diminished his chances of promotion and a better pension.

Notwithstanding that the report exonerated us, both Mr Justice Anyangwe and I appeared before the Higher Judicial Council sitting as a disciplinary body. By this date Mr Itoe had skillfully worked his way up politically and was now the Minister of justice and consequently, the Vice-President of the Council.

---

[39] Article 47(c) to (j)
[40] 47 (e) – reduction by one or more incremental positions.

I have never been as furious and insensed to appear before a tribunal that was, *prima facie*, biased against me and my colleague in its composition. An obviously interested party was going to participate in deciding my cause and future career. A typical case of someone being a judge in his own cause. That's what it was in so long as Mr Itoe had been our principal accuser or at least the person who had set in motion what had led to a whole court being put on trial. My conscience was fighting between doing one of two things. Firstly, to challenge the Vice-President's participation in the decision making process that meant so much to anyone in my position. And secondly, to be contemptuous of the entire exercise and declare that what was going on was an inquisition because none of us had had the opportunity to cross-examine our accusers, a practice so dear to the common law system under which I had been schooled. Then I decided that the circus was put in place when a field report was before Council; with the Head of State personally presiding, any of the scenarios would be of no effect. So, just adopt whatever statement was made *ante*. That was it!

As earlier stated, Justice Anyangwe and I appeared before the Council on the same date. In fact, at the same time. There was a comic side as we walked up the steps leading to the Hall where the Council was holding. We were driven from the gate to the foot of the steps, by one of the usual black cars that ferries very important personalities for Presidential audience or other business. A guard of Honour was mounted. As we emerged from the car, the command was given for the official salute. We nodded in response. A few steps away Justice Anyangwe turned to me and said: President, meaning President of the Court, we have had our own today. Thanks to Mr Itoe. The routine of the salute was repeated as we walked out of the Palace. Needless to say that the hearing lasted a few minutes since we had adopted to decide and rely on our statements during the visit of the rogatory commission.

When the decisions were eventually pronounced, I was reprimanded while Justice Anyangwe was warned. The measures taken against us unlike Itoe's were announced over Radio. I remember very well a passing comment made by Shasha Ndimbie the announcer for the evening and one of the best at the time. After reading the sanctions, she interjected:

"*No reason has been given*"

I there and then learnt to accept that *the cobwebs of the law in my country are there to catch the small flies while the big ones would break through at will and with impunity*. My fury would take me nowhere in proceedings presided over by the Head of State.

After several years and ignoring the invocation of the provisions of the Statute of Magistrature[41] I decided to put something on record. The relevant sections stipulate:

"(1) Judicial and Legal officers against whom disciplinary action other than dismissal has been taken shall automatically be rehabilitated upon the expiry of the periods fixed below, on condition that no other action is taken against them within the said periods.
- one year for a warning;
- two years for a reprimand, and three years for other measures.

(2) Rehabilitation shall mean the withdrawal from the personal file of the judicial or legal officer of all the documents relating to the disciplinary action in question. Rehabilitation shall not give entitlement to the reconstitution of a career or to salary arrears."

The result of my decision to have these things recorded was a petition I wrote. The Presidency's reaction was as per the Secretary General's reply signed by Paul Tessa dated 10 April 1989 and referenced No. B1104/SG/PR. That's what I needed and today I can speak authentically about the event(s).

Prior to these events, my young friend did not give up. 1983 was the year when the Higher Judicial Council was due renewal. In accordance with the Provisions of the legal enactment establishing that body, the Supreme Court is empowered to nominate three (3) members chosen from members of the bench.

I was highly honoured by my colleagues to name me one of the three members to represent the corps in the Council. This did not go down well with the Minister before the voting. He carried out an intensive campaign against me using his good friend – supposedly, who was then the Secretary to the Council. My admirers in the Court kept me fully briefed. In fact one of them told off Mr Minister's emissary during one of these visits. I was voted overwhelming by my colleagues. Whether it was a rebuke vote to the Minister or not remains a dilemma. The next day, I was working till late, say right down to 18h00 when a colleague well connected in the circle of the Secretary to Council bombed into my office to tell me I would be transferred to the Ministry in the transfers that were being awaited. It came to pass. This was intended to prevent me from becoming a member of the Council since I would no longer be said to represent the judicial corps.

---

[41] Decree No 82-467 of 4 Oct. 1982, S. 65(1) – (2)

In the new appointment I was designated as Technical Adviser in the Ministry of Justice and directly under the Minister. I showed my resentment by refusing to fill the annual confidential forms. I maintained the position even when I was transferred back to the Court until my retirement in 1990. He tried to recommend me for a decoration. I refused to complete the Form to the consternation of the Francophones who worked with me.

To every one, I was an enigma.

REPUBLIQUE DU CAMEROUN	**REPUBLIC OF CAMEROON**
Paix – Travail – Patrie	Peace – Work – Fatherland
Présidence de la République	**Presidency of the Republic**
SECRETARIAT GENERAL	SECRETARIAT GENERAL
N° ..../SG/PR	Yaoundé, le .... 19 ....

Objet: _____   **Le Secretaire General**
        Subject: The Secretary General
Réf. : Votre requête du
21 November 1988.-   a M.__onsieur NYO WAKAI
                                                   Magistrat
                                     to Ministèere de la Justice
                                                    Yaounde

Monsieur,

J'ai le regret de vous faire connaître qu'il n'a pas été possible au Chef de l'Etat, de réserver une suite favourable à votre requête de référence, *étant observé du reste, que suivant l'article 65 paragraph 1 du décret no 82/467 du 04 Octobre 1982 portant statut de la magistrature, le magistrat frappe de la sanction de reprimande bénéficie de la réhabilitaion de plein droit au bout de deux ans.*

Veuillez agréer, Monsieur, l'expression de ma considération toute distinguée./-

Sgd: Paul TESSA

Chapter XII
Signature

At this moment in time I thank Almighty God for having sustained me so far. Now I can let the world share in my reflections which have given me the opportunity to experience the wisdom of Shakespeare of life being likened to a stage where we are all actors with each one of us having his entrances and exits.

What we always forget is the principle enunciated by Paul J. Lindell, namely; that *between these exits and entrances, we live in encircling gloom, an envelope of pain and distress, afflictions and illness, disorder and conflict are ever with us.*

I found in my library correspondences that remind me of the fact that with the entrances and exits, some people only see their entrances and never their exits. Entrances and exits belong to others and not to themselves. I believe that there can be no entrance without an exit or no exit without an entrance. I have had my entrances with their exits. Many like me, have had. The difference is in how we individually have experienced the entrance and exit. No matter the length of time-space the *between* has its own gloom, pain and distress, and affliction as well as illness.

Like Job in the Bible, it is in the nature of men to suffer for *man is born to trouble as the sparks fly upwards. Pain does not come in the same measure to all people alike, but it does come to all. It goes down to the roots of our human nature and life. We can feel it in our bones.*

So far I have narrated my own personal encircling gloom during the period of my entrance and exit in the legal and judicial service of my country. While I enjoyed my entrances and my exits, they have made me believe that *there are evil powers that trod the earth untamed.*

I have earlier mentioned that a resort to my reading archive has produced some revealing documents and documentation. Besides decided cases examined on the basis of how efficient our justice system has worked and is working, several examples of the abusive use of administrative and quasi-judicial powers have been noted or observed. The last word should make interesting reading for those who will follow the correspondence hereafter. You will have food for thought by the time the last word is read. It concerns the invitation from the American Bar Association to attend the bicentennial of the Constitution of that country. I have, in my life, refused to be embroiled in *appointment politicking*.[42]

---

[42] Book of Job, 5.7

April 20, 1987,

Mr Nyo Wakaii
Technical Counselor
Supreme Court
Yaounde, Cameroun

Dear Mr Wakaii:

As Chairperson of the Appellate Judges Conference of the American Bar Association, I would like to extend to you an invitation to participate in a twelve day program celebrating the bicentennial of the U.S. Constitution. The program will take place in San Francisco, California during the period of August 1 – 12. This program is being funded by the American Bar Association, the United States Information Agency (USIA) and the New York Times Foundation.

A daily schedule of the program along with travel arrangements is enclosed. A brief description of the program follows.

Appellate judges from fifteen of the world's democracies are being invited to participate in a twelve day program centering around the ABA Annual Meeting in San Francisco. The theme of the program is to celebrate the Bicentennial of the U. S. Constitution by demonstrating on an international basis the crucial role an independent judiciary plays in a constitutional democracy. We wish to explore the doctrines of separation of powers, the extent to which an independent judiciary is a democratic necessity, the constitutional protection of human rights, and the ways and means by which the independence of the judiciary is guaranteed. The countries invited to participate are: Argentina, Australia, Brazil, Cameroun, Colombia, Egypt, Federal Republic of Germany, France, India, Israel, Japan, Nigeria, Philippines, United Kingdom and Zimbabwe.

The cornerstone of the Program will be a three-hour presentation at the American Bar Association (ABA) Annual Meeting. Time and format will not allow participation by all fifteen countries, therefore, only justices from six of the countries will participate in the presentation. The countries chosen for the presentation are: Argentina, Federal Republic of Germany, France, India, United Kingdom and Zimbabwe. These countries were chosen because either their constitution has served as a basis for many constitutions or their constitution is representative of that of a developing nation.

Although you will not be a speaker in the formal presentation, you will be an active participant in all other program segments. You will be involved in many ABA events as the distinguished guest of the ABA President, Eugene Thomas. In addition, several local activities are being arranged in San Francisco and a special two-day program in Reno, Nevada at the National Judicial College will be held. We are hopeful that the program will offer you a wide range of educational and social benefits.

Given the intense nature of this working program, this invitation can be extended only to the participants themselves and cannot include spouses or other family members.

I sincerely hope that you will accept this invitation. Please address your response to our staff director, Mary Ellen Donaghy, American Bar Association, 750 N. Lake Shore Dr, Chicago, IL 60611, telex 270593.

Very truly yours,

Sgd: Joseph T. Sneed
      Chairperson

5364A
PROPOSED DAILY SCHEDULE FOR BICENTENNIAL PROGRAM

Saturday August 1	Arrival in San Francisco. Foreign judges will be met by ABA staff and escorts. Overnight stay at airport hotel.
Sunday August 2	Flight to Reno; foreign judges will be met by College staff. Orientation session and welcome reception. The National Judicial College was founded in 1963 and is the leading residential judicial education institution in the U.S. Each foreign judge will be assigned a host who will be an U.S. judge attending the summer session of the college. A private dinner for the foreign judges will end the day.
Monday August 3	Educational program at college conducted by Prof. Jeffrey Hackney, Oxford University; topic is: "Role of the Judge in a Parliamentary Society". U.S judges will participate in afternoon session. Dinner with faculty of program.
Tuesday August 4	Visit to Washoe County Courthouse. Judges will view criminal arraignments, trials and sentencing hearings. An educational program on comparative criminal constitutional principles will follow at the courthouse. Lunch will be hosted by the Governor of Nevada at the Governor's Mansion. A sightseeing trip to Virginia City and Lae Tahoe will follow concluded by dinner at the home of the President of the

International Visitors Club of Nevada. Leaders of the Reno bar and the justices of the Nevada Supreme Court will attend.

Travel to San Francisco. Full orientation session. Cultural program sponsored by San Francisco Bar Association is planned for the afternoon followed by reception. Each foreign judge will be assigned a host who will be a U.S. appellate judge attending the ABA Annual Meeting.

Wednesday
August 5

Educational program at US Court of Appeals, 9th Circuit. Foreign judges will view oral argument and judicial conferencing. Discussion with members of the court will follow.

Thursday
August 6

Friday
August 7

ABA Annual Meeting begins. At the annual meeting, approximately 10,000 lawyers will gather for two weeks of educational meetings and social programs. The judges will be the distinguished guests of the ABA President and will be invited to a number of exciting events. Today, the luncheon of the Judicial Administration Division will be held. U.S judges from all levels of the judiciary will be in attendance. Justice Antonin Scalia, the newest member of the U.S. Supreme Court, has been invited to speak. Throughout the annual meeting, the foreign judges will be able to attend any educational program being offered by the ABA that they wish to attend. Evening: Judicial Administration Division Reception.

ABA orientation session. The foreign judges will participate in the Appellate Judges Conference's Annual Business Meeting where a debate will be held on the value of oral argument. A reception for members of the Conference in honor of the foreign visitors will follow. In the evening, the President's reception for distinguished guests will be held.

ABA President's prayer breakfast; Red Mass; personally scheduled programs balance of day.

Saturday
August 8

Morning: Opening General Assembly of ABA;
Afternoon: Bicentennial of U.S. Constitution Program;
Evening: International Law Section's reception; Annual Dinner in Honor of Judiciary. President Reagan has been invited to be the speaker for the annual dinner. At this dinner, the Chief

Justices of the fifty states, the Chief Judges of the eleven federal circuits and the officers of the ABA are the honored guests. The foreign judges will be seated on the dais along with the other dignitaries.

Sunday
August 9

Monday
August 10

Program evaluation session, educational program at California Court of Appeals to view case management processing with a focus on the latest technology, experiments and use of non-judicial staff. In the evening, the ABA President's Annual Dinner will be held.

Tuesday
August 11

Departure

Wednesday
August 11

5037A/18-9

TRAVEL AND HOTEL INFORMATION

Hotel accommodations in Reno and San Francisco will be made by the ABA staff as follows:

Saturday, August 1: Sheraton Airport Hotel, San Francisco

Sunday-Tuesday Aug. 2-4: Hilton Hotel, Union Square, San Francisco

Airtime reservations and ticketing for both international and domestic travel will be handled by the ABA's travel agency, Ask Mr Foster. Tickets will be mailed to USIA post for delivery to participants. Once your acceptance is received, Mr Foster will arrange a travel schedule for you.

Ask Mr Foster Telex Number: 5106009154

ABA Telex Number: 270593

Any travel done before or after August 1-12 will be at the judge's own expense.

5037A/20
May 19th, 1987
Mr Nyo Wakai
Technical Counselor to
the Supreme Court of
Cameroon
YAOUNDE

DEAR Mr Wakai,

I have been instructed by our offices in the United States to invite you to participate in a special program and conference organized by the American Bar Association to celebrate the bicentennial of the American Constitution. The conference and program will be organized by the American Bar Association and will take place in the State of Nevada between August 1st and 12th of this year.

The American Bar Association will send you a formal invitation, care of the Ministry of Justice, if you should be able to attend. They have asked me to approach you and inquire if you are interested and if you believe you can attend. If your response is positive, the formal invitation will be on its way to you in the very near future.

I am delighted to be able to make this offer and convey the Bar Association's invitation. Please contact me as soon as possible with your response.

Sincerely,
Sgd: Cornelius C. Walsh
Director

NOTE:
Discussed with Hon. BM. Itoe who had no objection to my acceptance of the invitation. 21st May 1987.[43]

---

[43] Personal note made after discussion with Hon. B.M. Itoe

May 22, 1987.
The Director,
American Cultural Centre,
B.P. 817,
<u>YAOUNDE</u>.

Sir,

With reference to your letter dated May, 19, 1987, conveying the invitation of your offices in the U.S. for me to participate in the celebration of bicentennial of the American Constitution, I accept the invitation with pleasure and thank you for the honour. I should, however, like to be informed of the conditions attaching thereto. A copy of this letter of acceptance is being sent to the Honourable Minister of Justice for information.

Sincerely yours,
Sgd. <u>NYO'WAKAI</u>.

<u>Copy to:</u>
The Honourable Minister of Justice,
Keeper of the Seals, Ministry of Justice,
<u>YAOUNDE</u>.
Above for information with reference to our discussion of yesterday.

Sgd. <u>NYO'WAKAI</u>.

EMBASSY OF THE
UNITED STATES OF AMERICA

N° 291

The Embassy of the United States of America presents its compliments to the Ministry of Foreign Affairs of the Republic of Cameroon and has the honor to inform the Ministry that it has been asked to transmit to the Technical Adviser of the Supreme Court, Justice NYO WAKAI, an invitation has been extended to the Justice by the American Bar Association which has asked the Embassy to act as its agent in this matter. Neither the Embassy nor the Government of the United States of America are participants of the conference or program. The Embassy would, however, appreciate any assistance the Ministry of Foreign Affairs might provide Justice Wakai in this matter to assure Cameroon of suitable representation at the conference.

Justices from fifteen of the world's democracies have been invited to participate in the conference which will take place in the first weeks of August in San Francisco, California.

All costs of the project, including air fare and per diem allowance, will be borne by the American Bar Association.

The Embassy of the United States of America takes this occasion to renew to the Ministry of Foreign Affairs the assurances of its highest consideration.

Embassy of the United States of America
Yaounde June 2, 1987.

DOUALA – CAMEROON
AT AMERICAN ASSOCIATION
TELEX DU 9/06/87
FOR THE ATTENTION OF MARY ELLEN DONAGHY – 750 N LAKE SHORE DR CHICAGO ILLINOIS 60611.
- YOUR INVITATION TO THE BICENTENNIAL CELEBRATION OF THE U.S CONSTITUTION IS GRATEFULLY ACCEPTED JUSTICE NYO WAKAI OF SUPREME COURT OF CAMEROON - YAOUNDE

SALUTATIONS.
J. NYO WAKAI.
AMERICAN BAR
CAPRICAM 6009KN

June 12, 1987

The Staff Director
(Mary Ellen DONAGHTY),
American Bar Association,
750 North Lake Shore Drive/10th Floor
CHICAGO, Illinois 60611.

Madam,

Thank you for the invitation dated April 20, 1987, to participate in the bicentennial celebration of the U.S. Constitution from August 1 – 12, 1987.

I wish to convey by this letter my ready acceptance of the invitation as I regard it not only as a personal honour but that of my country.

Sincerely yours,

Sgd. *NYO' WAKAI*.

Copy to:
The Director,
American Cultural Centre,
B.P. 817,
YAOUNDE.
Above for information.

June 16, 1987

The Honourable Minister of Justice,
Directorate of General Administration,
Ministry of Justice,
YAOUNDE.

Your Excellency,

TRAVELING WARRANT

I have the honour to refer to my letter dated May 22, 1987, addressed to the Director of the American Cultural Centre and copied you by which letter I accepted the invitation of the American Bar Association to participate in the bicentennial celebration of the United States Constitution. I enclose herewith a copy of the formal invitation with the request that you apply on my behalf for an 'Ordre de Mission' to enable me travel to and fro the U.S.

2. Accept, Your Excellency, my regards for your office and person.

Sgd. *NYO' WAKAI*.

C.C.
The Director,
American Cultural Centre,
Yaounde.

Above for information.

June 22, 1987

MEMORANDUM FOR: PAO – USIS Yaounde
FROM: E/P – Russell Bikoff

SUBJECT: ABA Program

Please deliver the enclosed letter to the judge participating in the ABA program.

Thank you.

June 17, 1987

Honourable Nyo Wakai
Supreme Court
Yaounde, Cameroon

Dear Justice Wakai:

    I have prepared a tentative agenda for the ABA Program for Judicial Leaders which is enclosed. We are most anxious to make your trip a memorable one and we would like to incorporate into the program any activities of interest to you that are not presently included.
    These activities may include legal programs, visits to law firms, mediation centers, cultural programs, visits to law schools, educational programs in a specific area of the law, etc.
    The time blocks set aside for these special events follow:
August 7, Friday: morning; August 8, Saturday:
Morning; August 9, Sunday: afternoon; August 11,
Tuesday: morning.
    We would appreciate it if you would request no more that two special events.
    Please let me know by July 10 what activities you would like scheduled. We will do our best to incorporate your request into the agenda. My telex number is 270593.

Sincerely,

Sgd. Mary Ellen Donaghy
      Staff Director

TENTATIVE AGENDA

ABA PROGRAM FOR JUDICIAL LEADERS

<u>Saturday, August 1</u>
Arrival in San Francisco. Hotel accommodations at Embassy Suites Hotel, 150 Anza Boulevard, Burlingame, CA, telephone: 415/342-4600. each judge will be met at the airport by ABA Staff.

<u>Sunday, August 2</u>
Departure by train to Reno, Nevada. Orientation session on board. Hotel accommodations in Reno at Airport Plaza Hotel. Dinner and National Judicial College Orientation Session at hotel.

<u>Monday, August 3</u>
Program at National Judicial College: "Role of the Judge in a Democratic Society" with an exploration of three areas: comparative constitutional issues, separation of powers and an independent judiciary and the role of the judiciary in the protection of human rights. The program will include discussion groups with U.S. judges attending the College. Breakfast and lunch will be at the College. In the evening, a reception will be held at Harrah's Hotel in honor of this group. Dinner for the group will be held at a local Reno restaurant, Rapscallion's.

<u>Tuesday, August 4</u>
Morning: A visit to the Reno Criminal Court where a tour of the court will be held including the opportunity to witness trials, arraignments and sentencing hearings.

Afternoon and Evening: A bus tour to Virginia City (an old west frontier town), Carson City (the capitol of Nevada) for lunch with the Governor and on to Lake Tahoe for reception and dinner at a private home.

<u>Wednesday, August 5</u>
Morning: Departure by air for San Francisco

Afternoon: Check in at hotel, the Hilton Hotel, 333 O'Farrell St., telephone: 415/771-1400. Bus tour of San Francisco

Evening: Dinner at Judge Sneed's home. Judge Sneed is Chairperson of the Appellate Judges Conference and a member of the U.S. Court of Appeals, 9th Circuit.

Thursday, August 6
A visit to the California Intermediate Appellate Court will be held where oral arguments and judicial conferencing will be viewed. Lunch at a local restaurant with the members of the court will end the program. In the afternoon, a boat trip to Sausilito will be scheduled. In the evening, a dinner at a restaurant in Chinatown will be held where the judges will meet the U.S. appellate judges who will be their hosts.

Friday August 7
Morning: Free.

Afternoon: Visit to the U.S. Court of Appeals, 9th Circuit to learn about case management experiments and the use of technology in appellate courts.

Evening: Reception sponsored by the San Francisco Bar Association.

Saturday, August 8
Morning: Free

Afternoon: ABA Orientation Session, President of the ABA Reception, Appellate Judges Conference Annual Business Meeting including a program on the pros and cons of oral argument ending with a reception honoring the foreign judicial leaders.

Sunday, August 9
Morning: ABA Prayer Breakfast

Afternoon: Free
Evening: ABA President's Reception

Monday, August 10
Morning: Opening of ABA General Assembly
Afternoon: Showcase program: "The Role of the Judiciary in a Modern Society"
Evening: Section on International Law Reception; Annual Dinner in Honor of Judiciary

Tuesday, August 11
Morning: Free
Afternoon: Critique Session
Evening: ABA President's Annual Dinner

Wednesday, August 12

Departure for home

5458A

July 23, 1987

Justice NYO' WAKAI
Supreme Court
B.P. 980
Yaounde

Dear Justice WAKAI:

I am sorry that I was not able to speak with you yesterday when you visited the Centre to pick up your airline ticket for the American Bar Association special program. Yesterday was one of those days where the office is so busy that you barely have time to think. I hope that we will have the opportunity to meet before you leave for the U.S.

Today I received a telex from Washington which includes a message for you from Mary Ellen Donaghy, Coordinator of the American Bar Association's Special Bicentennial Project for Appellate Judges. The text of the message is as follows:-

I am writing to give you final details about the ABA Bicentennial Program. I am enclosing the itinerary which lists details about where you will be staying and what the appropriate dress will be.

You will be met at San Francisco Airport by either myself or Virginia Russell, another ABA staff person. We will be holding signs that say "ABA." We will be monitoring your flight arrival time so that if you are delayed, we will be aware of it. However, if there is a major delay and you arrive after midnight, we will not be able to meet you and ask that you take a taxi to the hotel which is located just a short distance from the airport.

We will be giving you your first per diem money in U.S. dollars on Sunday, August 2. Your per diem covers meal expenses and local taxis not prepaid by the program. For those of you with intermediary stops before San Francisco, you may wish to convert approximately dollars 100 into U.S. currency either in your country or at your arrival in the United States. For those of you traveling directly to San Francisco, it is possible to change money at the airport.

The average high temperature for San Francisco in August is 65 degrees Fahrenheit (18 C) with a low temperature of 54 degrees Fahrenheit (12 C). I would recommend that you bring a raincoat, some sweaters, a wool jacket and an umbrella.

Reno, Nevada, where we will be for three days, is much hotter with an average temperature of 89 degrees Fahrenheit (31 C) in August. However, it is in the mountains and does get cool at night.

We are very excited about this program and are looking forward to meeting you in a few weeks.

Sincerely,
Sgd. Judith A. Moon
Cultural Affairs Officer

AGENDA
FOR THE AMERICAN BAR ASSOCIATION'S

SPECIAL BICENTENNIAL PROGRAM FOR APPELLATE JUDGES

PARTICIPATING JUSTICES

Argentina - Justice PETRACCHI
Brazil - Justice REZEK
Cameroon - Justice WAKAI
Colombia - Justice MELO
Egypt - Justice AL-MARAGHI
India - Justice PATHAK
Israel - Justice SHAMGAR
Nigeria - Justice BELLO
Philippines - Justice HERRERA
Zimbabwe - Justice DUMBUTSHENA

SATURDAY, AUGUST 1
Arrival in San Francisco. Hotel accommodations at Embassy Suites Hotel, 150 Anza Boulevard, Burlingame, CA. Telephone: (415) 342-4600. Each judge will be met at the airport by ABA Staff.

SUNDAY, AUGUST 2
Morning: departure by train to Reno, Nevada. Orientation session on board. Hotel accommodations at the Airport Plaza Hotel, 1981 Terminal Way, Reno, Nevada. Telephone: (702) 348-6370. dress: causal.

    Evening: dinner and National Judicial College Orientation Session at hotel. Dress: causal.

MONDAY, AUGUST 3
Morning: Program at National Judicial College: "Role of the Judge in a Democratic Society" with an exploration of three areas: comparative constitutional issues, separation of powers and an independent judiciary and the role of the judiciary in the protection of human rights. The program will include discussion groups with U.S. judges attending the College. Breakfast and lunch will be at the College. Dress jacket and tie. Evening: a reception will be held at Harrah's Hotel in Honor of this group. Dinner for the group will be held at a local Reno restaurant, Rapscallion's. Dress jacket and tie.

TUESDAY, AUGUST 4

Morning: A visit to the Reno Criminal Court where a tour of the court will be held including the opportunity to witness trials, arraignments and sentencing hearings. Dress: jacket and tie.

Afternoon and evening: a bus tour to Virginia City (an Old West frontier town), Carson City (the capital of Nevada) for lunch with the Governor and on to Lake Tahoe for a reception and dinner at a private home. Dress: jacket and tie.

WEDNESDAY, AUGUST 5

Morning: departure by air for San Francisco

Afternoon: Check in at hotel, the Hilton Hotel, 333 O'Farrell Street. Telephone: (415) 771-1400. Bus Tour of San Francisco. Dress: casual

Evening: Dinner at Judge Sneed's home. Judge Sneed is Chairperson of the Appellate Judges Conference and a member of the U.S. Court of Appeals, 9th Circuit. Dress casual.

THURSDAY, AUGUST 6

Morning: a visit to the California Intermediate Appellate Court will be held where oral arguments and judicial conferencing will be viewed. Lunch at a local restaurant with the members of the court will end the program. Dress: Jacket and tie.

Afternoon: a boat trip to Sausilito will be scheduled. Dress: casual

Evening: a dinner at the Empress of China Restaurant in Chinatown will be held where the judges will meet the U.S. Appellate judges who will be their hosts. Dress: jacket and tie.

FRIDAY AUGUST 7

Morning: Free. Optional trip: visit to the law firm, Morrison and Forster, where a continental breakfast will be served. Dress: jacket and tie.

Afternoon: visit to the U.S. Court of Appeals, 9th Circuit, to learn about case management experiments and the use of technology in appellate courts. High tea will be served. Dress: jacket and tie.

Evening: reception sponsored by the San Francisco Bar Association. Dress: jacket and tie.

SATURDAY, AUGUST 8

Morning: free. Optional Visit (tentative): tour of San Quentin Prison.

Afternoon: ABA orientation session, President of the ABA reception. Appellate Judges Conference annual business meeting including a program on the pros and cons of oral argument ending with a reception honoring the foreign judicial leaders. Dress: jacket and tie.

SUNDAY, AUGUST 9
Morning: ABA Prayer Breakfast. Dress: jacket and tie.
Afternoon: free. Optional Visit (tentative): tour of San Quentin Prison.
Evening: ABA President's Reception. Dress: jacket and tie.

MONDAY, AUGUST 10
Morning: Opening of ABA General Assembly. Dress: jacket and tie.
Afternoon: Showcase program: "The Role of the Judiciary in a Modern Society." Dress: jacket and tie.
Evening: session on International Law; reception; Annual Dinner in honor of judiciary. Dress: black tie or national dress.

TUESDAY, AUGUST 11
Morning: critique session. Dress: casual
Afternoon: free. Optional Visit: tour of the University of California at Berkeley Law School; lunch with the Dean and several faculty members. Dress: casual.
Evening: ABA President's Annual Dinner. Dress: black tie or national dress.

WEDNESDAY, AUGUST 12
Departure for home

July 24, 1987

Mrs Kitt WALLACE,
International Visitors' Center,
312 SUTTER STREET,
SAN FRANCISCO,
California 94108.

Madam,
    Following our telephone conversation, I enclose herewith two copies of my biographical note.
    Looking forward to seeing you soon.
    Sincerely.
    Sgd. <u>NYO'WAKAI</u>

REPUBLIQUE DU CAMEROUN *Paix – Travail – Patrie* **MINISTERE DE LA JUSTICE** DIRECTION DE L'ADMINISTRATION GENERALE SOUS DIRECTION DU PERSONNEL SERVICE DU PERSONNEL MAGISTRAT **Objet:** Mission to SAN FRANCISCO Réf.: …………………………..	REPUBLIC OF CAMEROON *Peace – Work – Fatherland* **MINISTRY OF JUSTICE** N° 110/DAG/SPM/MJ *Yaoundé, le 31 JUIL 19 87* **Le Ministre de la Justice, garde des Sceaux** The Minister of Justice, Keeper of the Seals *a M. onsieur NYO WAKAI, Magistrat to COUNSELLOR AT THE SUPREME COURT* *Yaounde*

Following your letter dated 16ᵗʰ June 1987 on the matter under reference, I have been directed to inform you that the Presidency of the Republique has not deemed it necessary for you to travel to SAN FRANCISCO in CALIFORNIA for the meeting of the General Assembly of the AMERICAN BAR ASSOCIATION./-

Le Ministre de la Justice
Garde de Sceaux
Sgd. ITOE Benjamin

14ᵗʰ August, 1987

Miss Judith Moon,
Cultural Officer,
American Cultural,
YAOUNDE.

Madam,

You expressed the wish to have a copy of the enclosed letter. Herewith.
There is some misrepresentation therein. It was not a mission and it was not a meeting of the General Assembly of the American Bar Association but a conference jointly organized by the ABA, U.S. Information Agency, and the New York Times Foundation as part of the celebrations of the bicentennial of the U. S. constitution.
This is just to keep the record straight.
Sincerely,
Sgd. <u>NYO' WAKAI</u>

July 31, 1987

The Director,
American Cultural Centre,
B.P 817
Yaounde.

Sir,

ABA INVITATION

I have the honour to refer to the above matter which has been the subject of several correspondence between the ABA, your good office and myself and regret to say that I find myself unable to travel to San Francisco for the seminar/conference on the Bicentennial celebration of the U.S. constitution organised by ABA because I have not, up to now, obtained the authorisation to leave the country. I wish you to convey to the ABA my deep and sincere gratitude for the kind invitation and to wish it a successful seminar and conference.

Enclosed is an all round air ticket in my name for onward transmission to the American Bar Association.

Sincerely yours,
Sgd. <u>NYO'WAKAI</u>

July 31, 1987

The Chairperson,
American Bar Association,
750 North Lake Shore Drive,
CHICAGO, Illinois 60611

Sir,

INVITATION

I have the honour to refer to your kind invitation dated April 20 1987, by which you asked me to participate in a twelve-day programme celebrating the bicentennial of the U.S. constitution. I deeply regret to say that despite my ready willingness to participate in the programme I now find myself unable to avail myself at the seminar/conference due to the non-authorisation of my Government to travel out of the Country. The all round ticket in my name has accordingly been deposited with the Director of the American Cultural Centre, Yaounde.

I wish you a successful programme.
Sincerely yours
Sgd. <u>NYO'WAKAI</u>

All is well that ends well. So says the great Shakespeare. As the curtains were about to fall in 1989 for me to have a final exit in 1990, the door once more opened on me. Prior to that date a good working relationship had been established between the Canadian Bar Association and the Cameroon Bar, then led by Barrister Muna. After full discussions between the two bodies, it was agreed that a Project on Human Rights for Developing Countries should be initiated.

The committee consisted of the following members:-

For Canada:
- The Honourable Roberts Wells, Justice of the Supreme Court of Newfoundland and Chairman of the Committee;
- The Honourable Senator Gérald-A Beaudoin, G.C., Professor at the Faculty of Law at University of Ottawa vice - Chairman of the Committee;
- L. George Boros, Director, Resources and Professional Development, Canadian Bar Association, Project Co-ordinator.

For Cameroon:
- Bernard A. Muna, President of the Cameroon Bar Council;
- Nyo' Wakai, former Justice of the Supreme Court of Cameroon;
- Stanislas Melony (late), Doctor of Laws, Professor at Yaounde University.

The committee met twice, in Yaounde, Cameroon, and finally in Vancouver, Canada. The outcome of the work of the Committee was the production of the **Model Human Rights Charter for Developing Countries, 1989**. The Project was finalized by the meeting in Vancouver between 20 and 23rd August 1989 about one year and two months to my retirement. In hindsight, I consider this a most befitting exit in my career.

A final footnote. I am satisfied and proud with my contribution in the drafting of the Criminal Procedure Code which is an attempt to harmonise the two legal cultures and more so that it is the product of purely Cameroonian jurists. The proceedings from the beginning in 1974 to the end in 1981 when it was submitted to the Presidency further enriched my experience. It deals with a very important area of law in the administration of a criminal justice system.

Life must come to an end. When that happens, it is realized that the rest thereafter is darkness and a void. He who has passed on is completely forgotten. Those who realize this fact nearly always seek to leave a legacy behind by which they are immortalized and maybe either venerated or condemned forever.

Were life to be as those whose faith propagates incarnation, it would be most exciting to return to our original state when we traversed this earth and read one's epitath by those who outlived us.

It is this reminiscence that has inspired me to bring to the attention of the reader what I consider to be my epitath by two personalities with whom I have had to interact in the course of my professional life. Let them speak for themselves.

UNIVERSITE DE YAOUNDE
THE UNIVERSITY OF YAOUNDE

FACULTE DE DROIT	FACULTY OF LAWS
ET DES SCIENCES	AND ECONOMIC
ECONOMIQUES	SCIENCES

B.P.1365. YAOUNDE–TÉL: (237) 23-12-55
P.O. BOX 1365 – YAOUNDE– TÉL. (237) 23-12-55

Le 23rd January, 1991

Réf.:

Chief Justice Nyo' Wakai
Bamenda
Mezam Division

Dear Chief Justice Nyo' Wakai,

It is a pity that it was impossible to reach you before the second launching ceremony of the four books at Hilton Hotel in Yaounde. I am pleased to inform you that the event went on smoothly.

As I did inform you, the bills for the four books are colossal. In fact I hate quoting the figures since they go to remind me of my indebtedness. I therefore felt that I should make a small gesture to you of a few copies of the book, Law in Action, in which your most enviable article appears. I am herewith forwarding to you a carton containing 32 copies.

It is my fervent wish that you would find your "youthful retirement" very rewarding. Since you have a good pen, it may not be a bad idea if you decide to do some writing. If you need my assistance, I would gladly and willingly do so.

You must have heard that I was made Assistant Director of Administration and Personnel in the new university set-up. I am thankful for it. But one thing is clear, I am bent on completing my major academic project, namely, a complete text-book in Family Law. It has been going on now for over six years. It must be out before the end of the year.

Please, extend greetings to your beloved wife. Bye for now.

Yours Sincerely
Ephraim Ngwafor

P.O. BOX 2200
BAMENDA
28 October 1995

Mr Justice N. Wakai

Just a short note to let you know that of all the Heads of Department I had in my career in the Cameroonian Magistracy, you were the most fair minded and broad minded.

I will go down to my grave remembering, appreciating, thanking and treasuring all the understanding and help you gave me in my time under you in our country's magistracy.

Since enrolling at the Cameroonian Bar, I have met with nothing but unsolicited hostility and obstruction from all and Sundry and especially from members of the Bar in practice in the North West Province and that is why I have decided to mind my own business and keep myself to myself.

For my part, I have nothing against any member of the Legal Profession, any other Profession or indeed the general public.

Once more, many thanks for all that you have ever done for me and may God bless you, your family and all your endeavours.

Yours very sincerely,
Robert Ndoping

Justice R.T.N. Ndoping's letter was written five years after my retirement when I was not in a position to influence his service career. I consider it as coming from his heart and greatly flatters me beyond my expectation. He passes as one of the ninety-nine in the Bible who returned to say "thank you" for restoring my health.

Bob, thank you for this living tribute.

www.ingramcontent.com/pod-product-compliance
Lightning Source LLC
Chambersburg PA
CBHW011139290426
44108CB00020B/2689